*A*dventure Guide to
New
Mexico

*A*dventure Guide to
New Mexico

Rankin Harvey, Dave Houser & Steve Cohen

HUNTER
PUBLISHING

Hunter Publishing, Inc.
300 Raritan Center Parkway
Edison NJ 08818
Tel (908) 225 1900
Fax (908) 417 0482

ISBN 1-55650-727-5

Maps by Kim André

Cover photo: *Collared lizard cooling body off hot rock*
(John Cancalosi)

About the Authors

Rankin Harvey

A travel writer and photographer, Rankin is an avid sports and outdoor enthusiast. He is a PSIA-certified ski instructor at Ruidoso's Ski Apache and is a trained rock climbing instructor. His photography has appeared in magazines and newspapers ranging from *Trailer Life* to the *Los Angeles Times*.

Dave G. Houser

One of America's most widely published travel journalists, Dave G. Houser's work appears regularly in dozens of leading magazines, newspapers and books. In 1985, he was named runner-up for the Lowell Thomas Travel Journalism Award and in 1992 received the Pacific Area Travel Association's Grand Award for "best travel story with an article on Baja." That same year, he won a Lowell Thomas award for "best self-illustrated article." Dave has travelled to more than 125 countries and specializes in offbeat/adventure, cruise, and luxury travel. He is co-author of two other guidebooks: *Hidden Coast of California* and *Hidden Mexico*. To market photos from their far-flung adventures, Dave and his wife Jan manage their own stock photo agency based in New Mexico, presently listing almost 300,000 images.

Steve Cohen

Steve is author of more than a dozen travel books, including the outdoor classic, *Adevnture Guide to Jamaica*, first published in 1988 and now in its third edition. An adventure-seeking travel writer and photographer specializing in the unusual and offbeat, his self-illustrated articles appear regularly in America's largest newspapers and magazines. While reporting on life and cultures around the world, he has lived in the High Southwest for the last decade with his wife Jodie and his son Sean. He is a member of the Society of American Travel Writers.

Adventure Guide to Arizona, Morris & Cohen, 725-9, $12.95

Adventure Guide to the Alaska Highway,
Readicker-Henderson, 457-8, $15.95

Adventure Guide to Baja California, Morrison, 590-6, $13.95

Adventure Guide to the Bahamas, Howard, 705-4, $12.95

Adventure Guide to Barbados, Pariser, 707-0, $15.95

Adventure Guide to Belize, Pariser, 647-3, $14.95

Adventure Guide to Bermuda, Howard, 706-2, $12.95

Adventure Guide to the Catskills & Adirondacks,
Morrison, 681-3, $9.95

Adventure Guide to Coastal Alaska & the Inside Passage,
Readicker-Henderson, 731-3, $14.95

Adventure Guide to Colorado, Casewit & Cohen, 724-0, $12.95

Adventure Guide to Costa Rica, Pariser, 722-4, $16.95

Adventure Guide to the Dominican Republic,
Pariser, 629-5, $14.95

Adventure Guide to the Great Smoky Mountains,
Howard, 720-8, $13.95

Adventure Guide to the High Southwest, Cohen 723-2, $15.95

Adventure Guide to Jamaica, Cohen, 499-3, $17.95

Adventure Guide to Oregon & Washington, Booth, 709-7, $11.95

Adventure Guide to Puerto Rico, Pariser, 628-7, $14.95

Adventure Guide to Utah, Osberger & Cohen, 726-7, $12.95

Adventure Guide to the Virgin Islands, Pariser, 597-3, $14.95

Contents

is, mountain men and desert rats, amid powerful
ing and undeniably attractive. It's a hard coun-
ners but resistant to easy change. That is exactly
isistibly challenging.

n as the "Land of Enchantment" because of its
rich history, New Mexico is a veritable paradise
seeking traveler. Covering an enormous 121,593
ie nation's fifth largest state. Only Alaska, Texas,
itana have a greater area. And with a population
people, there's plenty of room to roam without

sical grandeur − which ranges from Chihua-
 to sweeping plains and snow-capped alpine
nicled. But few visitors realize that New Mexico
al experience as it is a great place to hike, bike,
Iexico has a higher percentage of Indian and
than any other state − roughly 45% − and the
roups is strikingly evident in terms of place
itecture, foods and customs. One could make a
r New Mexico being the most "foreign" of all

versity is the cornerstone of the American epic,
al about New Mexico's Indian, Hispanic and
wer can be found in the collision and co-min-
t has for more than 450 years dominated New
e state's tri-culturalism is quite simply older
e country. The Spanish explorer Coronado was
o in search of the Seven Cities of Cibola in 1540
 birth of George Washington and nearly seven
Inglish laid the foundations of Jamestown in

ever found the fabled cities of gold, the Span-
 primarily to converting Indians to Christian-
heir first mission colony at **San Juan Pueblo**
f the Chama and Rio Grande Rivers in 1598.
apital was moved to **Santa Fe**. Still the capital
Mexico, Santa Fe is the oldest seat of govern-
tates. Actually, Spain governed New Mexico
r than it's been part of the United States. For
anic colonists, mostly Franciscan missionar-
sing their culture on the rugged land and the
The legacy of their work survives to this day
an anything else, endows the modern state
 flavor.

In the 1990s,
longer considered
classic hang-by-
ture, although th
Mexico. You wor
you try a samplir
your chances of
doesn't need to b
the juices flowir
lenges that any
mind can enjoy.

Inside this b
many of which
remoteness, and
stressful, while
to-accomplish s
devil capers tha
find them here
week, or a mor
in the remarkal
drive, an India
offers thousan
and ride on h
lure you into a
trout or troll f
explore by jee
the gondola o
Indian and c
wild flowers
explore cany
nings are coo
tryside with

Assumir
New Mexico
out and do t
bolts inform
as well as sp
to do.

The tru
way being

of cowboys, Indiar
geology that is tes
try, open to all cor
what makes it irre

Forever know
scenic beauty and
for the adventure-
square miles, it is th
California and Mor
of just 1.6 million
feeling crowded.

The state's phy
huan desert basins
peaks – is well-chro
is as much a cultur
ski or fish. New M
Hispanic residents
influence of both g
names, art and arch
pretty good case fo
states.

Multicultural di
so what's the big de
Anglo mix? The ans
gling of cultures tha
Mexico's history. Th
than in the rest of th
combing New Mexic
– 192 years before the
decades before the
1607.

Although they n
ish stayed. Dedicated
ity, they established
near the confluence
In 1610 the colonial c
of present-day New
ment in the United S
almost 80 years longe
nearly 225 years Hisp
ies, toiled here, impos
Indians occupying it.
and, perhaps more th
with an exotic, foreig

Others will say that New Mexico's persistent and vital Indian cultures, healthier than perhaps anywhere in the country, have contributed most toward defining the state's unique character. Certainly the Indians were here before anyone else – and in this instance we are not speaking of the Anasazi, whose cliff dwellings and many-storied apartments of stone we can still visit today.

Thousands of years earlier, nomadic hunters were tracking down woolly mammoths, giant bison and saber-toothed tigers on the plains of New Mexico. In fact, the continent's oldest known Indian sites have been discovered here. At **Folsom** the remains of Folsom man, dating back 10,000 years, were uncovered. Later, near **Clovis**, remnants of the Clovis culture pushed back the antiquity of human occupation in New Mexico to more than 11,000 years. More recently, researchers from the Massachusetts-based Andover Foundation for Archaelogical Research discovered artifacts in Pendejo Cave on the Army's Fort Bliss firing range near **Orogrande** in Southern New Mexico that establish human presence in the area at least 25,000 years ago. There may be evidence, in fact, to place Orogrande man – America's oldest, without a doubt – here as long as 40,000 years ago.

Eventually Anglos began making their imprint as well. Not, however, while the Spanish retained power. Insular and protective of its New World dominion, Spain refused to allow its New Mexican colonists to trade with foreigners, especially French and British trappers and traders who were swarming westward from the upper Mississippi and Missouri Valleys. But, once Mexico wrested its independence from Spain in 1821 and made New Mexico a province, the pipeline was opened at last. Settlers and traders poured into New Mexico along the **Santa Fe Trail**. Braving the rigors of a harsh land and beset by hostile Indians, miners and ranchers struggled to develop and utilize the area's rich resources. Inevitably, too, they were soon caught up in a conflict with Mexico. In a one-sided affair known as The Mexican War of 1846, the United States prevailed and in 1850 Congress declared New Mexico a US territory, then including Arizona and part of Colorado.

The arrival of the railroads in the 1870s brought on an economic boom, with cattle and ores being shipped to the north and east where there was a ready market for them. Fortunes were made and many lives were lost during those lawless and violent days of the Wild West. Groups of cattlemen and merchants fought for economic and political control of **Lincoln County**, the largest county in the nation at the time. The bitterness burst into open violence with the murder of merchant John Tunstall. Notorious outlaw **Billy the Kid** took sides as a mercenary in the fighting that came to be known as the **Lincoln County War**.

Violence and the lack of law and order persisted in New Mexico Territory right into the 20th century, dissuading the federal government from granting statehood until 1912. Lawlessness – some would call it frontier independence – seemed destined to remain the Anglo's most notable contribution to the tri-cultural equation until World War II. It was then that New Mexico became the epicenter of America's weapons research and development program. Shrouded in secrecy, the world's first atomic bomb was developed at **Los Alamos Laboratory** and on July 16, 1945, it was detonated in dramatic fashion at **Trinity Site**, near **Alamogordo**. In August, 1945, US planes dropped two of the bombs on Japan, bringing an end to the War in the Pacific. To this day, New Mexico remains at the forefront in research and development for the defense industry.

To help you get your geographic bearings, it is useful to remember New Mexico has four main land regions: the **Rocky Mountains**, the **Great Plains**, the **Basin and Range**, and the **Colorado Plateau**.

These physical regions correspond rather closely to the chapter divisions in this book. For example, the North Central chapter, which includes **Albuquerque**, **Santa Fe** and **Taos**, pretty much overlays the Rocky Mountains. The Northeast chapter covers the Great Plains region from the Rockies east to the borders of Texas and Oklahoma. It was this section of the plains that was crossed by two of the West's most historic byways, the **Santa Fe Trail** and **Route 66**. The area addressed in the Southeast chapter is almost evenly divided between the Great Plains on the eastern side of the Sacramento and Guadalupe Mountains and Basin and Range country to the west. The Southwest chapter deals entirely with Basin and Range topography, featuring the rugged mountains of the **Gila National Forest** (the state's largest) and the **Gila Wilderness**, near **Silver City**, which was the first area in the country to be set aside as a national wilderness. Steve Cohen's Northwest New Mexico chapter takes place on the Colorado Plateau, home to many of the state's most outstanding remains of ancient Indian civilizations.

The **Rocky Mountains**, according to most geographers, penetrate north-central new Mexico to a point near Santa Fe. Others suggest the Rockies run to the borders of Texas and Mexico and that the **Salinas**, **San Mateo**, **Mimbres**, **Mogollon**, **Organ**, **Guadalupe** and **Sacramento Mountains** in the southwest and central part of the state are really a continuation of the great cordillera.

While New Mexico's tallest mountain, **Wheeler Peak** (13,161 feet), is situated in the north-central area near the Colorado border, one of the state's highest elevations is 12,003-foot **Sierra Blanca**

Peak in the Sacramento Mountains near **Ruidoso** – more than 250 miles south of Wheeler Peak.

Almost 100 miles due west of Sierra Blanca, **Whitewater Baldy** rises 10,895 feet in the Mogollons. So, whether you consider them part of the Rockies or Basin and Range, there are some big mountains in Southern New Mexico. There are also some splendid examples of broad desert basins lying between the southern mountain ranges. The two largest are *Jordana del Muerto* (Journey of the Dead) and the **Tularosa Basin**, which is home to the magnificent gypsum dunes of **White Sands National Monument**.

Intersecting New Mexico's mountainous backbone like a vital nerve, the **Rio Grande River** flows down from Colorado, providing water for crops in the fertile **Rio Grande Valley** and for the state's best water sports and recreation. A section of the river known as **Taos Box** offers spectacular whitewater sport and, to the south, where the Rio Grande feeds **Elephant Butte Lake**, you'll find some of the finest fishing waters in the Southwest. The Rio Grande served for centuries as the source of life to both Indians and Spaniards, so much of the state's colorful history unfolded in its valley.

Part of the vast interior plain that carpets the country's mid-section from Canada to Mexico, the **Great Plains** covering the eastern third of New Mexico are not, for the most part, awave with tall grass as you might picture them. Long committed to ranching and dry farming – and severely overgrazed in the past – most of the eastern plains appear to be barren. This is particularly true of the high plains or *Llano Estacado* along the eastern edge of the state, south of the **Canadian River**. Dramatic skies and sunsets, however, lend a special beauty to these plains. The entire southern border of the state fringes the great **Chihuahuan Desert**. This high desert landscape is especially evident and accessible around **Carlsbad Caverns National Park**. What lies beneath the scrubby surface here is, of course, another story entirely.

The **Colorado Plateau** in northwestern New Mexico is a broken country of high, wide valleys, deep canyons, jagged cliffs and rugged mesas. Sitting atop the most famous of these mesas, **Acoma Pueblo**, has been occupied by Anasazi and later Pueblo Indians for more than 1,000 years. Some say it is America's oldest continuously inhabited community. The plateau is home as well to **Chaco Culture National Historical Park**, southwest of **Farmington**. At one time, Chaco was the epicenter of the Anasazi culture and remains perhaps the best-preserved of all ancient environments in the Southwest. Other important features in Northwest New Mexico include a 40-mile strip of extinct volcanoes and lava beds known as the *Malpais* (Spanish for badlands) and **Shiprock**, a classic example of a volcanic neck, which is the result of a tremendous up-swelling of molten rock magma from the earth's core. Known to the Navajo as *Tse Bi Dahi*, the Rock With Wings, Shiprock is an improbably steep hill that rises 1,678 feet out of surrounding flatlands and distinctly resembles the bow of a ship. Preserving a page from more recent history is the **Cumbres & Toltec Scenic Railroad**. Daily, from June to October, it chugs passengers between **Chama** and Antonito, Colorado, making it the longest (64 miles) and highest (over 10,015-foot-high Cumbres Pass) narrow-gauge steam railroad in the United States.

How To Use This Book

This book divides New Mexico into regions – North-Central, Northeast, Southeast, Southwest and Northwest. The order of these chapters describes a large circle, presuming that you will likely begin your journey through the major gateway of Albuquerque.

Each chapter starts with an introduction to the region. This covers climate, history, and culture, along with the main sites and activities. It is followed by a section called Touring, which outlines the main roads and transportation options as well as the general route the chapter will follow. Each region is then broken down into touring sections listed in the same order as they appear on the selected route. These sections provide information and useful contact numbers such as chambers of commerce, regional US Department of Agriculture Forest Service offices, Bureau of Land Management offices, National Park Service offices, and airline and rental car services.

After the general touring sectionr, a separate section detailing specific adventures within each region follows. These include options for independent travelers or those seeking guided tours. There are many activities to choose from and many more limited only by your imagination. For example, you can generally experience an enjoyable hike on a listed bike trail, or bike on a jeep road.

The following is a brief description of the range and nature of activities covered under the Adventure categories.

ON FOOT

(Hiking/Backpacking/Rock Climbing)

Whether you want to go it on your own or with a guided tour, this category will show you where to go and how to do it. There are hundreds and hundreds of miles of hiking trails in New Mexico. Some are strenuous, requiring specialized rock climbing skills and equipment; others are more like a walk in the park. It is impossible to list them all, but you will find a cross-section of the hikes for all levels of ability, from short walks over easy trails to multi-day routes through rugged mountain or canyon country.

When hiking in backcountry, the more popular short trails are usually well worn and marked, but it's still remarkably easy to get lost. Don't head out into the wilds on your own without some preparation. Figure out where you want to go, then consult the Forest Service, BLM, or Park Service for up-to-date topographical maps and information. Discuss with them the difficulty of various trails and technical climbing skills or specialized equipment that may be required. USGS (US Geological Service) maps can be purchased for around $3 each. They show contour lines that indicate the relative steepness of the terrain. Some adventures in this area can be accomplished easily alone, while others require special gear, permits, and expertise. If you're short on equipment or in doubt about your skills, seek help from the professionals before attempting a demanding adventure. The USDA Forest Service suggests that all users of the backcountry remember the following:

❑ Take no chances. Assistance can take hours or days.

❑ Be aware of conditions. Varied terrain exposes you to hypothermia, dehydration, and lightning hazards on exposed ridges. There can be snow fields in early summer.

❑ Start hiking early in the day – mornings are generally clear. Later in the afternoon you may encounter storms of varying intensity. An early start gives you time to get to your destination and set up your camp in comfort, not while fighting the elements.

❑ Travel with a companion. File a hiking plan with someone who is staying behind and check in with revisions so you can be found if something goes wrong.

- ❏ Be in shape. Don't push past your limits. Allow time to acclimate to altitude.

- ❏ Always take fresh water with you, especially in the desert where heat can be deceiving and water may not be available. A gallon of water per person, per day, is recommended for summertime desert travel.

- ❏ Pack extra food just in case something goes wrong and you're out there longer than you planned.

TRAVEL WITH LLAMAS OR HORSES

Let's say you want to get out on your own two feet but you don't want to lug heavy gear. An alternative if you'd rather not be burdened with packs but want to travel into some of the most improbable terrain imaginable is hiking with packstock. Llamas are employed by a few operators. They're not strong enough to carry the weight of an adult human but they are prodigious hikers and can easily tote 75 pounds or so of food and equipment in specially designed packs. Other hiking trips are run with horses or mules to carry the gear. Without weight restrictions imposed by the strength of your own back, you can experience deep backcountry with a case of beer or a few bottles of wine, an extra pair of dry shoes, and other heavy and awkward items to make your trip more enjoyable.

Harder on your bottom than your feet is the venerable primary mode of transportation – horseback riding. Horses are still common out here and trips on well-trained, tractable mounts or high-spirited animals are easily arranged for an hour, a day, or overnight. A number of guest ranches and resorts also offer horseback riding. These are listed under accommodations.

ON WHEELS

(Railroads/Jeeps/Bicycles)

There is a steam train trip offered in New Mexico on one of the most scenically compelling and historic rail lines in the world. We're not talking about Amtrak here, though one of its trains does make several stops along the I-40 corridor.

A jeep or other four-wheel-drive may sometimes be the only motorized vehicle able to negotiate the hundreds of miles of remote, minimal roads that are among the most scenic in the Southwest. Please stay on established roads and don't chew up the backcountry by carving your own route.

Mountain biking has really blossomed as a mainstream activity throughout New Mexico. New high-tech bikes, with 18, 21, or more speeds, make it possible for just about anyone who can ride to negotiate at least some of the terrain. Mountain bikers move faster than hikers, and knobby tires can transport you into certain regions where motorized vehicles cannot go.

Throughout the region, the topography for biking is testing and picturesque. The assortment of logging roads, jeep routes, and single-track trails on public lands is immense, offering something for everyone, from easy paved bikeways to world-class backcountry excursions.

Again, it's impossible to include all the great biking routes here. The selection offered in this book will suit varying skills and abilities. Guided bike tours suggested here will generally handle logistical arrangements. On a tour or on your own, every rider needs to carry extra food and water, a head lamp, maps, and rain gear. Of course, a helmet is essential.

Local bike rental operators, repair shops, and tour resources are included throughout the text. An excellent single source of detailed information on bike routes throughout this region is *The Mountain Biker's Guide to New Mexico* by Sarah Bennett, Falcon Press, 1994. Other valuable sources of information are the experts in local bike shops who know the terrain.

Although bike riding is generally supported in New Mexico, continuing access to backcountry trails is partly dependent on the goodwill you and other outdoor folk inspire. The International Mountain Biking Association has established rules of the trail to help preserve mountain bikers' trail rights:

❏ Ride on open trails only. Respect trail and road closures, private property, and requirements for permits and authorization. Federal and state wilderness areas are closed to cyclists and some park and forest trails are off-limits.

❏ Leave no trace. Don't ride on certain soils after a rain, when the ground will be marred. Never ride off the trail, skid your tires, or discard any object. Strive to pack out more than you pack in.

❏ Control your bicycle. Inattention for even a second can cause disaster. Excessive speed frightens and injures people, gives mountain biking a bad name, and results in trail closures.

❑ Always yield. Make your approach known well in advance to others using the trail. A friendly greeting is considerate and appreciated. Show respect when passing by slowing to walking speed or even stopping, especially in the presence of horses. Anticipate that other trail users may be around corners or in blind spots.

❑ Never spook animals. Give them extra room and time to adjust to you. Running livestock and disturbing wild animals is a serious offense. Leave ranch and farm gates as you find them, or as marked.

❑ Plan ahead. Know your equipment, your ability, and the area in which you are riding and prepare accordingly. Be self-sufficient at all times, keep your bike in good condition, carry repair kits, and supplies for changes in weather. Keep trails open by setting an example of responsible cycling for all to see.

As for the terrain, even routes classified as easy by locals may be strenuous for a flat-lander. Most downhill routes will include some uphill stretches. Pay particular attention to your personal limits if you're on your own.

ON WATER

(Whitewater Rafting/Canoeing/Kayaking/Boating/Fishing)

From around mid-May to mid-June rivers rise dramatically and the flows are at their highest, fastest, and coldest. Sometimes by August things are pretty sluggish. It all depends on the winter's snowfall, spring rains, and summer thunderstorms.

In general, at high or low water levels, it takes an experienced hand to negotiate the rivers of New Mexico. Unless you really know what you are doing, it is highly recommended that you consider a river tour rather than an independent river trip. Tour operators also handle any permits that may be necessary for certain popular stretches. A number of operators offer half-day and full-day whitewater trips through the famous **Taos Box** section of the **Rio Grande** and multi-day float trips on the **Chama River**. You also can raft, canoe or kayak independently on the **Gila River** in southwest New Mexico.

For any river trip, the smaller the vessel, the bigger the ride. Be sure to inquire about the size of a raft and how many people it holds. Ask if you'll need to paddle or simply ride along while guides do the work. Listings that mention paddleboats mean you will have to paddle. Oar boats mean a guide does the work. Kayaks accommodate one person, who will obviously do all the paddling.

CLASSIFYING WHITEWATER RAPIDS

Class I	Easy
Class II	Intermediate
Class III	Difficult
Class IV	Very Diffcult
Class V	Exceptionally Difficult
Class VI	Impossible

Lakes and reservoirs throughout New Mexico offer boat ramps for your vessel. Larger bodies of water feature marinas offering boat rentals where you can probably secure a rowboat, a canoe, a motorboat, a windsurfer, or other equipment.

If you're seeking fishing waters rather than rapids, lakes and reservoirs are suitable for canoe and boat excursions. In addition, there are innumerable places to fish from the shores of streams, rivers, and alpine lakes. Many waters are well-stocked with a variety of fish including several species of trout, striped, large and smallmouth bass, crappie, bluegill, walleye and catfish.

ON SNOW

(Downhill & Cross-Country Skiing/Snowmobiling/Dog Sledding)

You'll find New Mexico's most reliable and sophisticated downhill skiing operations at **Taos** in the north and **Ski Apache**, near Ruidoso, in the south. There are other areas, too, notably at **Santa Fe**, **Sandia Peak**, **Red River**, **Angel Fire** and **Snow Canyon** (Cloudcroft) where, when the snow is good, skiing is great. Winter skies here are often sunny and temperatures generally run 10 to 15° warmer than at Colorado ski areas.

There are a few cross-country skiing areas as well, offering a more peaceful and less crowded experience than at downhill areas. But you should stick to groomed trails unless you know what you are doing. You can ski the backcountry for an hour or for days, but snow conditions are often unstable and avalanches are possible in certain areas or under certain conditions. To help match your abilities with appropriate terrain, it is highly recommended that you consult with ski shop personnel or regional information sources before approaching the backcountry.

The listings in each chapter are some of the safest cross-country routes. Remember that conditions are completely unpredictable and depend entirely on weather that can and does change rapidly. For current snowpack and wind conditions, on-the-spot research is essential before any backcountry ski trip. Dress warmly and carry high-energy foods. Though less physically demanding, the same rules apply if you're snowmobiling or dog sledding.

IN AIR

(Scenic Flights/Ballooning/Soaring)

If you think New Mexico looks impressive from the ground, then you might want to consider seeing it from the air. A range of options are available, including fixed-wing aircraft, helicopters, gliders, and balloons.

ECO-TOURS & CULTURAL EXCURSIONS

Adventure travelers as a group are becoming increasingly sensitive to the environment. Consequently tour operators are now offering more and more trips devoted to ecological themes. Closely related and growing in popularity are a profusion of cultural excursions aimed at growing the mind.

In addition to local offerings described in the ensuing chapters, the following tour operators conduct eco-travel, cultural and other educational programs in New Mexico and throughout the Southwest.

Nature Expeditions International
PO Box 11496
Eugene, OR 97440
☎ 800-869-0639

Four Corners School of Outdoor Education
PO Box 1029
Monticello UT 84535
☎ 800-525-4456

Earthwatch Expeditions
680 Mt. Auburn St.
PO Box 403
Watertown, MA 02272
☎ 800-776-0188

WHERE TO STAY & EAT

Although not expressly an adventure, finding good places to stay and eat in New Mexico can be a challenge.

In some remote areas, there may be only a campground with a fire grill, or a single, shabby motel for many miles. In other places you'll find a number of excellent establishments. All listings are subjective and are included for some good reason, whether for exceptional service, ambiance, great food, or good value. Rates range from inexpensive to deluxe choices. Because these services may change rapidly, local information sources will come in handy for updates.

CAMPING

Public campgrounds and information sources are included in this section. You will also find details regarding camping on Indian reservations and remote backcountry campsites.

CLIMATE

The diverse topography of New Mexico causes wide variations in climate. The season you visit will depend on what sort of activities you wish to pursue, but be aware that summer is not necessarily the most comfortable time. Summer weather is considerably milder the higher you go into the mountains, and is certainly quite spectacular on an 80° blue sky day in the Sacramentos. Down below, in the flatlands and arid deserts, it can get dangerously hot, especially if you're hiking or biking around Las Cruces in August. Just the reverse is true in winter. While skiers are snowbound in Ruidoso, you may want to head to Carlsbad Caverns, only 150 miles or so south. It may not only be warmer, but it's likely to be devoid of tourists at that time. There are always trade-offs. Certain outfitting or adventure tour businesses are only open during particular seasons; some lodgings even close during the winter.

If you come in the spring, you need to be prepared to deal with mud in the lowlands or dust storms in the deserts. Fall is considered by many to be the perfect season. The air is cooler, but not yet cold. Desert areas are once again tolerable after the scorching summer, while mountains boast colorful foliage and fewer crowds. Because of the great ranges in elevation, fall lasts several months (from September in the high mountains, to November in the deserts).

Count on daytime temperatures of 100° or more in the deserts by July and August. At the same time, temperatures are likely to be 75-85° in Santa Fe, Taos or Ruidoso. A temperature drop of 25-30° after the sun goes down is common throughout the state. January through March may be cold in the region, with below freezing temperatures in the high mountains.

CLOTHING & GEAR

New Mexico is a casual place. Shorts and T-shirts are fine for summer days but long pants and a sweater or jacket may be needed at night, particularly at higher elevations. Because conditions can change very quickly, layering your clothes is the best idea so you can remove or add clothing as it gets hotter or colder.

Sneakers may not be rugged enough footwear for backcountry hiking, so heavier, lug-soled boots are recommended. A broken-in pair of cowboy boots may be a good idea for extended horse travel. Hiking boots with heels to catch in your stirrups will probably do for short rides.

Find out in advance everything you can about your destination, such as water supplies, restroom facilities, fireplace availability and restrictions on camping, group size, fires, and wood cutting. Plan your gear accordingly; bring shovels, cook stoves, water jugs, or saws as needed.

Outfitters and tour operators can usually supply any special gear that may be required for specific activities, so you may want to check with them about rental equipment before buying expensive items.

Always carry extra food and water on any backcountry excursions. You may be out there longer than expected.

Depending on the activities you wish to pursue, special clothing and gear may be needed. Rafting in spring may call for a wetsuit. In winter, if you're cross-country skiing in the backcountry, special touring skis with metal edges are highly recommended. Cross-country skiing produces a lot of heat so you can easily work up a sweat, but when you stop moving you will feel how cold it really is. Again, layers are the answer. And even in mid-summer, on a backcountry bike ride you might start out in 80° weather, then run into a thunderstorm that drops the temperature dramatically. If you plan for the most severe conditions you will be able to weather these changes in fine form.

At any time of the year the sun can be quite strong. Wear a hat, sunscreen, and bring sunglasses.

Insect repellent is a good idea in the summer, particularly at lower elevations and around lakes or reservoirs.

DRIVING

To really get out and experience the plains, mountains and deserts of New Mexico you need a car, and some of the best places to go are not on main roads. Always inquire of locals about current road conditions. Some back roads may be marked for four-wheel-drive vehicles only. Do not test local wisdom in your Oldsmobile sedan. You will be in deep trouble if you travel several miles down an ultimately impassable dirt road and discover you cannot turn around. After rains, dirt roads can become dense, muddy tracks from which there is no easy escape. In the desert, sandy roads can swallow a car up to its hubcaps before you know what hit you. Snow sometimes closes main highways (though generally for short periods) and unmaintained back roads may disappear until spring.

Those cowboys in their pickups know what they're doing. A truck or a four-wheel-drive with high ground clearance are clearly the vehicles of choice but, with or without one, precautions are de rigueur. The farther out you plan to go, the more important it is to carry spare fuel and water for your radiator. Top up the gas tank wherever you can. The next gas station may be 100 miles away. Smart backcountry winter travel means good snow tires, windshield wipers that work, a couple of blankets, and a shovel in your car.

Local people understand the conditions and will probably help you out if you have trouble, but there may be nobody around for many miles or many hours. A cellular phone or CB radio could make a big difference in getting help. And don't forget to travel with the most up-to-date maps. Reliable maps are available from offices of the Forest Service or BLM. Auto clubs and outdoor stores are also good sources.

WEATHER & ROAD CONDITIONS

Always check with local offices of the state patrol and the National Weather Service for current information. Don't be lazy about this. Just because it looks okay where you're standing does not mean it's going to be that way where you're going. Conditions can change quickly.

SPECIAL CONCERNS

The areas covered in this book are here for all to enjoy and special care should always be taken to insure their continued existence. There are designated wilderness areas with seriously enforced rules of etiquette, including restricted access limited to those on foot or with pack animals only. Throughout New Mexico, fishing and hunting are subject to state or tribal law. Certain areas have restrictions on campfires and, even where fires are allowed, dry weather may lead to prohibitions on open fires. It's always safest to cook on a camp stove. If you need to make a fire, do not cut standing trees but burn dead wood only. And do not be tempted to pocket an arrowhead or a pottery shard you may find on your travels. Think of the next person who'll be coming along, and remember that artifacts are protected by strictly enforced laws.

It's a sound policy to take only photographs and leave only footprints. Before leaving a campsite, replace rocks and scatter leaves and twigs to restore the area to a near-natural condition. Pack out all your garbage and any other trash you may find. Take care with human waste; it should be buried 100 feet or more from any water source and not near possible campsites. Use only biodegradable soap and, whenever possible, wash from a bucket of water far from running sources.

Do not travel into a fenced area. The Forest Service or BLM may be protecting it for re-vegetation or protecting you from dangerous conditions, such as extremely wet roads. Private landowners do not need a reason to keep you out; respect private property. Cross streams only at designated crossings.

Watch out for lightning. Especially avoid exposed areas above the tree line during thunderstorms. If you are in a thunderstorm, don't hide under trees or in your tent. Get back into your car, if you can, or look for a cave or a deep protected overhang. If none of these is possible, crouch down as low as you can and hope for the best. Avoid narrow canyons during rainy weather; check weather reports for thunderstorm predictions. Disastrous flash flooding is a real danger.

Drinking water in lakes, rivers, and streams is not exactly the same wilderness treat it once was. Now it's more likely to provide a nasty trick – *Giardia lamblia,* a tiny protozoan that can cause big problems. Animal waste found in many water sources can give you diarrhea and violent stomach cramps, while medical attention could be far away. To avoid problems, make sure you always have adequate fresh water. On longer trips, this usually means boiling all lake and stream water for five to 10 minutes or carrying effective water purification paraphernalia, which can be purchased from area sporting goods stores.

INFORMATION SOURCES

Local information sources, including Chamber of Commerce and tourist bureaus, are included in the chapter texts that follow, but the federal and state sources below can be a big help in getting you started. All of them provide free information.

New Mexico, Tourism & Travel Division, Montoya Building, Rm 106, 1100 St. Francis Dr., Santa Fe, NM 87503, ☎ 505/827-0291.
National Forest Service, Southwestern Region, 517 Gold Avenue SW, Albuquerque, NM 87102, ☎ 505/842-3292.
National Park Service, Southwest Regional Office, 1100 Old Santa Fe Trail, Santa Fe, NM 87501, ☎ 505/988-6340.

North-Central New Mexico

North-Central New Mexico has a higher concentration of biggests and bests than any other region in the state. Most visitors begin touring this area in **Albuquerque**, the state's largest city, arriving through **Albuquerque International Airport**, again the state's largest. A spin around the city finds several fine museums, the **Rio Grande Zoo**, one of the best in the Southwest and the **Sandia Peak Tramway**, the world's longest unsupported span. The **Kodak Albuquerque International Balloon Fiesta** also calls the city home and, billed as the most photographed event in the world, is the largest balloon festival on the planet.

Just an hour north, **Santa Fe** is the oldest state capitol in the nation, having been a seat of government since 1610. But much more goes on here than politics. This is without a doubt New Mexico's premier cultural center. Santa Fe began attracting world class artists and painters in the early 1900s and, with over 150 quality galleries concentrated in the historic **Plaza** and along **Canyon Road**, has grown to become one of the largest art markets in the world. Also a leader in performing arts, the city's internationally renowned **Santa Fe Opera** stands as the finest among a number of excellent music and theater companies.

Nearby **Los Alamos**, home to **Los Alamos National Laboratory** where the first atomic bomb was developed, is the state's most affluent city, with both the lowest unemployment rate and the highest per household annual income. Just south of the "Atomic City," **Bandelier National Monument** protects one of the most important and complex ruin sites in the Southwest.

In the northern section of the region near the Colorado Border, **Chama** serves as the western depot for the **Cumbres & Toltec Scenic Railroad**, America's longest and highest narrow gauge steam railway. The **Rio Grande Gorge Bridge**, almost 100 miles to the east, is the second highest in the US, with the **Rio Grande River** running underneath. It provides the highest waves for the most intense whitewater rafting in the state.

Taos is the headquarters for all of the top rafting guides in New Mexico and is also one of the state's best destinations for all other outdoor recreation as well. The incomparable **Taos Ski Valley**

offers some of the best skiing in the world and its ski school consistently wins top honors as the #1 school in the nation.

The **Enchanted Circle**, one of the prettiest drives in New Mexico, connects the resort communities of Taos, **Red River** and **Angel Fire**, passing through some of the best hiking, biking and fishing wilderness in the state.

North-Central
New Mexico

Taos Pueblo is the largest multi-storied pueblo structure in the US. It is also the best known and most accessible of New Mexico's 19 active pueblos, 16 of which are located in the north-central region of the state. While most allow visitation, some close periodically for private ceremonies; others are only open for feast days, and a few allow no tourists whatsoever. If you visit a pueblo, it is common courtesy to check with the tribal office first upon arrival. Remember that, while on Indian land, you are subject to Indian laws, and the tribal office is the best place to inform yourself of pueblo visitor regulations. When attending dances, remain silent and respectful; these are religious ceremonies, not shows put on for your entertainment.

The areas described in this chapter range in elevation from 5,000 feet in Albuquerque to 13,161 feet at the summit of New Mexico's highest mountain, **Wheeler Peak**. If visiting from lower elevations, expect to tire quickly during your first few days in the area. Be sure to exercise special caution when engaging in vigorous outdoor activities until your body has a chance to acclimate.

North-central New Mexico is the most mountainous region of the state. Be prepared for the unexpected when participating in outdoor wilderness activities. Late summer thunderstorms develop quickly in the mountains and can drop temperatures considerably in just a few minutes. In winter, blizzards are capable of dumping more than four feet of snow a day and often shut down all travel on roads and highways, not to mention backcountry trails. Thoughtful preparation, warm layered clothing and a reasonable amount of common sense are imperative when traveling in this region.

Touring

Touring in North-Central New Mexico begins in Albuquerque. From there, head north on Interstate 25 to Santa Fe, where US 84 leads north to Chama with a side trip on NM 502 to Los Alamos. At Chama, take US 64 to Taos. There, NM 522, NM 38 and US 64 form the Enchanted Circle to Red River, Cimarron and Angel Fire, then returning to Taos.

Albuquerque

New Mexico's largest city is a sprawling metropolis of near 500,000 people on the banks of the Rio Grande River. It is sheltered by the spectacularly high cliffs of the Sandia Mountains to the east. Albuquerque lies at the junction of Interstate 25, once the heavily traveled Camino Real between Santa Fe and Mexico City, and

Interstate 40, better known as America's Old Route 66. It is a uniquely diverse blend of the antique and the contemporary, frontier town and cosmopolitan city, and man-made and natural environments, flavored by both indigenous and imported cultures, cuisines, and styles.

Perhaps the best place to begin exploration of this intriguing city is in **Old Town**, just south of Interstate 40 on the west side of town. Most of the buildings in the historic plaza date back to 1706 and Albuquerque's official founding as a Spanish colonial villa named after the Duke of Alburquerque (the first "r" was dropped in the late 1800s after the United States took over the New Mexico Territory). The magnificent **San Felipe de Neri church** dominates the square, while more than 150 shops and galleries occupy Old Town's plaza and narrow backstreets.

About one block east of Old Town, **Albuquerque Museum of Art, History and Science**, 2000 Mountain Road, ☎ 505/243-7255, documents 400 years of New Mexico's history and houses the largest collection of Spanish Colonial artifacts in the nation. The museum is open Tuesday through Sunday from 9 AM to 5 PM.

The Spanish, however, were not the first to inhabit the area. More than 200 million years ago, New Mexico's San Juan Basin was part of a flood plain with dense tropical forests and was home to thousands of dinosaurs. Just across the street from the Albuquerque Museum, a life-sized dinosaur guards the entrance to the **New Mexico Museum of Natural History**, 1801 Mountain Road, ☎ 505/841-8837. A Quetzalcoatlus with a 35-foot wingspan soars above the lobby floor of this museum that provides a vivid look at 12 billion years of history. Visitors can explore an Ice Age cave and an erupting volcano or watch the activity in a 3,000-gallon shark-infested aquarium. The museum is open daily from 9 AM to 5 PM.

Some evidence suggests man was present in the region as far back as 10-25,000 years ago. More recently, Anasazi Indians inhabited the valley during the 12th, 13th and 14th centuries.

Petroglyph National Monument, Unser Boulevard Northwest, at the foot of a lava escarpment in west Albuquerque, includes an estimated 17,000 images chipped into the rock by Anasazi and other cultures. The park is open daily from 8 AM to 5 PM, September through March, and 9 AM to 6 PM, April through August.

When the Spanish explorer-conquistador Francisco Vasquez de Coronado passed through the area in 1540, there were a number of thriving Indian pueblos along the Rio Grande. In fact, Coronado and his enormous entourage of troops, cooks and priests were guests at the now-deserted Kuaua Pueblo during the winter of

1540, while they searched for the fabled "Seven Cities of Gold." The **Coronado State Monument**, 15 miles north of Albuquerque via Interstate 25 and NM 44, preserves the ruins of the Kuaua Pueblo, which offers one of the best places to explore an authentic restored kiva (sacred ceremonial chamber – normally off-limits to non-Indians). The monument is open daily from 9 AM to 5 PM. For information, ☎ 505/867-5351.

Of New Mexico's 19 active pueblos, 16 are located in the north-central region of the state and several are quite near Albuquerque. Most allow visitation, some close periodically for private ceremonies, others are only open for feast days, and a few allow no tourists whatsoever. If visiting a pueblo, it is common courtesy to check with the tribal office first upon arrival. Remember that, while on Indian land, you are subject to Indian laws, and the tribal office is the best place to inform yourself of pueblo visitor regulations, such as admission fees, speed limits, photography allowances and use of alcohol. When attending dances, remain silent and respectful. Do not applaud, ask questions or disturb the dancers in any way, as dances are a form of prayer. These religious ceremonies are not shows put on for your entertainment and should be observed with respect.

A better place to learn about Native American culture is the **Indian Pueblo Cultural Center**, 2401 12th Street, ☎ 505/843-7270. A museum, restaurant, art galleries and gift shops exemplify the best of New Mexico's 19 pueblos. Representatives of each are usually on hand and are always happy to answer questions. Traditional dances and art demonstrations are performed every weekend and photography is allowed. The center is open daily from 9 AM to 5:30 PM.

Salinas Pueblo Mission National Monument, about 50 miles southeast of Albuquerque via Interstate 40, NM 337 and NM 55, offers another look into the history of New Mexico's pueblos. Three remarkably well-preserved pueblo ruins – Abo, Gran Quivira and Quarai – make up the monument near the town of Mountainair. They each offer visitor centers with museum-quality displays. Self-guided walking trails afford exploration of the actual pueblos. The monument is open daily from 9 AM to 5 PM. There is a general visitor center in Mountainair at the intersection of NM 55 and US 60. For information, ☎ 505/847-2585.

Albuquerque, however, is not all fossils and artifacts. As mentioned above, it is also a city of varied and sophisticated culture. The downtown skyline with its impressive skyscrapers hints at Albuquerque's cosmopolitan character, but the best illustration of the city's progressive nature lies within the prestigious halls of the

University of New Mexico. Nearly 10,000 employees and 25,000 students make this the state's largest and most influential educational facility. This prominent university offers more than 130 bachelor's degrees, just as many master's degrees and near 70 Ph.D.s, and it features outstanding medical and scientific research facilities. Several museums and galleries on campus highlight the work of the university's most promising students. The most visually entertaining of them is the **University Fine Arts Museum**, Cornell Street, ☎ 505/277-4001. It exhibits wonderfully innovative paintings, photography and sculpture by university students, as well as a fascinating permanent collection of early experimental photography, 17th-century Italian paintings, three Georgia O'Keefe paintings and photography by Ansel Adams. Other museums of interest on campus deal with anthropology, geology and biology. University museums are generally open weekdays from 9 AM to 4 PM. For information, call the University Operator at ☎ 505/277-0111.

Follow Central Avenue east to Wyoming Boulevard and the gate of Kirtland Air Force Base to find the **Atomic Energy Museum**, ☎ 505/845-6670. A guard at the gate will issue a pass and direct you to the museum. New Mexico labs have played some of the most important rolls in the development of atomic energy. This museum documents breakthroughs of Einstein and Oppenheimer, the first atomic detonation at Trinity Site, the dropping of "Fat Man" and "Little Boy" on Nagasaki and Hiroshima, as well as the latest advancements and issues of today, from energy research to nuclear waste disposal. The museum is open daily from 9 AM to 5 PM.

The **Rio Grande Zoological Park**, 903 10th Street Southwest, ☎ 505/843-7413, offers an escape from the standard museum tour. It is the state's largest, with more than 1,000 animals, and is also one of the finest in the Southwest. It is comparable to the renowned San Diego Zoo, if not in size or scope, at least in quality, cleanliness and creativity of natural habitat design. A pack of Mexican lobos, a rare wolf subspecies extinct in the wild, are the zoo's most unusual residents. The most popular are the seals and sea lions, especially at feeding time when they put on a boisterous and active show for their trainers and zoo patrons. The park also features one of the best reptile centers in the nation, boasting a rare Komodo dragon, which will one day grow to longer than 15 feet. In the wild, its preferred dinner menu might include full-grown cattle or even humans. The zoo is open daily from 9 AM to 5 PM.

Albuquerque is also home to the world's longest unsupported tram. The **Sandia Peak Tramway**, 10 Tramway Loop Northeast,

☎ 505/298-8518, carries passengers 2.7 miles in 15 minutes from the eastern edge of the city limits to a 10,378-foot peak in the Sandia Mountains, affording access to one of the area's finest restaurants (see below, under Where to Stay & Eat), the **Sandia Peak Ski Area** and excellent hiking, climbing and biking opportunities. The tram operates daily from 9 AM to 10 PM during summer, after Labor Day from 9 AM to 9 PM Monday, Tuesday, Thursday and Sunday, 9 AM to 10 PM Friday and Saturday, and 5 PM to 9 PM on Wednesday.

Other than viewing spectacular sunsets from Sandia Peak, evenings in Albuquerque center around a lively performing arts scene. The University of New Mexico's **Popejoy Hall**, ☎ 505/277-3121, saw extensive remodeling and renovation in 1995 and now plays host to various Broadway roadshow companies, the **Albuquerque Civic Light Opera Association**, ☎ 505/345-6577, and the **New Mexico Symphony Orchestra**, ☎ 505/881-8999. The **KiMo Theater**, 423 Central Avenue Northwest, ☎ 505/764-1700, is another important Albuquerque performing arts hall, hosting performances by various ballet and acting troops.

Every October, Albuquerque is the site of the world's largest gathering of hot air balloon enthusiasts. The **Kodak Albuquerque International Balloon Fiesta** attracted more than 1.5 million spectators and nearly 700 balloons in 1995. Mass ascensions are held every morning during the week-long festival. Evenings and afternoons are filled with balloon glows and special balloon rodeos – the Cheshire Cat, a fire-breathing dragon, the Energizer Rabbit and the space shuttle were some of the favorite balloons at the '95 fiesta. Interested spectators can pay to go aloft in participating balloons during the week or volunteer to join one of the chase crews, enjoying all the excitement of the week while keeping feet planted firmly on the ground. There are also several balloon companies in Albuquerque and throughout north-central New Mexico who provide ballooning adventures year-round. (See below, under Adventures In the Air.)

INFORMATION SOURCES

Albuquerque International Airport provides national and worldwide service through several commercial airlines.

America West Airlines, ☎ 800/235-9292.
American Airlines, ☎ 800/433-7300.
Continental Airlines, ☎ 800/525-0280.
Delta Airlines, Inc., ☎ 800/221-1212.

Frontier Airlines, Inc., ☎ 800/4321-FLY.
Mesa Airlines, ☎ 800/MESA-AIR.
Southwest Airlines, ☎ 800/435-9792.
Trans World Airlines (TWA), ☎ 800/325-4933.
USAir, ☎ 800/428-4322.

Rental cars are available at the airport through various agents.

Advantage, 2200 Sunport, ☎ 505/247-1066.
Avisr, 2001 Randolph Southeast, ☎ 505/842-4080 or 800/331-1212.
Budget, ☎ 505/768-5900.
Dollar, ☎ 505/842-4304 or 800/369-4226.
Hertz, ☎ 505/842-4235 or 800/654-3131.

Amtrak *provides rail service from 500 cities nationwide to Albuquerque's Santa Fe Station, 214 1st Street Southwest,* ☎ *505/842-9650 or 800/USA-RAIL.*

For more information, contact:

Albuquerque Chamber of Commerce, 401 Second Street Northwest, ☎ 505/764-3700.
Albuquerque Convention and Visitors Bureau, PO Box 26866, Albuquerque, NM 87125-6866, ☎ 505/243-3696 or 800/284-2282.

Santa Fe

New Mexico's state capitol, Santa Fe, is the oldest capital city in the United States, established 10 years before English pilgrims founded Plymouth Colony. Don Juan Peralta, governor of Spanish Colonial Nuevo Mexico, built the settlement known as La Villa Real de la Santa Fe here in 1610 as an adobe fortress and plaza designed to protect area missions involved in converting Pueblo Indians to Catholicism. The town soon evolved as the headquarters for provincial political and military leaders and the plaza's fortress became known as the **Palace of the Governors.** It is the oldest continuously used public building in the US, serving as the seat of power for both Spanish and US territorial governors from 1610 until 1881. Located on the north side of the plaza, it is now a museum, housing more than 17,000 historical objects. Display items include Jemez pottery dating to 1300, accounts of Spanish expeditions, 17th-19th-century wagons and 18th-century Spanish maps of the New World (one showing California as an island). The museum is open daily from 10 AM to 5 PM. For information, ☎ 505/827-6463.

The first 200 years of Santa Fe's history were under Spanish rule, whose isolationist policies discouraged any contact with other European settlers. Often, travelers arriving from the east were arrested for trespassing and sent to prison in Durango, Mexico. The New Mexico territory did not open to trade with the US until Mexico won its independence from Spain in 1821. Soon after, the famous Santa Fe Trail was established as the life-line for trade between Mexico and the United States. At its peak, this 1,000-mile-long dusty highway saw more than 5,000 freight wagons a year, not to mention countless covered wagons filled with prospective settlers hoping to strike it rich in this newly opened frontier. In fact, 100-year-old wagon ruts are still visible on various stretches of the trail through New Mexico's eastern prairies.

With the outbreak of the Mexican American War in 1846, General Stephen Kearny arrived in Santa Fe with 1,700 troops and claimed the territory for the United States. Mexican Governor Manual Armijo, giving in to America's "Manifest Destiny," fled to Chihuahua before any battles were fought. New Mexico was officially recognized as a US territory in 1851, and in 1879 the railroad arrived, pumping increased prosperity into the already thriving community.

By the time New Mexico was granted statehood in 1912, its capitol was already well on its way to becoming internationally known as America's premier art city. The area's magnificent landscapes and powerful skies were especially attractive to painters, and in 1921 a group known as Los Cinco Pintores banded together to pursue their artistic visions and to make their art more accessible to Santa Fe's working people. Galleries soon took over most of the buildings in the **Plaza**, spreading out from there to encompass **Canyon** and **Cerrillos Roads** as well. Today, Santa Fe is one of the largest art markets in the world, boasting more than 150 galleries within the city limits.

If you don't have time to visit hundreds of galleries but would like to see a sampling of New Mexico's best, visit the **Museum of Fine Arts**, 107 West Palace Avenue, ☎ 505/827-4468. Works by the state's foremost 20th-century artists, including Peter Hurd and Georgia O'Keeffe, are displayed on a rotating basis, along with traditional and contemporary works by prominent international artists. The museum is open daily from 10 AM to 5 PM.

Santa Fe is not, however, dedicated only to the art of painting and many area galleries feature various media from photography to sculpture or even furniture. The **Museum of International Folk**

Art, 706 Camino Lejo, ☎ 505/827-6350, illustrates this well, housing the world's largest collection of folk art. On display are more than 125,000 miscellaneous artifacts from around the world, including toys, textiles and religious art. The Hispanic Heritage Wing of the museum houses a collection focusing on the Spanish Colonial era and its influence on New Mexico's art. The museum is open daily from 10 AM to 5 PM

Of course, Native Americans inhabited the area long before the Spanish. The best way to experience their colorful and intriguing culture is to attend Santa Fe's **Indian Market**, held the third weekend in March. Collectors from all over the world converge on the city to inspect the wares of the Southwest's 500 finest artists. Rugs, jewelry, pottery, paintings, baskets, dolls – you name it; it's here. The week-long festivities also include various reenactments of ceremonial dances, which would normally only be performed during feast days on the pueblos. Note: this is one of Santa Fe's busiest times and most accommodations are booked solid a year or more in advance.

If you can't visit in August, the **Museum of Indian Arts and Culture**, 710 Camino Lejo, ☎ 505/827-6344, and the **Wheelwright Museum of the American Indian**, 704 Camino Lejo, ☎ 505/982-4636, give an impressive look into the history and culture of this area's native people. Year-round exhibits include clothing and spear point collections dating to 550 A.D., Anasazi pottery and 16th-20th-century pueblo dioramas and artifacts. Resource centers with rotating exhibits feature hands-on displays portraying such characteristics of Native American life as rug making, art, jewelry and music. The Museum of Indian Arts and Culture is open daily from 10 AM to 5 PM The Wheelwright Museum is open Monday through Saturday from 10 AM to 5 PM and Sunday from 1 to 5 PM

The Palace of the Governors Museum, Fine Arts Museum, Museum of International Folk Art and Museum of Indian Arts and Culture comprise the **Museum of New Mexico**. An entry pass for one is good at all four.

The grand rotunda at the **State Capitol Building**, Paseo de Peralta and Old Santa Fe Trail, ☎ 505/986-4589, also features exhibits on loan from the New Mexico Museum. The **Governor's Gallery** there displays work by local artists. The Capitol is open to visitors Monday through Saturday from 8 AM to 5 PM. The Governors Gallery, however, is closed on Saturday.

A number of other interesting sites around town are worth a look if you have time to do a little exploring. Just off the Plaza, **Cathedral of Saint Francis of Assisi**, 131 Cathedral Place, ☎ 505/982-5619, was built in 1869 on the site of Santa Fe's original mission, Our Lady of Assumption, built in 1610. The cathedral was designed by a team of French architects commissioned by Archbishop Jean Baptiste Lamy, perhaps the city's best-known historical figure, made famous by Willa Cather's book, *Death Comes to the Archbishop*. Its Romanesque style and stained glass stand in sharp contrast to the pueblo buildings surrounding it. The church is open daily from 6 AM to 6 PM.

Loretto Chapel, 211 Old Santa Fe Trail, ☎ 505/988-5531, was built in 1878 for the sisters of Loretto, six women who arrived with Archbishop Lamy. Modeled after Sainte Chapelle in Paris, it is one of Santa Fe's most interesting historical churches. Legend has it that the original craftsmen completed the building without installing any way to access its elevated choir loft. Short on funds, the nuns gathered to pray for a solution. Soon, an unknown carpenter arrived and single-handedly constructed a beautiful spiraling staircase that completes two 360-degree turns, but has no visible means of support. When he finished, the man mysteriously disappeared without ever asking for or receiving any payment for the job. The chapel is open daily from 9 AM to 4:30 PM

San Miguel Mission, 401 Old Santa Fe Trail, is the oldest surviving mission in the area and the longest continuously used church in the United States. It was built in 1610 to serve the overflow from Santa Fe's first mission and still contains religious artifacts created by Spanish Colonists and converted Pueblo Indians, including buffalo and deer-hide painted depictions of Jesus. The mission is open May to October, Monday through Saturday from 9 AM to 4:30 PM and Sunday from 1 to 4:30 PM. The rest of the year, it is open Monday through Saturday from 11 AM to 4 PM and 1 to 4 PM on Sunday.

Just around the corner, two small adobe rooms, believed to have been built in 1250, stand preserved as the **Oldest House in the US**, 215 East De Vargas Street, ☎ 505/983-8206. A number of galleries and shops surround the historic site, taking advantage of its tourist draw.

As if Santa Fe's history and visual arts aren't enough for its visitors, the city has also attained international acclaim through music, boasting a symphony, orchestra, and world-class opera. The **Santa Fe Symphony**, ☎ 505/983-3530, performs roughly 15 concerts a year, featuring both classical and contemporary works. **Santa Fe Pro Musica**, ☎ 505/988-4640, presents orchestral and chamber ensemble concerts from September through May. Works performed range from contemporary Hispanic pieces to Mozart, Bach or Haydn.

Each summer, from mid-July to mid-August, some 50 acclaimed soloists collaborate to present a concert and lecture series known as the **Santa Fe Chamber Music Festival**. The festival actually celebrates a wide variety of musical genres, with one night a week reserved for concerts geared specifically to younger audiences. Performances are always splendid, and rehearsals at St. Francis Auditorium are usually open to the public, offering a fascinating look into the intense preparation required to perform the world's finest music. For information, ☎ 505/983-2075.

The world-renowned **Santa Fe Opera** is the pinnacle of the city's performance art scene. Its beautifully designed outdoor amphitheater hosts one of the country's finest summer opera companies. Established in 1957, the opera runs from late June through August, presenting both classic favorites and delightful premieres. You may also attend gourmet dinners or tours of the grounds before each night's performance, during which a representative from the company will tell about and answer questions relating to the evening's selection. The amphitheater is located seven miles north of town via US 84/285. For information, contact the Santa Fe Opera, PO Box 2408, Santa Fe, 87504-2408, ☎ 505/986-5900 or 505/986-5955.

But Santa Fe is not all classical music aficionados, art collectors and historians. The city still conforms to the casual New Mexico standard and, while tuxedos and evening gowns are often worn to many of the city's productions, so are blue jeans and cowboy boots. Summer on the plaza sees shoppers and even those visiting the most prestigious art galleries wearing comfortable T-shirts and shorts.

New Mexico's casual atmosphere stems from the amount of outdoor recreational options it offers and Santa Fe is no slouch in this arena either. The surrounding **Sangre de Cristo Mountains** and **Santa Fe National Forest** present copious opportunities for year-round hiking, biking and jeep touring. During winter, the **Santa Fe Ski Area** attracts thousands of visitors, and during summer, rafters, kayakers and fishermen flock to the nearby **Rio Grande River**. (See below, under Adventures.) Santa Fe is also home to one of the state's largest horse tracks. Every summer from June through Labor Day, thoroughbreds and quarter horses race against the spectacular backdrop of the Sangre de Cristo Mountains at **The Downs at Santa Fe**, just minutes from town on Interstate 25 South. For information, ☎ 505/471-4037.

INFORMATION SOURCES

Most visitors to Santa Fe fly into the Albuquerque International Airport and drive up, but **Mesa Air**, ☎ 800/MESA-AIR, does provide passenger service into the capital city.

Rental cars are available in Santa Fe through **Ugly Duckling**, ☎ 505/989-8100, **Adopt A Car**, ☎ 505/473-3189, and **Thrifty Car Rental**, ☎ 505/984-1961.

For information, contact **Santa Fe Chamber of Commerce**, PO Box 1928, Santa Fe, NM 87504-1928, ☎ 505/983-7317. Or contact **Santa Fe Convention and Visitors Bureau**, PO Box 909, Santa Fe, NM 87501, ☎ 505/984-6760 or 800/777-City.

Los Alamos

One of America's most affluent communities, **Los Alamos** boasts the lowest unemployment rate and highest income in the state (49% of the households have income of $50,000 or more a year; nationally, only 13% earn that). This results directly from the fact that most of the town's residents are highly educated and employed by Los Alamos National Laboratory, which is one of the nation's foremost science and technology research centers. The laboratory's origins were as a top-secret closed compound for military weapons development during World War II. It was here in 1943 that General Leslie Groves gathered J. Robert Oppenheimer and a number of the world's most brilliant scientists to embark upon the Manhattan Project and thus create the world's most powerful weapon – the atomic bomb. Two bombs developed here, "Fat Man" and "Little Boy," were dropped on key cities in Japan, striking the final blows to end World War II.

Los Alamos remained a small, closed city for nearly a decade after the War but, since security dropped in 1957, it has grown to more than 18,000 people. Rather than hold onto its reputation as "The Atomic City," Los Alamos has instead evolved into a choice recreation and tourism destination.

Two museums in town help tourists appreciate the city's interesting past. **Los Alamos Historical Museum**, 1921 Juniper Street, ☎ 505/662-4493, is dedicated to preserving the area's civic history. The museum is open Monday through Saturday from 10 AM to 4 PM and Sunday from 1 to 4 PM. The **Bradbury Science Museum**,

15th and Central Streets, ☎ 505/667-4444, arranges exhibits to provide insight into events that took place in New Mexico during the 1940s with the development of the atomic bomb. The museum also provides an up-to-date look at current laser and computer technologies. The museum is open Tuesday through Friday from 9 AM to 5 PM and Saturday through Monday from 1 to 5 PM

The biggest draw in Los Alamos, however, is **Bandelier National Monument**, just 10 miles south of town via NM 4. The monument encompasses 32,737 acres of the Pajarito Plateau and several lush canyons, where a number of large Anasazi cliff dwellings and pueblo ruins were found in the 1880s. A three-mile drive from the entrance takes visitors past a scenic overlook and down into Frijoles Canyon and the park headquarters. From a visitor center there, several trails of varying lengths wander out into the wilderness, accessing ruins believed to have been inhabited from 1100 to 1550 A.D. The main Frijoles Canyon ruins are visited by a 1½-mile loop trail that passes every type of ruin found at the monument. Many of the ruins are extremely well-preserved and others have been carefully restored. Most are open to public exploration. Feel free to enter and poke around as long as you like, but remember that removal of any artifact carries a fine of up to $100,000. (See below, under Adventures on Foot.) For information, ☎ 505/672-3861. Camping is available.

The **Jemez Mountains** of the **Santa Fe National Forest** also entice visitors into the area for backpacking, biking, camping and cross-country skiing. The mountains are home to the **Pajarito Ski Area**, one of the state's better kept secrets. (See below, under Adventures.)

For information, contact **Los Alamos Chamber of Commerce**, PO Box 460, Los Alamos, 87544, ☎ 505/662-8105 or 800/444-0707.

Chama

Located at 8,000 feet in the San Juan Mountains just nine miles from the Colorado border, **Chama** is a sleepy old mining town that now survives with healthy lumbering, ranching and tourism industries. It's best known as the departure point for the **Cumbres and Toltec Scenic Railroad** (see below under Adventures on Wheels), but it is also close to two major recreation lakes (see below, under Adventures on Water).

For information, contact **Chama Chamber of Commerce**, PO Box 306, Chama, 88710, ☎ 505/756-2306 or 800/477-0149.

Taos

Nestled on the western edge of the Sangre de Cristo mountains, **Taos** is one of those wonderful little towns that people just fall irresistibly in love with. The town is steeped in history and is quite a prominent artist colony, but most visitors are drawn to the area by its year-round recreational opportunities, including snow skiing at **Taos Ski Valley**, fishing on the **Rio Grande** and high alpine lakes, whitewater rafting through the **Taos Box**, and hiking, biking and camping in the wilderness of the surrounding **Carson National Forest**.

According to a Taos Indian legend, their ancestors were led into the valley by an eagle more than 800 years ago. Whether that's true or not, inhabitants of the **Taos Pueblo** were here to greet the Spanish when they arrived in 1540. Their pueblo stands as the largest existing multi-storied pueblo structure in the US and is one of the oldest continually inhabited communities in the country – more than 700 years. Located two miles north of Taos, the Taos Pueblo is the northernmost of 19 active pueblos and is New Mexico's best-known Indian village. The community is open to non-Indian visitors most of the year and pueblo artisans operate several shops and galleries where they display and sell beautiful handcrafted pottery, tanned buckskin clothing, and silver and turquoise jewelry. If you visit, remember this is not a shopping mall but a living community and home of the Taos Indians. Be respectful of their privacy and cultural differences. Check in at the visitor office before entering and pay photography, sketching and video camera fees. No photography is allowed on Feast Days or during ceremonial dances, and you should always ask permission before photographing people. For information, ☎ 505/758-9593.

Like most of New Mexico's native people, the Taos Indians were living peacefully when the Spanish arrived in 1540 and initial contact was friendly. But by 1650, relations had strained due to increasing numbers and frequent intermarriages. The Taos Pueblo became one of the key instigators of the 1680 Pueblo Revolt that drove the Spaniards out of New Mexico completely. The revolt only lasted 12 years, though, and the Spaniards returned to Taos in 1692.

Their influence is easily visible in much of Taos' art and architecture, especially in the downtown **Plaza** area. Several quality museums are dedicated to documenting the area's Spanish history. The **Martinez Hacienda** is a completely restored Spanish Colonial home built in 1804. The 21 rooms are furnished to recreate the look and feel of when Don Antonio Severino Martinis, an early Taos mayor and prominent merchant, lived there with his family. The hacienda has two large patios enclosed by thick adobe walls, creating a type of fortress to protect residents from the dangers of living on the wild New Mexican frontier. Costumed interpreters are usually on hand, presenting demonstrations on Hispanic culture and 19th-century frontier life. The museum is located two miles south of the plaza via NM 240 and is open daily from 9 AM to 5 PM. For information, ☎ 505/758-1000.

The best known remnant of Spanish culture, however, is **San Francisco de Assisi Church** in Ranchos de Taos, just south of Taos proper. The church is found in the middle of Ranchos de Taos' old plaza on the east side of NM 68. Impressive because of its towering four-foot-thick adobe walls and interesting lines, it has long been a favorite of local artists and visiting photographers, and may well be the most photographed structure in New Mexico.

As for artists, Taos has been attracting them since the mid-1800s and by the turn of the century the Taos Society of Artists had attracted the attentions of important East Coast buyers and collectors. In 1917, the wealthy East Coast patroness, Mable Dodge, moved to the growing artist colony and, enticing her well-known artist friends to join her there, she cemented Taos' reputation as one of the best artist communities in the West. Notables who joined Dodge in New Mexico included Andrew Dasburg, Georgia O'Keefe, Ansel Adams, John Marin and D.H. Lawrence.

The **Blumenschein Home and Museum**, 222 Ledoux Street, ☎ 505/758-0330, is a restored 1790 adobe home that was purchased and remodeled in 1919 by Ernest Blumenschein, one of the co-founders of the Taos Society of Artists. On display are original works by Blumenschein and other early Taos artists as well as antique furniture and Spanish Colonial pieces. The museum is open daily from 9 AM to 5 PM.

The **Harwood Foundation Library and Museum**, 238 Ledoux Street, ☎ 505/758-3063, is housed in a complex of Spanish Colonial adobe buildings and encompasses a museum, library and research center. A large collection of books by D.H. Lawrence, contemporary paintings, Indian sculpture and Spanish religious carvings make up exhibits in the museum, which is open Monday through Saturday from 10 AM in summer and from noon in winter.

D.H. Lawrence fans will also be interested in visiting the **D.H. Lawrence Gallery** at **La Fonda de Taos Hotel** on the plaza. About a dozen of Lawrence's paintings, created while in Taos, are displayed in a tiny room behind the main desk. Also on display are a handful of letters, photos and other personal effects.

The **Millicent Rogers Museum** displays the personal collection of Indian and Spanish Colonial art amassed by Millicent Rogers, heiress to the Standard Oil fortune, who lived in Taos from 1947 until her death in 1953. Also on display are pieces donated by friends and other patrons, including 14th-century Zuni pottery, a Spanish Colonial "death cart" and works by Maria Martinez, the famous San Ildefonso potter. Take NM 522 four miles north of Taos, then make a sharp left turn around the gas station and follow the road paralleling the highway back toward town; look for the museum on the right side of the road. The museum is open daily from 9 AM to 5 PM, closed on Monday during winter. For information, ☎ 505/758-2462.

Taos was also greatly influenced by French trappers and colonial-American mountain men who came to town in the early 19th century to trade furs and what have you for other needed supplies. Kit Carson was the most well-known among that group and his name is given to the national forest surrounding the area. His house is now the site of the **Kit Carson Museum**, one block east of the plaza on Kit Carson Road, ☎ 505/758-4741. Displays in the 12-room adobe relate to Carson's role as a trapper, mountain guide and Indian fighter. Various items include saddles, firearms, clothing, utensils and tools from Northern New Mexico's rowdy 19th century. The museum is open daily from 9 AM to 5 PM in winter and 8 AM to 6 PM in summer.

The true charm of Taos, however, is found by exploring the plaza and the narrow backstreets, visiting galleries and studios of current artists or soaking up the laid-back atmosphere in little bookstores, restaurants and gift shops.

For information, contact **Taos County Chamber of Commerce**, PO Drawer I, Taos, NM 87571, ☎ 505/758-3873 or 800/732-8267.

Red River

Dating back to the early 1900s as a mountain camp for miners and trappers, **Red River** remains one of the most popular resort communities in New Mexico. With only 400 year-round residents and no museums or other citified tourist attractions, the town relies on sheer natural beauty and limitless outdoor recreation to draw visitors. Red River is enveloped by the Carson National Forest and serves as a fabulous headquarters for mountain biking, fishing, hiking, cross-country skiing, snowmobiling or what have you.

For information, contact **Carson National Forest-Supervisor's Office**, PO Box 558, Taos, NM 87571, ☎ 505/758-6200.

Red River Ski Area, however, is the town's largest visitor magnet and operates in various capacities to serve guests year-round.

For information, contact **Red River Chamber of Commerce**, PO Box 870, Red River, NM 87558, ☎ 504/754-2366 or 800/348-6444.

Cimarron

Cimarron was once an important stop along the Mountain Route of the Santa Fe Trail and a gathering place for traders, trappers, miners, ranchers, businessmen and homesteaders. In the late 1800s, it had even attracted such prominent New Mexicans as Lucien Maxwell, "Buffalo" Bill Cody and Henri Lambert. Early days here saw Maxwell, the largest landowner in the country, build a mansion that covered an entire city block (destroyed by fire in 1922) and Cody organize his famous Wild West Shows. Lambert, personal chef to both President Lincoln and General Ulysses S. Grant, created the elegant **St. James Hotel** which continues in operation today. But, when the Atchison, Topeka & Santa Fe Railroad passed this community by in favor of Raton, activity slowed dramatically. Home to fewer than 1,000 people, the town relies as much on the natural beauty of its surroundings as on historical sites to entice visitors. **Cimarron Canyon State Park**, between Cimarron and Eagle Nest via US 64, is one of the state's best areas for fall color. Also, the **Cimarron River** and its tributaries present superb fishing waters and its banks through the canyon are lined with picturesque national forest campgrounds.

Most outdoor enthusiasts have heard of **Philmont Scout Ranch**. Donated to the Boy Scouts of America by oil magnate Waite Phillips in 1938, the ranch encompasses 137,493 acres and is the BSA's National Training Center and High Adventure Base. More than 25,000 Scouts, Explorers and leaders visit here every year to participate in camping, hiking, fishing, rock climbing, rappelling and other mountain pursuits.

Two museums on the ranch are open to the public. The **Philmont Museum**, four miles south of Cimarron via NM 21, incorporates Villa Philmont, a separate building, home to Waite Phillips from 1922 to 1927. Modeled after buildings Phillips saw while on cruises in the Mediterranean, the sprawling villa is furnished mostly with items bought overseas, yet the floors are covered with rugs made from the skins of indigenous bears and mountain lions. The highlight of the museum proper is the **Seton Library**, featuring the works of Ernest Thompson Seton, naturalist, writer, sculptor, and painter. His 3,000 paintings of birds, rabbits, elk, and other wildlife are on rotating display here year-round. The museum is open daily from 8 AM to 5 PM during summer, but only on weekends the rest of the year.

Kit Carson Museum, 10 miles south of Cimarron via NM 21, is an interpretive history museum run by Philmont staffers who live on the premises. Dressed in 19th-century garb, staffers give blacksmithing, candle-making, and other craft demonstrations. They also lead room-by-room tours of Carson's old adobe compound. The museum is open daily from 8 AM to 5 PM during summer only.

For information regarding the ranch or either museum, ☎ 505/376-2281.

In Cimarron, the **Old Mill Museum**, NM 21, ☎ 505/376-2913, houses historical photos and documents, Native American tools and weapons, early surgical equipment and musical instruments, and various other items relating to local history. The museum is open May to October, Monday through Saturday from 9 AM to 5 PM and Sunday from 1 to 5 PM.

For information, contact **Cimarron Chamber of Commerce**, PO Box 604, Cimarron, NM 87714, ☎ 505/376-2417.

Angel Fire

Established in 1965 as a family ski area, **Angel Fire** has recently grown into a quality year-round resort, featuring an 18-hole PGA-rated championship golf course, a number of fine tennis facilities and a small fishing lake.

Just outside of town on US 64, the **DAV Vietnam Veterans National Memorial** pays tribute to those who fought and died in Vietnam. The 24-acre monument is one of the largest in the country and stands stark and strong against the majestic backdrop of the Sangre de Cristo Mountains. There's an interdenominational chapel and a visitor center at the monument. Both are open daily from 8 AM to 5 PM.

For information, contact **Angel Fire Chamber of Commerce**, PO Box 547, Angel Fire, NM 88710, ☎ 505/377-6611 or 800/446-8117.

Adventures

On Foot

Albuquerque's eastern horizon is dominated by thousand-foot cliffs on the Sandia Mountains' west face. More than 70 specific rock formations are recognized on the western face and together they comprise the most spectacular rock climbing area in the state. The **Shield** is the largest formation in the range and is, perhaps, the most popular among climbers. It rises more than 1,000 feet at the north end of the Sandias and offers 20 designated routes ranging from 5.4 to 5.11a in difficulty and two to 13 pitches in length (a pitch is usually 100 to 150 feet). The **Needle**, originally called the pyramid, is the next major formation south of the Shield and was probably the site of the first climb in the Sandias back in the 1930s. Climbers may choose from 10 routes on this impressive spire, ranging from 5.4 to 5.8 in difficulty and from three to 15 pitches in length. Tombstone, Sentinel, Torreon and Muralla Grande are names of other popular formations in the range. *Hikers & Climbers Guide to the Sandias*, by Mike Hill, University of New Mexico Press, 1993, is the best climbing guide for this area and should be required reading for anyone considering technical climbing in the Sandias. It also provides a comprehensive list and descriptions of general hiking and backpacking trails in the area.

Piedra Lisa Spring Trail is a popular trail along the base of the Sandias at the northern end of the range. It travels five miles from the Juan Tabo Picnic Area, off Tramway in northeastern Albuquerque, to Piedra Lisa Spring, where a car shuttle is possible via Interstate 25, NM 165 and Forest Road 445. Several spurs branch from this trail leading to the base of the Shield, a waterfall and an abandoned mine. La Luz and Pino Canyon Trails are the two most popular hiking routes from Albuquerque to the crest of the range. **La Luz** gains more than 3,700 feet over seven miles and is a strenuous trek for even the most physically fit hikers. It departs from a trailhead at Juan Tabo Picnic Area and joins South Crest Trail just 0.8 miles north of the upper tram terminal, where exhausted adventurers may opt for a leisurely 15-minute return to the base. Or ride the tram up and hike La Luz Trail down to enjoy its spectacular views with much less strain. Allow three to five hours to walk the trail one-way and expect to be on the trail most of the day if hiking the full circuit. **Pino Canyon Trail** only climbs 2,680 feet from a start at Elena Gallegos Picnic Area to where it joins South Crest Trail 4½ miles from the trailhead. It is a much easier hike than La Luz Trail but finishes nearly three miles south of the tram terminal. **South Crest Trail** is the longest in the Sandias, climbing 4,000 feet over 16 miles from a trailhead at Canyon Estates, just off Interstate 25, to its end at a parking area just past the intersection with La Luz Trail. Cross the parking area to continue along the ridge on **North Crest Trail** 12 more miles to Tunnel Spring at the end of the range. The Tunnel Spring trailhead can be reached via Interstate 25, NM 165, and Forest Road 231 for a convenient car shuttle at the end of the 28-mile hike. This combination is a popular two-or three-day backpacking trip. Plan to carry plenty of water when hiking in the Sandia Crest as springs are few and often unreliable. NM 14 and NM 536, off Interstate 40 east of Albuquerque, afford access to numerous other hiking opportunities in the Sandias. Use the topo map that accompanies *Hikers & Climbers Guide to the Sandias* or the Placitas, Sandia Crest and Tijeras 7.5-minute USGS quads when hiking in this area.

Cochiti Mesa, roughly 10 miles northeast of Cochiti Lake via Dome Road 289, offers some of New Mexico's best sport climbing. Established routes are well bolted, often featuring solid two-bolt anchors, although there is limitless rock for developing new ascents. Most climbs range from 60 to 75 feet tall and from 5.6 to 5.13 in difficulty. A climber's guide entitled *Sport Climbing in New Mexico*, by Randal Jett and Matt Samet, copyright 1991, is available in Albuquerque bookstores or climbing shops.

For those interested in rock climbing, but who are smart enough not to attempt anything untrained, **Albuquerque Rock Gym**, 3300 Princeton Northeast #S-30, ☎ 505/881-3073, presents the best indoor climbing and instruction in the area. They also schedule outdoor climbing seminars at various area locations. Rental shoes and harnesses are available for use in the gym and ropes are provided.

REI (Recreational Equipment Inc.), 1905 Mountain Road, ☎ 505/247-1191, is Albuquerque's (and New Mexico's, for that matter) best supplier of outdoor gear, clothing and information. They also feature a fine rental department and offer various free clinics during the year.

The **Sangre de Cristo Mountains** stretch from Santa Fe north to the state's border with Colorado. Most of the best hiking around New Mexico's capital city is in these mountains, encompassed by the **Santa Fe National Forest** and offering more than 1,000 miles of mapped trails.

Take Hyde Park Road/NM 475 northeast of Santa Fe 15 miles to a parking area just below the ski area, where a sign indicates the trailhead to **Santa Fe Baldy**. This is probably the most popular hike in this part of the forest, covering about seven miles from the parking lot to the 12,622-foot peak of one of the highest peaks in the region. The trail is well worn and easy to follow the entire way. Begin on **Windsor Trail #254** and follow it about three miles to a juncture with **Trail #160**. Continue along these combined trails about a quarter-mile until the intersection with **Trail #251**. Trail #254 continues to **Spirit Lake**, but a left onto the new trail leads up to the crest of an 11,600-foot ridge. Again turn left, leaving the trail you were on, and follow the ridge to the summit of Santa Fe Baldy. This last section is the steepest and most strenuous of the hike, climbing more than 1,000 feet in less than one mile, but the 360° views of the surrounding wilderness are well worth the effort. On clear days, Wheeler Peak, New Mexico's highest at 13,161 feet, will be visible to the north and Albuquerque's Sandia Mountains will rise in the south. Backtrack the way you came to complete this 14-mile trek, which can be done as a strenuous day hike or moderate overnighter. The only reliable water is found in the Rio Nambe about 2½ miles from the trailhead – be sure to boil or treat any water taken in the backcountry before use.

For extended backpacking, remain on Trail #251 to **Lake Katherine** at the northeastern foot of Santa Fe Baldy. Camp here, then continue on #251 past **Stewart Lake** to a juncture with **Trail #288**. Turn right, paralleling Cave Creek to find the **Cave Creek Caves**. The stream actually flows through a long section of the caves. If you enter the caves, be sure to wear hardhats, carry three sources of light and never enter alone. The caves are wet, slippery and have a number of steep drops. Whether entering the caves or not, the lush forests in this area are beautiful enough to make this trek worthwhile. From here, return the way you came or continue on Trail #288 to **Panchuela Campground**, near Cowles about 25 miles north of Pecos via NM 63, where a pre-arranged car shuttle can end your hike.

Always carry rain gear and warm clothes when hiking in this region, as even in summer quickly developing thunderstorms can drop temperatures 20 to 30° in a matter of minutes.

Use the Santa Fe National Forest and Pecos Wilderness maps; the Aspen Basin and Cowles 7.5-minute USGS quads further detail trekking excursions in this area.

For information, contact the **Santa Fe National Forest office**, 1220 St. Francis Drive, PO Box 1689, Santa Fe, NM 87504, ☎ 505/988-6940.

For light day hikes in the Santa Fe Area, head to **Santa Fe Ski Area**. The main chairlift there runs during summer to take sightseers to the 12,000-foot summit. Ride up, enjoy the views and stroll down one of the trails back to the base. For information, ☎ 505/982-4429.

Bandelier National Monument, 10 miles south of Los Alamos via Route 4, has more than 70 miles of maintained trails, leading through beautiful canyons and over impressive plateaus to various ancient Indian ruins. The **Main Ruins Trail** is a 1½-mile loop leaving from the visitor center in Frijoles Canyon. The ancient dwellings visited on this trail are representative of every type of ruin found in the monument. The first structure encountered will be Tyuonyi or "Meeting Place," a circular pueblo foundation believed to have been more than three stories tall. A little further up the canyon, the stone walls of Talus House need only a roof to restore them to their original state. Next, Long House is thought to have been the largest settlement in the area. Nestled under a cliff, many of the rooms here are natural caves, while others were actually carved out of the cliff wall's soft volcanic tuff. From Long House, the loop trail continues back to the visitor center, passing through a pretty picnic area on the way. The trail to **Ceremonial Cave** proceeds past Long House, crossing a permanent stream and following it up the canyon. About half a mile from the creek, crossing signs indicate the climb up to the cave high in the north wall of the canyon. A series of Indian-style ladders access the natural shelter, which contains a restored kiva – the highlight of the cave. Return via the same route. Because of heavy trail use, obtaining water from the creek is not recommended. It is best to carry all that you will need.

To get away from the crowds that usually mob the main ruins during summer and on weekends, try an extended backpacking trip to some of the lesser known but equally impressive sites in the monument. The hike to the **Shrine of the Stone Lions** is a strenuous two- or three-day affair covering 18 miles, but is well worth it for the solitude found in the heart of the Bandelier Wilderness. A marked trailhead is found at the picnic area across the creek from the visitor center, beginning with a steep climb out of Frijoles Canyon. The first third of the trip is the hardest and most exposed, crossing several steep canyons and arid plateaus but getting easier and more scenic the farther you go. Alamo Canyon is roughly halfway to the lions. Although visually spectacular, the steep trail across the 600-foot deep canyon is one of the toughest obstacles on the hike. From there, you will cross one more small canyon before passing **Yapashi Ruins** on the left side of the trail. The ruined walls of this ancient pueblo make for some interesting exploration, but please try not to disturb or remove any artifacts as the site has not officially been excavated. The Shrine of the Stone Lions is just down the trail from Yapashi Pueblo, about six miles from the trailhead. Two carved lions (barely recognizable, due to years of erosion) stand in the center of a stone ring, creating a shrine like none other found in the Southwest. Local Indians still visit and consider the site sacred, so no camping is permitted within a quarter-mile of it or the pueblo ruins. No water will be available until the Upper Alamo Canyon crossing, about nine miles into the hike, where you will find a usually reliable creek (you should check at the visitor center first to see if it's flowing). In the heat of summer, you will need about a gallon of water per person per day, so plan accordingly. Three miles further, the trail drops back down into Frijoles Canyon and the remaining six miles are an easy stroll beside a permanent stream, leading past Ceremonial Cave and into the Main Ruins area, where reappearing crowds heighten your appreciation of the just completed adventure.

Upper and Lower Falls Trail follows Frijoles Canyon south from the Bandelier visitor center to two large waterfalls about 1½ miles down the trail. The hike, from the trailhead at the backcountry parking area, descends a well-marked trail through lush riparian vegetation to the falls and returns the same way. The uphill return leg is more strenuous and may be quite hot during summer. Heavy trail use necessitates boiling or treating any water taken from Frijoles Creek. Since the hike is relatively short, it is easier just to carry an adequate water supply. Use Bandelier National Monument's "Trails Illustrated" topo map (available at the visitor center) or the Frijoles 7.5-minute USGS quad for these hikes in the Bandelier Wilderness.

Tsankawi Ruin is also part of Bandelier National Monument, but is located 11 miles north of Frijoles Canyon via NM 4, detached from the main body of the park. From an information station and marked trailhead on the east side of the road, a 1½-mile loop trail leads to the ruins atop a high mesa overlooking the Rio Grande Valley. Thousands of ancient feet have worn sections of the trail more than two feet deep into the soft rock of the mesa – one of the more interesting details of the trek. At the crown of the loop, visitors must climb an Indian-style ladder to reach the ruins of the crumbling 350-room pueblo. Also interesting are the numerous petroglyphs adorning the rock on the mesa, while views across the valley to the Sangre de Cristo Mountains in the east are quite spectacular, especially at sunset when the mountains blaze with bright reds and oranges. This trail is shown on Bandelier National Monument's "Trails Illustrated" topo map (available at the visitor center in Frijoles Canyon) and there is a trail guide available at the trailhead information station. The White Rock 7.5-minute USGS quad also shows this route.

For information, contact Bandelier National Monument, ☎ 505/672-3861.

A good number of choice crags for rock climbing are located in the general vicinity of Taos. There are no printed guidebooks on these areas, but **Mountain Skills**, PO Box 490, Taos, NM 87571, ☎ 505/758-9589 or 800/584-6863, offers technical rock climbing trips and instruction to people of all ages, fitness levels and commitment levels.

Hiking in the Rio Grande Gorge at the **Wild Rivers National Recreation Area**, 35 miles north of Taos via NM 522 and NM 378, ☎ 505/239-7211, is a fun alternative to the mountain hikes which dominate north-central New Mexico. An 800-foot-deep canyon has been sliced through the plains of northern New Mexico by the Rio Grande or "Great River," creating an area of rugged beauty and exciting recreational opportunities. The recreation area is located at the confluence of the Rio Grande and the Red River, two of America's nationally designated Wild and Scenic Rivers. A variety of hiking options are available here on 22 miles of trails. Five campgrounds are located on the canyon rim and a six-mile loop trail connects them with the recreation area visitor center. Each rim site has a corresponding riverside campground and each of these is connected via a hiking trail paralleling the river. Big Arsenic Springs, Little Arsenic Springs, La Junta and El Aguaje rim campgrounds feature trails connecting them to their riverside alter-egos. Descent trails into the canyon are steep and switchbacking, ranging from 560 feet to 800 feet. Combine these descent/ascent routes with the rim and riverside trails to create fun down-and-back day hikes or extended overnight backpacking trips. Water is available at the rim campgrounds and at Little Arsenic and Big Arsenic Springs by the river. Boil or treat any water taken from the springs. "The Wild Rivers Recreation Area" brochure, available at the visitor center, shows these trails in adequate detail, or use the Guadaloupe Mountain 7.5-minute USGS quad.

The hike to the summit of **Wheeler Peak**, New Mexico's highest at 13,161 feet, is one of the most popular treks in the Carson National Forest. The trailhead is marked by a large Wheeler Peak Wilderness sign in the upper parking lot at Taos Ski Valley. The first two miles of the trail are steep and rocky, crossed several times by old roads and other trails, but the route to Wheeler Peak is well-worn and easy to follow, especially on weekends in summer when you can simply follow the other people on the trail. At two miles, the trail forks near the edge of Bull-of-the-Woods Pasture. A sign points to the right fork as the correct route to the peak, following an old road for the first mile from the pasture. After that, the road becomes an obvious trail and is easy to follow for the remaining four miles to the summit. This last stretch, however, traces an exposed ridge and is very susceptible to lightning. If storms are brewing, do not continue past Bull-of-the-Woods Mountain. Seven miles from the trailhead, you will reach the summit of Mt. Walter at 13,133 feet. Don't let this one fool you; Wheeler Peak lies another half-mile ahead. From New Mexico's highest peak, spectacular views extend well into Colorado. Linger too long, though, and you're liable to be caught in an afternoon hail or thunderstorm. Complete the 15-mile journey by returning to the trailhead the way you came. With an early start, this hike can be done in one day but is quite exhausting as it climbs nearly 4,000 feet from bottom to top. If planning an overnight, the best campsite along the way is found at about five miles, when the trail drops into a small valley with a good stream for water. Use a Carson National Forest map or the Wheeler Peak 7.5-minute USGS quad for this hike.

If it's standing room only on the trail to Wheeler Peak, consider climbing **Gold Hill** instead. At 12,711 feet, the views from its summit are almost as stunning as from Wheeler's. Hike the first two miles of the Wheeler Peak Trail to the fork at Bull-of-the-Woods Pasture, turn left, go 50 feet and turn left again onto Forest Service Trail #64 to Gold Hill. The route is easy to follow all of the way, covering about 10 miles there and back. Yet, it remains a strenuous trek as it climbs nearly 3,500 feet. Again, get an early start if you want to complete this hike in a day. Use a Carson National Forest Map or the Wheeler Peak and Red River 7.5-minute USGS quads when hiking here.

An easier hike in the Carson National Forest is found seven miles south of Red River via NM 578. Take the turn-off to the **East Fork of the Red River** marked by a bridge 6.2 miles from town at the end of the pavement. The road splits in several directions across the bridge. Turn right, following Forest Road 58-A 1¼ miles to a marked trailhead at road's end. Trail #56 parallels the East Fork of the Red River 3¼ miles to the eastern boundary of the Wheeler Peak Wilderness. Return the way you came to complete a fun day-hike. Create a 14-mile loop for a good overnighter by incorporating Trail #91 and Forest Service Road 58 and 58-A. Lost Lake, about three miles west of the wilderness boundary, offers the best camping possibilities. Trail #91 follows the Middle Fork of the Red River down to Forest Road 58 and on to the bridge at the East Fork turn-off. Water, if boiled or treated, is available from both forks of the river, from Lost Lake and from several streams along the way.

Use a Carson National Forest map or the Wheeler Peak 7.5-minute USGS quad to further detail this hike.

From Memorial Day Weekend through Labor Day, the scenic summer chairlift at **Red River Ski Area** carries hikers to an elevation of 10,350 feet, offering 1,525 vertical feet of descent without the struggle of an uphill climb. For information, ☎ 505/754-2223.

Rock climbing and camping are permitted at **Cimarron Canyon State Park**, between Eagle Nest and Cimarron via US 64, with a special use permit (available at the park). For information, ☎ 505/377-6271.

OUTFITTERS ON FOOT

Guided backpacking and hiking trips can be arranged through the following outfitters.

Taos

Native Sons Adventures, 715 Paseo del Pueblo Sur, ☎ 505/758-9342 or 800/753-7559.
Taos Fitness Adventures, ☎ 800/455-4453.

Week-long to half-day horseback adventures are available through these area outfitters.

Albuquerque

Llano Bonito Ranch, 129 Upper Llano Road, Llano, 87543, ☎ 505/587-2636.
Sandia Trails Horse Rentals, 10601 North 4th Street, ☎ 505/898-6970.

Santa Fe

The Bishop's Lodge, ☎ 505/983-6377.
Rocking S Ranch, ☎ 505/438-7333.

Taos

Adventures in the Great Outdoors, PO Box 1618, Ranchos de Taos, 87557, ☎ 505/758-7332.
Native Sons Adventures, 715 Paseo del Pueblo Sur, ☎ 505/758-9342 or 800/753-7559.
Rio Grande Stables, PO Box 2122, El Prado, 87529, ☎ 505/776-5913.

Red River

Bitter Creek Guest Ranch, PO Box 310, ☎ 505/754-2587 or 800/562-9462.
Bobcat Pass Wilderness Adventures, PO Box 454, ☎ 505/754-2769.

Angel Fire

Roadrunner Tours, CS Ranch, ☎ 505/377-6416 or 800/377-6416.

The following operators offer guided llama trekking day hikes and overnight excursions.

Taos

Adventures in the Great Outdoors, PO Box 1618, Ranchos de Taos, 87557, ☎ 505/758-7332.
El Paso Llama Expeditions, PO Box 2672, Taos, 87571, ☎ 800/4-LLAMAS.
Taos Llama Adventures, PO Box 2879, Taos 87571, ☎ 505/776-1044 or 800/565-LAMA.

Quality outdoor equipment, information and maps can be obtained through these area retailers.

Albuquerque

REI (Recreational Equipment Inc.), 1905 Mountain Road, ☎ 505/247-1191.
Sandia Mountain Outfitters, 1700 Juan Tabo, ☎ 505-293-9725.
Snowy River Outfitters, Hoffman Shopping Center, 8210 Menaul Northeast, ☎ 505/298-7151.
Sportz Outdoor, 6915 Montgomery Boulevard Northeast, ☎ 505/837-9400.

On Wheels

The **Sandia Mountains**, east of Albuquerque, offer wonderful mountain biking opportunities. Most of the trails in the mountains, however, are at elevations higher than 9,000 feet. Visiting riders from lower elevations may want to acclimate first by riding **Foothills Trail** on the eastern outskirts of town. Trailheads near the Lower Tramway Terminal, at Elena Gallegos Picnic Area and at the end of Glenwood Hills Drive open the door to a maze of more than seven miles of single-track at the 6,500-foot base of the Sandias. The trail features many dips, arroyos and jumps, making it a great place for riders of all levels to get out, do some exploring and test their lungs at moderate altitude. When ready for the higher elevations, head east on Interstate 40 to the **Sandia Peak Ski Area** exit. NM 14 and NM 536 wind their way up into the mountains and to the base of the ski area. Mountain bike rentals are available at the ski area and the main chairlift operates during the summer carrying mountain bikes and riders to the top of the area for a minimal fee. From there several riding opportunities unfold. If you don't mind pedaling uphill, **NM 536**, **10K Trail** and **Tree Spring Trail** combine single-track and double-track to make a nine-mile loop that can be ridden from the ski area without the use of the lift. Ride uphill, north and east from the ski area on NM 536 past the Balsam Glade, Capulin Spring and Ninemile Picnic Areas into a steep section of switchbacks. The 10K Trail leaves from the uphill side of the seventh switchback, a right-turn switchback. The trail crosses under three ski area chairlifts before the intersection with Tree Spring Trail. A left turn onto this trail takes you back down to NM 536 south of the ski area. It should take intermediate to advanced riders in good shape about three hours to complete this ride. Just before the intersection of Tree Spring Trail and NM 536, a right turn onto **Oso Corridor Trail** presents an opportunity to extend this ride onto 2½ more miles of downhill single-track ending at Doc Long Picnic Area on NM 536. Use the Placitas, Sandia Crest and Tijeras 7.5-minute USGS quads for determining other rides in this area. Remember that mountain bikes are not permitted in wilderness areas.

The **Santa Fe National Forest**, north and east of the state capital, offers hundreds of great biking trails. A combination of forest service trails known as the **Windsor Trail System** comprises some of the best single-track riding in the area. Take Washington Street/NM 590 north out of Santa Fe, looking for a dirt road on the right about five miles from the city limits. Turn here and follow the road through a housing settlement to its end at the trailhead. Windsor Trail climbs 3,100 feet in nine miles from the start to its finish at the Aspen Basin Campground near Santa Fe Ski Area. The trail surface is excellent hard-packed alpine soil but does have several water bars. It is often crossed by encroaching tree roots, making the somewhat steep climb a good challenge even for advanced riders. Several trails branch off to the right, connecting with Hyde Park Road, which also leads to Aspen Basin Campground. Intermediate riders may choose to exit via one of these, ride the paved road to the top and then return down the exciting single-track. This trail system is shown on Santa Fe National Forest maps, but the Aspen Basin 7.5-minute USGS quad provides the greatest detail.

From Aspen Vista Campground, 13½ miles northeast of Santa Fe on Hyde Park Road, Forest Road 150 climbs more than 2,000 feet to the 12,300-foot **Tesque Peak**, overlooking Santa Fe Lake and the ski area. There is a locked gate about two miles up the trail, but it is only there to prevent unauthorized motorized vehicle use of the road. Simply ride around it and continue to the summit, where views become truly spectacular. The trail is sustained double-track the entire way and, while technically suitable for beginning riders, high altitudes encountered here require riders to be in superb physical condition. Up and back, the ride covers 12 miles and can take two to four hours to complete. The Aspen Basin 7.5-minute USGS quad shows this road in good detail.

For information, contact the **Santa Fe National Forest office**, 1220 St. Francis Drive, PO Box 1689, Santa Fe, NM 87504, ☎ 505/988-6940.

Most of the good mountain biking in the Los Alamos area takes place west of town in the Jemez Mountains, actually closer to the La Cueva settlement at the intersection of NM 4 and NM 126. The majority of rides are on double-track Forest Service Roads. In fact, the only good single-track is found at the **East Fork Cross-Country Area**, just off NM 4, seven miles east of La Cueva. From the parking lot at the recreation area, East Fork Ridge Trail and Mistletoe Canyon Trail head east into the forest and a number of trails branch from these. Limitless hours of exploration are possible by riding any number of combinations in this veritable web of trails. Elevation gain is minimal and riders of all skill levels will be able to navigate any path in the area. The riding season here is limited, however, to summer and fall, as trails are maintained for cross-country skiing in the winter and spring, holding snow until mid-to late April.

From Fenton Lake State Park, just northwest of La Cueva via NM 126, NM 126 and Forest Service Roads 314, 380, 144, 376 and 378 combine for several loop options. Scenery is the main reason for riding in this area and the roads basically connect the beautiful **San Antonio**, **Oat** and **Barley Canyons** of the Santa Fe National Forest. Most loop combinations will be about 15 miles long and will be suitable but strenuous for beginning and intermediate riders in good shape. Expert riders will find this area a good place to get out and stretch their legs.

Both the Santa Fe National Forest map and the Silver Springs 7.5-minute USGS quad will show these roads in adequate detail.

For information, contact the **Santa Fe National Forest-Jemez Ranger District office**, ☎ 505/829-3535.

Forest Road 9 joins NM 522 15 miles north of Taos. Park at the intersection for an easy seven-mile out-and-back ride across **Cebolla Mesa**. The edge of the 800-foot-deep Rio Grande Gorge will let you know when to turn around and head back to the car. Cebolla Mesa Campground is also located at the turn-around point. Plan to spend some time there. Views over the gorge are spectacular and a mile-long hiking trail descends to a good picnic spot on the river. There is one major fork in the road on this ride. Stay to the right, following the signs to the campground. Cebolla Mesa is a wide sagebrush-covered expanse on the Taos Plateau. Views extend for miles in every direction, with the impressive Sangre de Cristo Mountains rising in the east. It would be very difficult to get lost out here but, if you feel the need, use a Carson National Forest map or the Arroyo Hondo 7.5-minute USGS quad to locate this route.

If you didn't come to Taos to pedal placidly along forest service roads crossing scenic mesas but would rather challenge yourself on extreme sections of technical, lung-busting single-track, try the **Devisadaro Loop**. Find the trailhead, four miles southeast of Taos across from the El Nogal Picnic Area on US 64. This five-mile loop has a total elevation gain of 1,100 feet. Advanced and intermediate riders in excellent physical condition will enjoy this ride's steep uphills, exhilarating downhills and technical, rocky sections. The ride begins with a short access trail from the road. Bear left when the trail joins the loop. As a rule, the loop is ridden clockwise – follow the rules to avoid head-on collisions. The Carson National Forest map and the Taos 7.5-minute USGS quad show this trail.

For a full day's mountain bike adventure, **South Boundary Trail** connects the towns of Angel Fire and Taos on 20 miles of single-track through the Carson National Forest.

Beginning right from Red River city limits, NM 578, Forest Road 488 and NM 38 combine to make an exceptional 10-mile loop up to **Old Red River Pass**. The route will gain just over 1,000 feet, and will take about two hours to complete. Even though one section of switchbacks on FR 488 is fairly steep, the route keeps to pavement and well-maintained dirt roads the entire way. The ride is considered fairly easy by those in good physical condition and is a great way to acclimate to the higher elevations encountered here. From the pass at 9,854 feet, beautiful views are afforded over the Red River Valley and to Wheeler Peak, New Mexico's highest, seen piercing the southwestern sky.

From the top of the pass, Forest Road 490 heads south down **Fourth of July Canyon** to rejoin NM 578, creating another fun loop route. The ride covers 12 miles if ridden from town and back. Again, it will take about two hours, gain just over 1,000 feet and is considered fairly easy for riders in good physical condition.

Both of these loops are shown on the Carson National Forest Map.

Intermediate and advanced riders looking for more of a challenge, not to mention some single-track, will find all they can handle in a loop-ride to **Goose Lake** and back. Less than one mile south of Red River via NM 578, Forest Road 486 heads west into the mountains. Park at the intersection and begin your ride here. The forest road climbs almost 3,000 feet in eight miles up to Goose Lake at 11,600 feet and is guaranteed to make even top riders sweat. Stop and rest at the lake to enjoy the views of 12,711-foot Gold Hill to the north, but mainly because you will need to be as sharp as possible for the return trip down an insane seven-mile stretch of single-track. (You should return via Forest Road 486 if, for some reason, you don't have a helmet or you're not feeling quite on top of your game.) Trail #65 is found on the far side of Goose Lake and is the single-track way down. Sometimes overgrown, it basically follows Goose Creek all the way down to NM 578. A left turn leads back to your car. Use a Carson National Forest map or the Red River 7.5-minute USGS quad to find this trail.

From Memorial Day weekend through Labor Day, the scenic summer chairlift at **Red River Ski Area** carries bikes and riders to an elevation of 10,350 feet, offering 1,525 vertical feet of descent without the struggle of an uphill climb. For information, ☎ 505/754-2223.

South Boundary Trail, connecting the towns of Angel Fire and Taos, is one of New Mexico's very best mountain bike rides. A 20-mile, one-way, single-track adventure in the Carson National Forest for intermediate and advanced riders with the stamina to endure a full day's ride, this is not to be embarked upon lightly. Riders should seriously and honestly assess their fitness levels before attempting this ride. Then, come prepared with plenty of water, lots of high energy snacks, a weatherproof outer shell, your tool kit, maps and a compass. You should also check with forest service rangers for weather forecasts and trail conditions – the trail is sometimes not clear of snow until summer. You may also want to advise rangers of your riding schedule and establish a contact time for after the ride.

Carson National Forest-Supervisor's Office,
PO Box 558, 208 Cruz Alta Road, Taos, NM 87571, ☎ 505/758-6200.
Carson National Forest-Camino Real Ranger District,
PO Box 68, Penasco, NM 87553, ☎ 505/587-2255.

The best way to ride South Boundary Trail is from Angel Fire to Taos with a car shuttle. This way, you will ride uphill the first five miles and then downhill the last 15. Go past Angel Fire Ski Area to the small town of Black Lake and turn right onto County Road B1. Bear right when the road forks and continue for almost two miles until the road makes a sharp left-hand turn. This is the trailhead, with the trail heading up from the elbow of the turn. The entire route is designated as Forest Service Trail #164 on maps and is fairly well marked with brown stakes and permanent markers on the trail. The trail does share itself with Forest Roads 438, 437 and 445 in places (closed to motorized vehicles). Consult your map carefully to navigate intersections correctly. The trail ends at the El

Nogal Campground, four miles southeast of Taos via US 64. Use a Carson National Forest Map or the USGS 7.5-minute quads for Osha Mountain, Shadybrook and Rancho de Taos.

BIKING OUTFITTERS

Mountain bike rentals are available through these reputable shops and tour operators.

Albuquerque

Old Town Bicycles, 2000 Old Town Road Northwest, ☎ 505/247-4926.
Rio Mountainsport, 1210 Rio Grande Boulevard Northwest, ☎ 505/766-9970.
Sandia Peak Ski Area, Sandia Mountains, ☎ 505/242-9052.

Red River

Sitzmark Sports, 416 West Main Street, ☎ 505/754-2456.

Taos

Bikemeister Mountain Bike Tours, PO Box 1281, El Prado, 87529, ☎ 505/758-1194 or 800/876-1194.
Gearing Up Bicycle Shop, just south of the plaza, ☎ 505/751-0365.
Hot Tracks Cyclery, 729 Paseo del Pueblo Sur, Suite D, ☎ 505/751-0949.
Native Sons Adventures, 715 Paseo del Pueblo Sur, Box 6144, ☎ 505/758-9342 or 800/753-7559.

These area retailers provide professional sales and service for both mountain and road bikes and accessories.

Albuquerque

Bike World, 3119 San Mateo Boulevard Northeast, ☎ 505/881-4233.
Cycle Cave, 5716 Menaul Boulevard Northeast, ☎ 505/884-6607.
Fat Tire Cycles, 1425 Central Avenue Northeast, ☎ 505/243-5900.
REI, 1905 Mountain Road, ☎ 505/247-1191.
Two Wheel Drive, 1706 Central Avenue Southeast, ☎ 505/243-8443.

Santa Fe

Santa Fe Schwinn, 1611 St. Michaels Drive, ☎ 505/983-4473.
Coyote Bikes, 1722 St. Michaels Drive, ☎ 505/471-1682.

Los Alamos

Trail Bound Sports, 771 Central Avenue, ☎ 505/662-3000.

Chama is the New Mexico depot for the **Cumbres and Toltec Scenic Railroad**, America's longest and highest narrow gauge steam railroad. Built in 1880 to serve the rich mining camps of the San Juan Mountains, the railroad ceased operations in the early 1900s around the same time mining busted in the area. But in 1974, the New Mexico and Colorado state governments purchased a 64-mile stretch of the old railway between Chama, NM and Antonito, CO, and restored it and its coal-fired steam train as an historic tourist attraction. The train leaves Chama daily and climbs a precipitous 4% grade to the 10,015-foot crest of Cumbres Pass. From there, it passes through two tunnels to the spectacular Toltec Gorge of the Los Pinos River and descends gently into Antonito. The train runs from Memorial Day Weekend to mid-October. Early summer trips pass through meadows and valleys bursting with iris, sunflower and Indian paintbrush, while end-of-season excursions are famous for the spectacular fall color displayed in groves of pinon, oak, aspen and juniper encountered along the way. The 64-mile, one-way journey takes 6½ hours. You may arrange to ride back to Chama in a van provided by the railroad or set up alternate transportation on your own. For information, contact **Cumbres & Toltec Scenic Railroad-Chama Depot**, PO Box 789, Chama, 87520, ☎ 505/756-2151.

The mountains in this region are webbed with prime jeep roads. You should obtain a **Santa Fe National Forest** map or a **Carson National Forest** map for exploration on your own or make reservations with one of the following tour operators.

JEEP TOUR OPERATORS

Santa Fe

Outback Tours, PO Box 961, Santa Fe, 87504, ☎ 505/820-6101 or 800/800-JEEP.

Taos

Adventures in the Great Outdoors, PO Box 1618, Ranchos de Taos, 87557, ☎ 505/758-7332.

Red River

Bitter Creek Guest Ranch, Main Street, ☎ 505/754-6378.
High Country Tours & Jeep Rentals, Main Street, ☎ 505/754-2441.
Jeep Trailways Rentals & Tours, Main Street, ☎ 505/754-6443.

On Water

Cochiti Lake, 50 miles north of Albuquerque via Interstate 25 and NM 22, provides the area's best recreation beach. Windsurfing, small boat sailing and swimming are among the most popular pursuits on the reservoir. Power boats are restricted to trolling speeds and are used primarily for fishing – bass, catfish and wall-eye are the most common pole-benders. There is a small marina and store on the lake. For information, ☎ 505/242-8302. Camping is available.

The **Santa Fe National Forest** contains a number of high alpine lakes which make for some great fishing if you're willing to endure the hike necessary to reach them. Some of the most popular are **Lake Katherine, Spirit Lake** and **Stewart Lake. Fenton Lake State Park**, 45 miles west of Los Alamos via NM 4 and NM 126, offers a 28-acre fishing lake stocked with trout. No swimming or boating is allowed, but camping is available. For information, ☎ 505/829-3630.

On the other hand, **Abiquiu Reservoir**, halfway between Espanola and Chama via US 84, presents more than 4,000 surface acres, allowing just about every water sport imaginable. For information, ☎ 505/685-4371.

El Vado Lake State Park, 30 miles southwest of Chama via US 84 and NM 112, surrounds a beautiful mountain lake popular for water-skiing, swimming and fishing. During winter, the surface freezes solid enough to allow for ice fishing. The park features picnic areas, playgrounds and boat ramps. Camping is available. For information, ☎ 505/827-7465.

Heron Lake State Park, 25 miles southwest of Chama via US 84 and NM 95, contains another popular ice fishing lake, famous for rainbow trout and Kokonee salmon. When the ice melts, fishermen take to the lake in boats, but those with motors are restricted to cruising at trolling speed as the lake is a designated "quiet zone." Sailboats, however, may navigate the lake as fast as their sails can take them. The park provides a fine marina and boat ramp. Camping is available. For information, ☎ 505/588-7470.

The **Rio Grande** or "Great River" provides excellent trout fishing in New Mexico all the way from the Colorado border south to Mexico. This is especially true near Taos, with the Red River National Fish Hatchery adding thousands of rainbows and browns to the waters just upstream.

The **Taos Box**, however, is the most famous feature of the Rio Grande in North-Central New Mexico. This 16-mile stretch of river passes through some of the tightest sections of the Rio Grande Gorge and offers Class III and IV rapids with names like Screaming Right, Screaming Left and The Rock Garden. With 1,000-foot sheer cliff walls towering on either side, there's no turning back and no easy escape. Do not attempt this on your own without proper training and experience.

Further down the river in the **Lower Gorge**, the Race Course is another popular whitewater section. Class II and III rapids like Albert Falls, Big Rocks and Sause Hole are sure to thrill, while remaining safe enough for less experienced river-runners.

Red River, near the town of the same name, stocks more trout than any other public river in the country. More than 20,000 German brown, cutthroat and rainbow trout are released into the river each year – all more than 12 inches long.

Lost Lake and **Goose Lake** are popular alpine fishing holes in the Red River area. Use a Carson National Forest map to plot access. (See above, under Adventures on Foot/Wheels.)

Eagle Nest Lake, roughly half-way between Red River and Angel Fire at the junction of US 64 and NM 38, is perhaps New Mexico's most accessible ice fishing destination and is a year-round favorite for lunker rainbow trout, Kokonee salmon and Koho salmon. For information, contact **Eagle Nest Chamber of Commerce**, PO Box 322, Eagle Nest, NM 87718, ☎ 505/377-2420 or 800/494-9117. The **Cimarron River** running through **Cimarron Canyon State Park**, eight miles east of Eagle Nest via US 64, is teeming with brown and rainbow trout. Camping is available. For information, ☎ 505/376-6271.

OUTFITTERS ON WATER

Several area outfitters provide professional fishing guides and instruction as well as sales and service.

Albuquerque

Charlie's Sporting Goods, 7401-H Menaul Boulevard Northeast, ☎ 505/884-4545.
Los Pinos Fly Shop, 3214 Matthew Avenue Northeast, ☎ 505/884-7501.
The Reel Life, 1100 San Mateo Boulevard Northeast Suite 10, ☎ 505/268-1693.

Santa Fe

Santa Fe Flyfishing School, PO Box 22957, ☎ 800/555-7707.
High Desert Angler, 435 South Guadaloupe, ☎ 505/988-7688.

Known World Guide Service, PO Box 22621, ☎ 505/988-9609 or 800/983-7756.

Taos

Adventures in the Great Outdoors, PO Box 1618, Ranchos de Taos, 87557, ☎ 505/758-7332.
Los Rios Anglers, 226C North Pueblo Road, ☎ 505/758-2798.
Taylor Streit Fly Fishing Service, PO Box 2759, ☎ 505/751-1312.

The following operators guide day-trips through the **Taos Box** *and the* **Race Course** *as well as guide multi-day floats on the* **Rio Grande** *and* **Rio Chama**.

Santa Fe

Known World Guide Service Inc., ☎ 505/988-9609 or 800/983-7756.
New Wave Rafting, Route 5 Box 302A, ☎ 505/984-1444 or 800/984-1444.
Rocky Mountain Tours, 1323 Paseo de Peralta, ☎ 505/984-1684 or 800/231-7238.

Taos

Far Flung Adventures, PO Box 707, El Prado, 87529, ☎ 505/758-2628 or 800/359-2627.
Los Rios River Runners, Box 2734, near the blinking light on Ski Valley Road, ☎ 505/776-8854 or 800/544-1181.
Native Sons Adventures, 715 Paseo del Pueblo Sur, Box 6144, ☎ 505/758-9342 or 800/753-7559.
Rio Grande Rapid Transit, Box A, Pilar, 87531, ☎ 505/758-9700 or 800/222-RAFT.
Rio Grande River Tours, Box 1D, Pilar Route, Imbudo 87531, ☎ 505/758-0762 or 800/525-4966.

On Snow

Sandia Peak, 20 miles northeast of Albuquerque via Interstate 40, NM 14 and NM 536, offers 25 runs on 1,800 feet of vertical drop in the spectacular Sandia Mountains. Ski season runs mid-December to mid-March on this mountain that caters mostly to beginner and intermediate skiers. Slopes are accessed by four double chairlifts and two surface lifts, while a full-service restaurant and a skier café provide a warm place to take a break. PSIA-certified ski instruction is available through the Sandia Peak Ski School and rental equipment can be obtained at the area or from several shops in Albuquerque. For information, ☎ 505/242-9052.

Cross-country skiing and snowshoeing are also popular winter activities in the **Sandia Mountains**. **North** and **South Crest Trails** and **10K Trail** are some of the most used winter routes. (See above, under Adventures on Foot/Wheels.)

Santa Fe Ski Area lies just 15 miles northeast of the state capital via Hyde Park/Ski Basin Road. Four chairlifts and four surface lifts carry 7,800 skiers per hour to the top of a 12,000-foot peak, where 39 runs offer beginners to experts challenging descents over 1,650 feet of vertical drop. An average of 250 inches of snow a year fall on these slopes every year and its proximity to one of the hottest tourist destinations in the country makes it a very popular place. There's always something going on as the area hosts numerous winter festivals with its **Celebrity Winter Ski Classic** and **Winter Fiesta** pulling in the largest crowds. A fine system of cross-country trails branches out from the ski area as well as a 4.6-mile groomed loop track for telemarkers. Santa Fe Ski School offers PSIA-certified instruction for all levels of skiers and snowboarders and full equipment rentals/sales services are available at the base of the mountain. For information, ☎ 505/982-4429.

Los Alamos' **Pajarito Ski Area**, eight miles west of town via NM 4, is a surprisingly challenging little mountain. Only open on weekends, Wednesdays and federal holidays, the area offers more than 30 trails, 1,200 feet of vertical drop and an uphill lift capacity of 5,000 skiers per hour. Six lifts (three doubles, a triple and a quad chairlift, as well as a rope tow) give access to this mountain, rated 40% expert, 35% intermediate and 25% beginner. A new modern lodge at the base has a cafeteria and rental shop, and there is a ski school for ages four and up. For information, ☎ 505/662-5725.

Many areas near Los Alamos are ideally suited for cross-country skiing. Scenic sites include **Water Canyon**, off West Jemez Road, and **American Springs Trail**, **Bandelier**, **Apache Springs Loop** and **Peralta Canyon**, off NM 4.

East Fork Cross-Country Area, seven miles east of La Cueva via NM 4 west from Los Alamos, offers a web of groomed cross-country trails. East Fork Ridge Trail and Mistletoe Canyon Trail head east from East Fork Campground and connect with numerous other trails, making for limitless trail combination options. For information, call the **Santa Fe National Forest-Jemez Office**, ☎ 505/829-3535.

New Mexico's most renowned Ski Resort is **Taos Ski Valley**, 15 miles northeast of Taos via NM 522 and NM 150. Created by Ski Hall of Famer Ernie Blake in 1954, Taos Ski Valley consistently ranks as one of the nation's top resorts through reader polls of *Ski* and *Snow Country* magazines. Famous for waist-deep powder and steep terrain, the resort's West Basin Ridge, Highline Ridge and Kachina Peak (12,481 feet) offer hike-in expedition-style extreme skiing that can challenge even the world's top skiers. In fact, the mountain has so much to offer advanced skiers that, at a glance, it may seem too intimidating for less-skilled vacationers. There are stories about prospective first-time skiers who have driven into the parking lot, taken one look at Al's Run (the most prominent run visible from the base area – very steep), turned around and driven away. A closer look, however, will show that Taos Ski Valley is also one of the finest recreational skier resorts in the country. Though 51% of the runs are rated for experts, with 72 named trails, that leaves 35 runs rated for intermediate and beginner skiers. Some other ski areas don't even have 35 runs in total. In fact, Taos Ski Valley is probably the best place in the US for beginning and intermediate skiers to visit. The Ernie Blake Ski School continues to receive the #1 ranking from national skier polls – year after year. PSIA-certified instructors offer half-day and full-day lessons for all levels, as well as week-long learn-to-ski and learn-to-ski-better programs.

Taos Ski Valley has more than 1,100 skiable acres with a 2,612-foot vertical drop, not counting areas that you have to hike to. There are 11 lifts capable of transporting 15,500 skiers per hour to the top of these slopes that receive more than 320 inches of snow a year. Taos Ski Valley does not, however, allow snowboards.

The Euro/New Mexico ski village at the base of the mountain has full equipment rental, sales and service areas as well as fine restaurants, lounges, snack bars and lodging.

For information, contact **Taos Ski Valley, Inc.** PO Box 90, Taos Ski Valley, 87525, ☎ 505/776-2291. Reservations: ☎ 505/776-2233 or 800/776-1111.

Ski Rio, 48 miles north of Taos via NM 522 and NM 196, is New Mexico's newest and most innovative ski resort. The area embraces just about every snow sport known to man in an effort to offer a complete winter experience rather than just another ski day. One of the hottest new sports to hit the slopes since snowboarding is snow skating, introduced to America in 1991. Part in-line skating, part snowboarding, part skiing and part ice skating, this bizarre hybrid has been accepted at more than 190 ski areas nationwide, but Ski Rio is the first in the country to build a park specifically for snow skaters. Called "Park Sled Dogs," the 40-acre area features kickers, table tops, steps and rail walls as well as 14 marked trails for skaters of all abilities. Similarly, Ski Rio offers a 20-acre park just for snowboarding. "Chutes & Ladders" has a number of gladed trails, side walls, kickers, jumps, table tops and a 300-foot half-pipe serviced by a separate surface lift. Both parks have spectator viewing areas and the snowboard park parallels one of the main chairlifts so that you can watch the action while riding back to the top of the area. Continuing the trend, there is a nordic touring area with more than 21 kilometers of groomed trails for freestyle and classical skiers. The rest of the mountain is open to everyone. Two triple chairlifts, one double chair and three surface lifts can carry 5,500 skiers an hour to the 11,650-foot summit of the area. From there, 64 named trails and the three specialized parks spread out over 810 skiable acres with a 2,150-foot vertical drop. While only 20% of the trails in the developed area are rated black diamonds, a snowcat will deliver experts to nearby Carmillo Peak for extreme backcountry powder skiing on Saturdays and holidays. For those who only dream of being able to ski the steep and deep, Ski Rio's Perfect Turn Ski School guarantees that first-timers will be skiing independently by the end of the day or their money back. They also offer PSIA-certified lessons for downhill and nordic skiers, snowboarders and snow skaters of all abilities. The Ski Rio Rental Shop provides equipment for all three of those disciplines as well as snowshoes. There are also several marked trails for snowshoeing. As mentioned above Ski Rio, is attempting to create a complete winter experience and non-skiers are not left out in the cold here. Those not on the slopes can still enjoy the beauty of the mountains in winter through various sleigh rides, dog sled tours, snowmobile tours and snowcat tours available at the base of the area. All lodging in the area is operated through Ski Rio Resort and is located at the base of the mountain within walking distance of the slopes. Condos, hotel-type rooms and cabins are all available and were all completely renovated in 1994. Ski Rio also operates a cafeteria-style restaurant at the Day Lodge, the casual Southwestern Silvertree Restaurant, and the Blue Moon Grill for fine dining as well as Pinates lounge for après-ski entertainment. For information, contact **Ski Rio**, PO Box 159, Costilla, 87524, ☎ 505/758-7707 or 800/227-5746.

Enchanted Forest Cross Country Ski Area, 3½ miles east of Red River via NM 38, offers 1,400 acres of aspen groves and sweeping meadows in the Carson National Forest. A map, available at the area, details an extensive network of 12-foot-wide groomed trails, which are monitored by a full-time safety patrol. Lessons are available for skiers of all abilities. There is also a warming hut, offering snacks and drinks, while rentals and area passes are obtained at **Miller's Crossing**, 212 West Main Street, in Red River. Enchanted Forest is open daily from 9 AM to 4:30 PM, November 23 to April 2. For information, ☎ 505/754-2374.

Red River Ski Area can almost guarantee excellent snow conditions from November 24 to March 26, as the area has snow-making covering 75% of the mountain. One surface lift, two triple chairs and four double chairs can send 7,920 skiers an hour to the 10,350-foot summit of the area. From the top, 57 runs descend 1,600 vertical feet on 270 skiable acres. A PSIA-certified ski school offers lessons for skiers of all abilities and a full service equipment rental shop is located at the base. For information, ☎ 505/754-2223.

Angel Fire Ski Resort, established in 1965 as a family-oriented ski area, has been described as "the best intermediate resort in the US." Angel Fire actually has something to offer skiers of all levels, with 52 trails rated 34% beginner, 48% intermediate, and 18% advanced. Lift lines are seldom very long, as two triple chairs and four double chairs can carry 7,900 skiers an hour to the 10,680-foot summit, where 2,200 vertical feet of skiing awaits. A PSIA-certified ski school offers a full range of lessons and all rental, restaurant and lodging services are available at the Legends Hotel at the base of the mountain. (See below, under Where to Stay & Eat.) For information, ☎ 505/377-6401 or 800/633-7463.

OUTFITTERS ON SNOW

Rental equipment can be obtained through these area suppliers.

Albuquerque

Action Sports, 7509 Menaul Boulevard Northeast, ☎ 505/884-5611.
Cottam's Ski Shop, 11100 Montgomery Boulevard Northeast, ☎ 505/293-8981.
REI, 1905 Mountain Road Northwest, ☎ 505/247-1191.
Sandia Mountain Outfitters, 1700 Juan Tabo Boulevard Northeast, ☎ 505/293-9725.
Sandia Peak Ski Area, Sandia Mountains, ☎ 505/242-9052.
The Wintermill, 2225 Wyoming Northeast, Suite A, ☎ 505/292-4401.

Santa Fe

Ski Tech, 905 St. Francis Drive, ☎ 505/983-5512.
The Wintermill, Santa Fe Ski Area, ☎ 505/982-4429.

Taos

Adventure Ski Shops, South Santa Fe Road, ☎ 505/758-1167 or 800/433-1321.
Adventure Ski Shops, North Santa Fe Road, ☎ 505/758-9744 or 800/753-7559.
Cottam's Ski Shop, Kachina Lodge Arcade, ☎ 505/758-1697.
Cottam's Ski Shop, South Pueblo Del Sur, ☎ 505/758-8242.

Cottam's Ski Shop, Mid-Town, ☎ 505/758-2822.
Native Sons Adventures, 715 Paseo del Pueblo Sur, ☎ 505/758-9342 or 800/753-7559.
White Water Ski Shop, ¼-mile from the blinking light on Ski Valley Road, ☎ 505/776-8854 or 800/544-1181.

Taos Ski Valley

Cottam's Ski Shop, Alpine Village, ☎ 505/756-8540.
Taos Ski Valley Rental Shop & Ski Lab, at the base of Lift #1, ☎ 505/776-2291 ext. 1265.
Terry Sports I, between the ticket window and the Inn at Snakedance, ☎ 505/776-8711.
Terry Sports II, between the Thunderbird Lodge and Sierra del Sol, ☎ 505/776-8292.

Red River

Miller's Crossing, 212 West Main Street, ☎ 505/754-2374.
Sitzmark Sports, 416 West Main Street, ☎ 505/754-2456.

Angel Fire

Mountain Sports, North Angel Fire Road, ☎ 505/3773490.

Snowmobile rentals and tours can be arranged through these area outfitters.

Taos

Native Sons Adventures, 715 Paseo del Pueblo Sur, ☎ 505/758-9342 or 800/753-7559.

Red River

Bitter Creek Guest Ranch, ☎ 505/754-2587 or 800/562-9462.
Bobcat Pass Wilderness Adventures, ☎ 505/754-2769.
Red Caboose Adventures, Main Street, ☎ 505/754-6363 or 800/542-0154.
Red Dawg, Main Street, ☎ 505/754-2721.

In Air

Albuquerque is home to the largest balloon festival in the world, the **Kodak Albuquerque International Balloon Fiesta**, and north-central New Mexico is the center for hot air ballooning adventures in the state. Several area operators provide FAA-certified balloon flights year-round, with most offering sunrise ascents complemented by full champagne breakfasts and many featuring hotel pick-up and return service.

BALLOON OPERATORS

Albuquerque

B&B Ballooning, 8405 Monitor Drive Northeast, ☎ 505/821-8537.
Balloon Rides-Hot Alternatives, 8400 Menaul Northeast #201, ☎ 505/269-1174 or 800/322-2262.
Braden's Balloons Aloft, 3212 Stanford Northeast, ☎ 505/281-2714 or 800/367-6625.
Hot Air Extraord-in-air, 3416B Constitution Northeast, ☎ 505/266-9744.
Naturally High Balloon Company, Inc., ☎ 800/238-6359.
Omega Balloons, Inc., 600 Comanche Northeast, ☎ 505/344-6612.
Rainbow Ryders, Inc., 10305 Nita Place Northeast, ☎ 505/293-0000 or 800/725-2477.
World Balloon Corporation, 4800 Eubank Northeast, ☎ 505/293-6800 or 800/351-9588.

Santa Fe

Rocky Mountain Tours, 1323 Paseo de Peralta, ☎ 505/984-1684 or 800/231-7238.

Taos

Paradise Hot Air Balloon Adventures, ☎ 505/758-2378.

Statewide

Naturally High Balloon Company, Inc., ☎ 800/238-6359.

Sundance Aviation, Inc., at the Moriarty Municipal Airport, 30 miles east of Albuquerque, ☎ 505/832-2222, offers three different styles of glider rides tailored to fit most any disposition. Experienced FAA-licensed pilots conduct peaceful scenic flights, exhilarating high-performance flights and heart-stopping acrobatic rides for both reservation and walk-in customers. Similar glider rides over the Taos Valley can be arranged through **Air Taos, Inc./Soar Taos, Inc.** at the Taos Municipal Airport, ☎ 505/758-9501.

Angel Fire Helicopters, ☎ 505/377-6898, offers flightseeing tours above the Moreno Valley or the entire Enchanted Circle.

Eco-Travel & Cultural Excursions

Pueblos **Del Norte-Nambe Tours** is owned and operated by the Indians of the Nambe Pueblo. Courteous and knowledgeable Native American guides lead tours of the Northern Pueblos, Bandelier National Monument, the Chama River Valley, Taos and the Taos Pueblo, offering their unique insight into the wonders of Northern New Mexico. For information, contact Pueblos Del Norte-Nambe Tours, 112 West San Francisco Street, Plaza Mercado Upper Level, Santa Fe, 87501, ☎ 505/820-1340.

Where to Stay & Eat

Accommodations

ALBUQUERQUE

Albuquerque, as you would expect, presents a wide variety of accommodation options.

Near the **airport**, the Best Western **Fred Harvey Hotel**, 2400 Yale Boulevard Southeast, ☎ 505/843-7000 or 800/227-1117, offers deluxe rooms and features two restaurants, an outdoor pool, a health club and tennis courts. **Holiday Inn Express Airport**, 2331 Centre Avenue Southeast, ☎ 505/247-1500 or 800/HOLIDAY, built in 1995, presents the freshest rooms in the area and offers a complimentary breakfast, indoor pool and hot tub. Less expensive airport lodging is found at **Sahara Motor Hotel**, 5915 Gibson Boulevard, ☎ 505/256-9803.

The only time that it is hard to find a room in Albuquerque is during Balloon Fiesta Week in October. Most hotels are completely booked about three months in advance. Make reservations extra early if you want to stay near **Balloon Fiesta Park**. The 10-story atrium with a 50-foot waterfall and glass elevators only begins to hint at the elegance found in the rooms at **Holiday Inn Pyramid**, 5151 San Francisco Road Northeast, ☎ 505/821-3333 or 800/544-0623. The hotel also features both an indoor and outdoor pool, a hot tub and sauna, a piano lounge and an aerobic fitness centre. **Budget Inn**, 7439 Pan American Freeway Northeast, ☎ 505/345-7500 or 800/428-3438, will accommodate those travelers who do not need that much glitz. It does have a pool and the rooms are clean and comfortable.

Downtown and **Old Town** are easily accessed from a number of fine hotels. **Doubletree Hotel Albuquerque**, 201 Marquette

Northwest, ☎ 505/247-3344 or 800/528-0444, and **Hyatt Regency Albuquerque**, 330 Tijeras Northwest, ☎ 505/842-1234 or 800/233-1234, cater to big-spending business executives visiting the downtown area. Both feature pools, fine restaurants, health clubs and spas, but you get free chocolate chip cookies at Doubletree. **Sheraton Old Town**, 800 Rio Grande Northwest, ☎ 505/843-6300 or 800/237-2133, offers luxury accommodations within walking distance of the shops and sites of the historic district. The hotel features two restaurants, two lounges, an outdoor pool and hot tub. At about half the price, Best Western **Rio Grande Inn**, 1015 Rio Grande Northwest, ☎ 505/843-9500 or 800/959-4726, offers nice rooms and a pool, just three blocks from Old Town. About five blocks west of the historic district, **El Vado Motel**, 2500 Central Southwest, ☎ 505/243-4594, remains as Albuquerque's purest surviving "Route 66" motel. It offers clean inexpensive rooms and a pool.

Most of Albuquerque's moderate to inexpensive motels are found along Interstate 40 running east-west through town. On the **West Side**, **Best Western Inn at Rio Rancho**, 1465 Rio Rancho Drive, ☎ 505/892-1700 or 800/658-9558, offers good-sized rooms, restaurant, lounge, hot tub, indoor pool and outdoor pool. **Days Inn**, 6031 Iliff Road, ☎ 505/836-3297 or 800/DAYS-INN, features nice clean rooms, restaurant, indoor pool, hot tub and sauna, as well as a free continental breakfast. On the **East Side**, **Horne's Howard Johnson**, 15 Hotel Circle Northeast, ☎ 505/296-4852 or 800/877-4852, features two restaurants, a gym, pool and hot tub. **Ramada Inn**, 25 Hotel Circle Northeast, ☎ 505/271-1000 or 800/272-6232, offers a lounge, restaurant, indoor and outdoor pools. **Park Inn International**, Interstate 40 & Juan Tabo (exit 166), ☎ 505/293-4444 or 800/437-PARK, has an indoor pool, hot tub and free continental breakfast.

There are 20 fine **Bed & Breakfasts** in Albuquerque and countless others in surrounding communities. **Casas de Suenos Old Town Bed and Breakfast Inn**, 310 Rio Grande Southwest, ☎ 505/247-4560 or 800/CHAT-W/US, merits mention. It was named New Mexico's best B&B in 1994. Located one block from historic Old Town, this famous inn was built in the 1940s by an artist from Georgia as his home, but became somewhat of an artist colony when 12 individual *casitas* were added around the courtyard and were rented to friends and artists. Recently an Albuquerque lawyer turned innkeeper bought the property and restored it as a B&B. The inn retains much of its original artistic ambiance; its bizarre exterior resembles a large snail when viewed from the street, and inside walls contain murals by locally commissioned artists. The interior courtyard is a beautifully landscaped garden with a red-brick walkway weaving around flowers and elms to connect the 12 separate adobe *casitas*. Guests may choose from 19 individually decorated suites, featuring contemporary and antique furnishings, original art and private hot tubs. A gourmet breakfast is prepared by the inn's chef every morning.

For more information about this and other fine Albuquerque B&B's, contact the **Albuquerque Bed & Breakfast Association**, ☎ 505/293-2890 or 800/916-3322.

RV travelers interested in visiting sites in town should try **Albuquerque Central KOA Kampground**, 12400 Skyline Road Northeast, ☎ 505/296-2729. Located within the city limits, this campground offers a pool, hot tub, miniature golf, playground and store, as well as full hookups and tent sites. **Albuquerque North KOA**, 555 Hill Road, Bernalillo, ☎ 505/867-5227 or 800/624-9767, provides more seclusion. Large trees shade a pool, grassy tent area and outdoor seasonal café. Free pancake breakfasts are served daily. **Turquoise Trail Campground and RV Park**, 22 Calvary Road, four miles north NM 14, ☎ 505/281-2005, provides the closest access to the Sandia Mountains. Tent sites, cabins and full RV hookups are available.

SANTA FE

Santa Fe has long been a stopping place for weary travelers. Since its days as the terminus of the Camino Real and the Santa Fe Trail, it has become quite a reputable host, offering some of the most elegant accommodations in the state. Lodging ranges from budget to ultra-deluxe with prices rising the closer you get to downtown.

Right on the plaza, **La Fonda Hotel**, 100 East San Francisco Street, ☎ 505/982-5511 or 800/523-5002, was the first "inn at the end of the Santa Fe Trail." Although the original 1610 adobe hotel is gone, the current reincarnation upholds its reputation as being the central meeting spot for area tourists. Its restaurant and *cantina* are always a bustle of excitement and reunions. Each of its 153 rooms and 23 suites are individually decorated with handmade wooden furniture and many offer private balconies and fireplaces. La Fonda also features a newsstand, art gallery and gift shop.

Inn on the Alameda, 303 East Alameda, ☎ 505/984-2121 or 800/289-2122, is a small luxury hotel nestled conveniently between the Santa Fe's historic plaza and the gallery-lined Canyon Road. Each of the 66 uniquely decorated rooms and eight suites exemplifies the true essence of Santa Fe, featuring traditional kiva fireplaces accented with colorful Spanish tiles, authentic Native American rugs, and handmade furnishings. A gourmet breakfast of fresh fruit, pastries and juices is provided each morning in the spacious Agoyo Room, Lobby Library or the privacy of the guest's own room. There are also two open-air hot tubs for guests to relax in after their day's adventures in Santa Fe's mountains and galleries.

Known for its high-brow afternoon tea, **Hotel St. Francis**, 210 Don Gaspar, ☎ 505/983-5700 or 800/666-5700, is actually one of the prettiest hotels in town. High ceilings, brass beds and cherrywood furniture adorn each of 83 elegant rooms and two spacious suites.

Two blocks west of the plaza, the **Hilton of Santa Fe**, 100 Sandoval Street, ☎ 505/988-2811 or 800/336-3676, is unique among downtown luxury hotels. Built around Casa de Ortiz, the ancestral home of one of Santa Fe's early prominent families, the Hilton reflects territorial-style architecture rather than the more common pueblo style. Its skylit Chamisa Courtyard Café was once an open courtyard in the Ortiz home and its 250-year-old walls echo the ambiance of an earlier era. Southwestern "Santa Fe" decor creates a comfortable atmosphere in the hotel's charming lobby, lounges, restaurants and rooms. Guests may also relax in Santa Fe's largest swimming pool or soak in the Hilton's luxurious jacuzzi.

There are also a number of fine bed and breakfasts in the area. **Dancing Ground of the Sun**, 711 Paseo de Peralta, ☎ 505/986-9797 or 800/645-5673, offers five one-bedroom adobe *casitas* with fully equipped kitchens and cozy fireplaces. Each unit is individually decorated by local artisans and reflects the Native American personality of the city through handcrafted furniture and striking wall murals.

Lodging for five couples is available at **Dos Cajas Viejas**, 610 Agua Fria Street, ☎ 505/983-1636. This three-building adobe complex dates back to the 1860s and each attractive room features a traditional kiva fireplace, private patio and classic Southwest furnishings. There is also a walled courtyard with a private pool for guests.

Santa Fe's most intimate accommodations, however, are found at **Dunshee's Casita and B&B**, 986 Acequia Madre, ☎ 505-982-0988. There are only two available units at this exquisite little inn and the proprietor often only books one party at a time so that her guests receive undivided attention. Fresh flowers adorn every room and the kitchen is always stocked with homemade brownies or cookies.

Those looking for more economical lodging will find the majority of Santa Fe's less expensive accommodations situated along

Cerrillos Road. In the moderate price range, **Holiday Inn**, 4048 Cerrillos Road, ☎ 505/473-4646 or 800/HOLIDAY, **Quality Inn**, 3011 Cerrillos Road, ☎ 505/471-1211 or 800/228-5151, and **Ramada Inn**, 2907 Cerrillos Road, ☎ 505/471-3000 or 800/272-6232, all feature pools, restaurants and lounges. **Budget Inn of Santa Fe**, 725 Cerrillos, ☎ 505/982-5952 or 800/288-7600, **Comfort Inn**, 4312 Cerrillos Road, ☎ 505/474-7330, and **Days Inn**, 3650 Cerrillos Road, ☎ 505/438-3822 or 800/325-2525, only offer pools.

Travelers on tighter budgets should seek shelter at **Cottonwood Court**, 1742 Cerrillos Road, ☎ 505/982-5571 or 800/221-2222, **Silver Saddle Motel**, 2810 Cerrillos Road, ☎ 505/471-7663, or **Western Scene Motel**, 1608 Cerrillos Road, ☎ 505/983-7484.

RV travelers should head for **Los Campos**, 3574 Cerrillos Road, ☎ 505/473-1949, or **Trailer Ranch**, 3471 Cerrillos Road, ☎ 505/471-9970. Both offer full hookups and close proximity to Santa Fe's historic and shopping districts. **Santa Fe KOA**, 11 miles east of Santa Fe via Interstate 25 North, Exit 290 or 294, ☎ 505/466-1419, offers 44 pull-through sites with full hookups

LOS ALAMOS

Los Alamos Inn, 2201 Trinity Drive, ☎ 505/662-7211 or 800/279-9279, is the area's largest hotel, offering spacious rooms, an outdoor pool, a hot tub and a restaurant. **Hilltop House and LA Suites**, 400 Trinity Drive, ☎ 505/662-2441 or 800/462-0936, features an indoor pool, spacious rooms, and deluxe suites with kitchenettes. The hotel also has a fine restaurant and lounge.

Bed and breakfasts are another way to go in Los Alamos. The **Orange Street Inn**, 3496 Orange Street, ☎ 505/662-2651, is the only one in town inspected and approved by the New Mexico Bed and Breakfast Association. Seven rooms decorated with antiques feature large wooden beds stacked high with handmade quilts. Four of the rooms share baths.

Appletree Inn, 858 45th Street, ☎ 505/662-7054, is within walking distance of downtown and beautiful city parks. Rooms are spacious and tastefully decorated. **Back Porch Bed and Breakfast**, 13 Karen Circle, ☎ 505/672-9816, actually does feature a wonderful back porch which opens onto pretty landscaped gardens and a forested arroyo. Rooms are large and have private baths. **Early Bird Bed & Breakfast**, 4756 Trinity Drive, ☎ 505/662-9581, is located in a quiet, forested neighborhood and features two rooms with queen-sized beds. Guests also have access to a living room with fireplace, CD player, TV and VCR.

If you're visiting Taos to ski, Taos Ski Valley, 15 miles northeast of town via NM 522 and NM 150, offers some of the finest, not to mention most convenient, lodging in the area. **The Inn at Snakedance**, near the main ticket sales area, ☎ 505/776-2277 or 800/322-9815, was constructed as a hunting and fishing lodge for a local copper mining operation in the 1890s. When Ernie Blake, the founder of Taos Ski Valley, arrived in 1954, the "resort" consisted of Ernie's trailer, the lodge (10 rooms and an outhouse) and the area's first ski run, Snakedance. Less than 10 yards from the chairlift, the inn has long been the favorite of Taos traditionalists. In 1993, a massive renovation added 60 rooms to this venerable Taos native. New construction was careful, though, to preserve the classic spirit of the old lodge, staying with huge pine timbers for ceiling supports and utilizing original stone walls and fireplaces. Rooms are comfortable, blending alpine and Southwestern themes with handcrafted pine furniture and Taos art. A number of rooms feature cozy fireplaces and sitting areas with plush sofas. The inn offers a gourmet restaurant, library, spa and hot tub.

Hotel St. Bernard, located right on the slopes, ☎ 505/776-2251, is a 28-room chalet-style lodge famous for its European charm and excellent cuisine. All-inclusive packages are available. **Hotel Edelweiss**, also on the slopes, ☎ 505/776-2301 or 800/I-LUV-SKI, offers a similar experience. There are 21 spacious rooms with charming bay windows overlooking the slopes, huge beds with down comforters and private tiled baths. Guests also have access to a sauna and outdoor hot tub with sunset vistas.

TAOS

If you're visiting Taos to ski, Taos Ski Valley, 15 miles northeast of town via NM 522 and NM 150, offers some of the finest, not to mention most convenient, lodging in the area. **The Inn at Snakedance**, near the main ticket sales area, ☎ 505/776-2277 or 800/322-9815, was constructed as a hunting and fishing lodge for a local copper mining operation in the 1890s. When Ernie Blake, the founder of Taos Ski Valley, arrived in 1954, the "resort" consisted of Ernie's trailer, the lodge (10 rooms and an outhouse) and the area's first ski run, Snakedance. Less than 10 yards from the chairlift, the inn has long been the favorite of Taos traditionalists. In 1993, a massive renovation added 60 rooms to this venerable Taos native. New construction was careful, though, to preserve the classic spirit of the old lodge, staying with huge pine timbers for ceiling supports and utilizing original stone walls and fireplaces. Rooms are comfortable, blending alpine and Southwestern themes with hand-crafted pine furniture and Taos art. A number of rooms feature cozy fireplaces and sitting areas with plush sofas. The inn offers a gourmet restaurant, library, spa and hot tub.

Hotel St. Bernard, located right on the slopes, ☎ 505/776-2251, is a 28-room chalet-style lodge famous for its European charm and excellent cuisine. All-inclusive packages are available. **Hotel Edelweiss,** also on the slopes, ☎ 505/776-2301 or 800/I-LUV-SKI, offers a similar experience. There are 21 spacious rooms with charming bay windows overlooking the slopes, huge beds with down comforters and private tiled baths. Guests also have access to a sauna and outdoor hot tub with sunset vistas.

Just 1½ miles down the road from Taos Ski Valley, **Austing Haus,** ☎ 505/776-2649 or 800/748-2932, is the largest European-style timber frame structure in the US. It has graciously appointed rooms with classic cherrywood furnishings. A central hot tub room makes a perfect place to relax after skiing or hiking, and the elegant glass dining room always gives a perfect gourmet finish to your day in the mountains.

In town, **The Historic Taos Inn,** 125 Paseo del Pueblo Norte, ☎ 505/758-2233 or 800/TAOS-INN, has been a meeting place for locals and an adventure for visitors since the early 1800s. A dramatic two-story lobby greets guests, who are accommodated in spacious rooms decorated with contemporary Southwestern charm. Doc Martin's Restaurant and the Adobe Bar are located at the inn. (See below, under Taos Restaurants.)

Sagebrush Inn, NM 68 South, ☎ 505/758-2254 or 800/428-3626, and Best Western's **Kachina Lodge,** 415 Paseo del Pueblo Norte, ☎ 505/758-2275 or 800/522-4462, have moderately priced contemporary rooms and suites. Both feature restaurants, lounges, pools and hot tubs.

The **Taos Bed & Breakfast Association,** ☎ 505/758-4747 or 800/876-7857, is one of the best in the country. Every one of the 16 member properties is exceptional in some way.

Orinda, 461 Valverde, ☎ 505/758-8581 or 800/847-1837, is a dramatic adobe estate, only a 10-minute walk from the Taos Plaza and yet surrounded by country privacy. Horses graze in pastures framed by giant elms and cottonwoods with the majestic Sangre de Cristo Mountains rising as the perfect backdrop in the distance. Three cozy rooms open onto a private courtyard. Each features traditional Southwestern furniture, kiva fireplaces and private baths detailed with Mexican tilework. Gourmet continental breakfasts start the day, served at a skylit table in a lovely gallery hung with the work of local artists.

Salsa del Salto, Taos Ski Valley Road, ☎ 505/776-2422 or 800/530-3097, is a truly exquisite contemporary Southwestern inn, halfway between town and the ski area. Individually designed rooms are bright and spacious with large windows affording spectacular views across either the mesa or over the mountains. Guests are welcome to use the inn's private tennis court, heated pool and hot tub. Breakfasts feature creative gourmet dishes highlighted with homemade jellies, jams and croissants.

CHAMA

Those who need to will find a clean, comfortable room at the **Branding Iron Motel,** ☎ 505/756-2162 or 800/446-2650.

RV travelers should pull into **Twin Rivers Campground and Trailer,** junction of US 64/84 and NM 17, ☎ 505/756-2218, or **Rio Chama RV Campground,** two blocks north of the Depot on NM 17, ☎ 505/756-2303. Both feature pull-through sites with hookups, restrooms, showers and tent areas.

RED RIVER

Lifts **West Condominium Hotel,** Main Street, ☎ 505/754-2778 or 800/221-1859, is Red River's largest resort hotel, offering both standard rooms and two-story deluxe units. Many of them feature kitchens and balconies; all of them have fireplaces. The hotel is within walking distance of the ski area and has a full-service ski rental facility, restaurant, heated pool and two hot tubs.

Right across from the main chairlift, **Alpine Lodge**, Main and Malette Streets, ☎ 505/754-2952 or 800/252-2333, is the second largest, featuring standard rooms with fireplaces and balconies. There is also a restaurant, hot tub and playground.

Roadrunner Campground, just outside of town, ☎ 505/754-2286 or 800/243-2286, offers 150 RV sites with full hookups. There is also a game room, tennis courts, private fishing area and grocery.

CIMARRON

The **St. James Hotel**, 7th and Collins Streets, ☎ 505/376-2664 or 800/748-2694, is perhaps the most significant historical building remaining in the Old West town of Cimarron. Built in 1873 by Henri Lambert, personal chef to both President Lincoln and General Ulysses S. Grant, the hotel's early guest register contains the signatures of Buffalo Bill Cody, Annie Oakley and outlaw Clay Allison, to mention a few. In its heyday, the St. James served as the central meeting place for area ranchers, traders, businessmen, politicians and outlaws alike. Restored in 1985, the hotel offers today's traveler first-class luxury with 19th-century Victorian splendor. Distinctively decorated rooms feature period antiques and as many pieces of original furniture as possible to recreate an authentic Old West atmosphere. This is a must stop for every history buff, even if only to stay long enough for a meal at **Lambert's**, the hotel's elegant dining room. Steak, chicken, seafood and pasta are served on candle-lit tables with fine tablecloths and upholstered chairs. Only the bullet holes in the ceiling remain as proof of the chamber's days as a saloon and gambling hall.

Cimarron Inn & RV Park, US 64 and NM 58, ☎ 505/376-2268 or 800/546-2244, has 12 rooms with queen-sized beds, 12 RV sites with full hookups and a large tent camping area with picnic tables and grills.

ANGEL FIRE

Legends Hotel, at the base of the ski area, ☎ 505/377-6401 or 800/633-7463, has 157 rooms and suites. From moderate to deluxe, all are spacious and comfortable, with bright contemporary Southwestern decor. Legends features a hot tub, lounge and restaurant.

A wide range of condos are also available, and most are within walking distance of the ski area. For information, contact **Angel Fire Chamber of Commerce**, PO Box 547, Angel Fire, 88710, ☎ 505/377-6611 or 800/446-8117.

Restaurants

ALBUQUERQUE

As one might expect from the largest city in the state, Albuquerque features a wide range of restaurant options from fine dining and international cuisine to Mom and Pop operations serving the best in home-cooked meals.

Albuquerque's most unusual dining experience is found more than 3,000 feet above the city at the **High Finance Restaurant**, ☎ 505/243-9742, atop Sandia Peak. Sandia Peak Tramway, #10 Tramway Loop Northeast, affords the only easy access to the restaurant, delivering patrons 2.7 miles from the base of the mountain to the dining room at 10,738 feet. Glorious sunsets and sweeping views of the city below complement an elegant atmosphere and world-class cuisine, including traditional steaks, chicken and seafood, as well as pastas and Mexican dishes. Although it is one of the finest (and most expensive) restaurants in the area, the dress code here is quite liberal. Since various trails in the Sandia Mountain Wilderness offer more adventurous patrons alternate access to the dining room, you may see anything from hiking shorts to evening gowns here. Guests with dinner reservations receive a discount on tram fare, so be sure to call ahead.

A little less expensive – but not too much, **Firehouse Restaurant**, at the base of the Tram, ☎ 505/856-3473, offers a lighter atmosphere and nightly entertainment with an excellent menu of seafood, chicken, prime beef, ribs, pasta and Southwestern favorites. Again, reservations will garner discounted tram tickets.

In Albuquerque proper, the **Rancher's Club of New Mexico,** at the Hilton, 1901 University Northeast, ☎ 505/884-2500, adds an interesting twist to fine dining. When ordering a steak, you not only choose the cut, but you pick the type of wood that it's grilled over – mesquite, hickory, sassafras or wild cherry.

At the **Japanese Kitchen**, 6521 Americas Parkway-Park Square, ☎ 505/884-8937, knife-wielding chefs prepare traditional Japanese meals right at your table. And, if you're in the mood for sushi, this restaurant has one of the top sushi bars in the state.

If you're having trouble deciding, drive down Central Avenue to where three of Albuquerque's best restaurants are found within a couple of blocks from each other – follow your nose to whichever tempts you the most. **Scalo, Northern Italian Grill**, 3500 Central Avenue Southeast, ☎ 505/255-8781, features pastas, grilled steaks and fresh seafood served in a contemporary, split-level dining room. Just across the street, **Yanni's Mediterranean Bar & Grill**, 3109 Central Avenue Northeast, ☎ 505/268-9250, serves spanakopita, leg of lamb and gyros in a classic Greek white-washed building. Patio seating is available almost year-round due to Albuquerque's mild climate. Bring on an ocean and you're in the Med. Next door, **Monte Vista Fire Station Restaurant**, 3201 Central Avenue Northeast, ☎ 505/255-2424, is housed in a restored 1930s fire station that is one of the city's finest surviving representatives of that period's "Pueblo Revival" architecture. An imaginative menu changes nightly, featuring both continental and international cuisine. After dinner, walk across the street to the **Double Rainbow Bakery Café**, 3416 Central Avenue Southeast, ☎ 505/255-6633, for a cappuccino or espresso and a sinful slab of cheesecake. The café features one of the largest and most diverse magazine stands in the city and is a favorite of area college students. This is also a good breakfast option, serving fresh-baked pastries alongside the morning newspaper.

For a budget-priced meal on Central Avenue, a number of fast food restaurants will do in a pinch, but the **66 Diner**, 1405 Central Avenue Northeast, ☎ 505/247-1421, offers much more atmosphere than Burger King or Taco Bell. Designed with Route 66 buffs in mind, this 1950s-style roadside diner serves up heaping doses of nostalgia as well as cheeseburgers, fries and shakes.

If you've not come to New Mexico for its fine Greek, Italian, Japanese or other gourmet cuisine, but for the spicy Mexican food that the area is known for, the Albuquerque phone book lists more than 50 restaurants offering authentic tastes of the region. Among them, **El Pinto Restaurant**, 10500 4th Street Northwest, ☎ 505/898-1771, has been serving Albuquerque for more than 30 years. Garden patios with cascading waterfalls and fountains provide the best in territorial New Mexican atmosphere. Menu items are all original recipes from the proprietor's grandmother and feature New Mexican-grown green chilies roasted fresh on the premises. The best way to enjoy a big plate of fiery Mexican food is with a large margarita in hand to cool any blazing taste buds. **Sadie's Dining Room**, 6230 4th Street Northwest, ☎ 505/345-5339, offers the best 'ritas in the city and their daily specials are definitely spicy enough to burn your buds. One of the most popular eateries in Albuquerque, **Garduno's of Mexico Restaurant & Cantina**, offers four convenient locations in town: 10551 Montgomery Northeast, ☎ 505/298-5000; 8806 4th Street Northwest, ☎ 505/898-2772; 5400 Academy Northeast, ☎ 505/821-3030; 2100 Louisiana Northeast, ☎ 505/880-0055. Standard margaritas, sopapillas, enchiladas and tacos share the menu with exotic twists on Mexican steaks, chicken and seafood.

If none of the above have struck your fancy, there are 23 McDonalds within the city limits.

SANTA FE

Santa Fe has more than 200 restaurants, many presenting art through their entrées just as impressively as the city's galleries do through paintings, photography and sculpture.

Coyote Café, 132 West Water Street, ☎ 505/983-1615, is probably Santa Fe's most famous restaurant and is ranked among the top 100 in the country. Chef/owner Mark Miller was a leader in popularizing modern Southwestern cuisine. His duck quesadillas, chili shrimp and other delectable creations have won the café a national reputation for reinterpreting regional cooking and vaulting it into the realm of high cuisine. Reservations are required. During high tourist periods they should be made two to three days in advance.

Located in an 1860s restored adobe, **La Casa Sena**, 125 East Palace Avenue, ☎ 505/988-9232, is another of Santa Fe's finest. Head chef Kelly Rogers uses only fresh ingredients to create the restaurant's exciting menu. Cuisine is continental with, of course, Southwestern accents, including salmon with chili and trout baked in adobe.

For continental cuisine with a Louisiana flair, try **The Pink Adobe**, 406 Old Santa Fe Trail, ☎ 505/983-7712. The menu is ever-changing, but emphasis revolves around lamb, pork, chicken and grilled yellow-fin tuna. New Mexico's influence is, however, ever-present; the restaurant's most famous entrée, Steak Dunnigan, is covered with home-grown green chilies and sautéed mushrooms.

Santacafé, 231 Washington Street, ☎ 505/984-1788, also features an interesting Southwestern menu, but this time with distinct Asian influences. Various East-meets-West minglings stretch from marinated rack of lamb to free range chicken or Chinese dumplings. A filet mignon with roasted garlic crowns Santacafé's diverse menu and has even been featured on the cover of *Bon Appétit* magazine.

Classic Tuscan-style Northern Italian dishes are emphasized at **Julian's**, 221 Shelby, ☎ 505/988-2355. All items are expertly prepared by chef Wayne Gustafson, who changes his menu seasonally and even daily depending on which ingredients are freshly available.

La Traviata, 95 West Macy Street, ☎ 505/984-1091, is the place for Southern Italian. Imaginative Sicilian dishes are created daily by chef Alberto Calascione, again with attention to only the freshest ingredients.

More moderately priced Italian food is found at **Pranzo Italian Grill**, 540 Montezuma, ☎ 505/984-2645. The restaurant features an attractive rooftop terrace and the menu, while much more conventional than its more expensive relatives, is still quite interesting. One of the most popular choices is the ravioli with grilled salmon and a parmesan cream sauce.

San Francisco Street Bar & Grill, 114 West San Francisco Street, ☎ 505/982-2044, offers affordable American food in a light, fun atmosphere. Homemade soups, pastas, salads and sandwiches round out the menu, and the owner claims to serve the "Best Burger in Santa Fe."

Reasonably priced New Mexican specialties are found at **La Tertulia**, 416 Agua Fria, ☎ 505/988-2769. Considered one of the most romantic restaurants in Santa Fe, it surprisingly resides in a restored adobe that was once a Dominican-order convent. Although the nuns are no longer present, the food remains heavenly, from home made tortilla soup to entrées such as Carne Adovada followed by a traditional Natillas custard.

For lunch, **The Shed**, 113½ East Palace Avenue, ☎ 505/982-9030, is a Santa Fe tradition that absolutely must not be missed. During the high tourist season, guests wait as long as 30-45 minutes for a table, but the famous blue-corn tortillas stuffed with cheese and pork are well worth it. Green chili "Shedburgers" and home-made posole are also extremely popular and, followed by lemon soufflé or mocha chocolate cake, usually induce instant siesta. The Shed is open daily from 11 AM to 2:30 PM

Reservations for breakfast? Yep, at **Café Pasqual's**, 121 Don Gaspar Street, ☎ 505/983-9340 – the most popular spot in town, featuring a breakfast quesadilla that can't be beat. Lunch and dinner are also served.

Cloud Cliff Bakery, 1805 Second Street, ☎ 505/983-6254, is another fashionable breakfast choice. Located next door to Second Street Studios, the bakery is decorated with the latest works by local artists and offers a great jump start if you're heading out for a day of gallery hopping. Pastries and coffee are the dominant morning delectables.

It's almost painful to admit in the light of Santa Fe's fine restaurant scene, but a drive down Cerrillos Road finds representatives of just about every fast food chain known to man.

LOS ALAMOS

Los Alamos' finest restaurants are found at its two hotels. **Trinity Sights Restaurant**, at Hilltop House, 400 Trinity Drive, ☎ 505/662-2552, offers breathtaking views of the Sangre de Cristos from its second story dining room. Aside from a good menu of steak, chicken and seafood choices, the restaurant has an excellent hot buffet, soup bar and salad bar.

Ashley's Restaurant and Pub, at Los Alamos Inn, 2210 Trinity Drive, ☎ 505/662-7211, also has a good basic menu, but is most popular for its succulent Sunday brunch. The pub features light sandwiches and complimentary hors d'oeuvres during happy hour.

A favorite gathering place for locals, **De Colores**, 820 Trinity Drive, ☎ 505/662-6285, presents an inviting atmosphere to accompany their menu of steak, chicken and northern New Mexican specialties.

Café Allegro, 800 Trinity Drive in the MariMac Mini Mall, ☎ 505/662-4040, serves cappuccino, espresso, soups, sandwiches and fresh-baked pastries, as well as newspapers, magazines, tapes and CDs.

McDonalds, 1247 Trinity Drive, and **Subway**, 15th and Central, handle the fast food duties for the community.

CHAMA

The **High Country Restaurant and Lounge**, at the "Y," ☎ 505/756-2384, serves everything from 15-oz. T-bones to Alaskan King Crab as well as standard New Mexican favorites and burgers. There is also a well-appointed salad bar and an extremely well-appointed antique saloon bar.

TAOS

Taos celebrates fine food as robustly as it does fine art, beautiful scenery and world-class skiing.

The Historic Taos Inn's award-winning **Doc Martin's**, 125 Paseo del Pueblo Norte, ☎ 505/758-1977, features one of the most innovative menus in town. Start with the smoked chicken appetizer on a homemade corn tortilla with black bean salsa, chicos and a roasted garlic-avocado cream. Follow it with a bowl of Yucatan lime soup, and then a main course of pecan-crusted sea bass, apple cider pork tenderloin or green chili-braised rabbit. Menus change seasonally and reservations are highly recommended.

The **Apple Tree Restaurant**, 123 Bent Street, ☎ 505/758-1900, is located in a charming Victorian-era home on one of Taos' most historic streets. Entrées include mango chicken enchiladas, shrimp quesadillas and grilled lamb with rosemary.

The second-story balcony at **Ogelvies** on the plaza, ☎ 505/758-8866, offers the best view of Taos' classic central plaza. Serving traditional Mexican dishes, pastas, steaks and contemporary nouvelle-Southwestern cuisine, the restaurant is sure to please every member of most any party. Entrées include a fresh pinyon trout, a carne adovada chimichanga and a bacon-wrapped filet topped with crab meat covered with a light bearnaise sauce.

Michael's Kitchen, 304 Paseo del Pueblo Norte, ☎ 505/758-4178, serves the heartiest Southwestern breakfasts in the state. One green chili and ham omelet will keep you going well into the evening or at least until the shops and slopes close. Burgers and traditional New Mexican dishes are served for lunch and dinner as well.

A fun alternative for dinner, **Eske's Brew Pub**, half a block off of the plaza, ☎ 505/758-1517, serves salads, green chili stew and battered club sandwiches. But the reason for going is the experimental home-brewed beers; get brave and throw down one of their specialties – a spicy New Mexican green chili beer.

At Taos Ski Valley, **Rhoda's**, ☎ 505/776-2005, presents prime rib, lobster quesadillas, cajun chicken etouffée, and coconut shrimp in a bright dining room just below Chair #1.

Across from the Thunderbird Lodge, **Dolomite**, ☎ 505/776-1868, serves wonderful pastas, calzones and specialty pizzas in a funky little café at the Taos Ski Valley.

RED RIVER

Most of the restaurants in town serve basically the same menu – steaks, chicken and limited seafood. **Angelina's**, Main Street, ☎ 505/754-2211, serves a nice grilled trout and Mexican specials as well as vegetarian entrées. It also features a large soup and salad bar.

ANGEL FIRE

Rocky Mountain BBQ & Grill, Pinewood Plaza, ☎ 505/377-2763, has one of the most diverse menus in town. From chicken fried steak to prime rib, homemade tortilla soup to chicken fajitas, and old-fashioned burgers to turkey croissants, there's going to be something for everyone.

Camping

Coronado State Park, just across from Coronado State Monument, 15 miles north of Albuquerque via Interstate 25 and NM 44, has a large developed campground with picnic tables, shelters, grills and RV hookups. The park also has modern restrooms and showers. For state park information, ☎ 505/867-5589.

Two campgrounds at **Cochiti Lake**, 50 miles north of Albuquerque via Interstate 25 and NM 22, provide picnic areas and developed camp sites.

Hyde Memorial State Park, seven miles north of Santa Fe via Hyde Park Road/NM 475, offers numerous campsites in the thick fir, pine and spruce of the Sangre de Cristos. RV hookups are available. For information, ☎ 505/986-0283.

The **Santa Fe National Forest**, north and east of Santa Fe, contains several public campgrounds. **Black Canyon, Little Tesque, Big Tesque, Aspen Vista** and **Aspen Basin Campgrounds** are all located along Hyde Park Road on the way to Santa Fe Ski Area, offering convenient access to the best hiking and biking in the area. Most sites have drinking water, grills, picnic tables and pit toilets. For information, contact the Santa Fe National Forest office, 1220 St. Francis Drive, PO Box 1689, Santa Fe, 87504, ☎ 505/988-6940.

Bandelier National Monument, 10 miles south of Los Alamos via NM 4, has more than 70 miles of maintained trails, giving numerous backcountry primitive camping possibilities. Campers with more equipment than will fit in a backpack should seek out the park's **Juniper Campground**. Near the entrance station above Frijoles Canyon, the campground offers 94 sites with picnic tables, grills, water and modern restrooms. There are no sites with utility hookups, but there is an RV dump station. ☎ 505/672-3861.

In the Santa Fe National Forest, west of Los Alamos, try **East Fork Campground**, seven miles east of La Cueva via NM 4, or **Fenton Lake Campground**, just northwest of La Cueva via NM 126. Most sites have tables, grills and pit toilets.

For information, contact the Santa Fe National Forest – Jemez Ranger District, Jemez Springs, 87544, ☎ 505/829-3535.

A campground at **El Vado Lake State Park**, 30 miles southwest of Chama via US 84 and NM 112, offers a modern restroom and several scattered sites with picnic tables, grills and shelters. ☎ 505/827-7465. **Heron Lake State Park**, 25 miles southwest of Chama via US 84 and NM 95, features a slightly more developed campground. Numerous sites are equipped with RV hookups, as well as tables, grills and shelters. A central comfort station provides modern restrooms and showers. ☎ 505/588-7470.

Big Arsenic Springs, Little Arsenic Springs, Montosa, La Junta and **El Aguaje Campgrounds** are located on the canyon rim of the Rio Grande Gorge in the **Wild Rivers National Recreation Area**, roughly 35 miles north of Taos via NM 522 and NM 378, ☎ 505/239-7211. Each features water, restrooms, picnic tables, shelters and grills, but no hookups. Each rim site has a corresponding riverside campground offering shelters, picnic tables and grills. Riverside sites are accessible by hiking down from the rim or by canoe, kayak or raft from the river. (See above, under Adventures on Foot/Water.)

Several free campsites are located along the creek paralleling **Taos Ski Valley Road** (NM 150). Most sites have picnic tables and grills; only about half offer pit toilets and drinking water.

There are numerous campgrounds in the **Carson National Forest** surrounding Taos, Red River, and Angel Fire. Most feature picnic tables, grills, water and pit toilets. For information, contact Carson National Forest-Supervisor's Office, PO Box 558, Taos, 87571, ☎ 505/758-6200.

Camping is permitted in **Cimarron Canyon State Park**, eight miles east of Eagle Nest via US 64, with a special use permit (available at the park). **Tolby**, **Maverick** and **Ponderosa** regular campgrounds in Cimarron Canyon all have pit toilets and water. At least one person at each campsite is required to have a fishing license.

Northeast New Mexico

Miles and miles of nondescript grassland seem to be the overriding feature of Northeastern New Mexico, not very exciting for those hunched in the back of a station wagon cruising along the Interstate. But only a century ago this was the Wild West, not Hollywood's version, but the true untamed American frontier, where soldiers from **Fort Union**, defending the **Santa Fe Trail**, fought hundreds of skirmishes and waged several major campaigns against Comanches and Apaches. During the early railroad days in old **Las Vegas**, outlaws like Doc Holiday and Billy the Kid would just as soon shoot you in your sleep for snoring as cheat you out of your wagon in a game of cards.

Three hundred or so years before that, Coronado and the Spanish were here searching east of **Pecos** for the fabled lost cities of gold. And millions of years ago, dinosaurs roamed the area on the shores of a vast ocean with its coastline stretching across what is now the eastern edge of the state. Footprints and fossils have been found along the banks of a small lake near present day **Clayton**. And, between Clayton and **Raton**, the 1,000-foot-tall cinder cone of now dormant **Capulin Volcano** stands as a national monument reminding us that 10,000 years ago these plains were ablaze with molten lava.

More recently, the Santa Fe Trail and even the railroads gave way to **Route 66**, perhaps America's most fabled highway. This memorable two-lane blacktop crossed the entire state of New Mexico, serving as the focal point for early tourism development. In the northeast, rivers all along the famous byway were dammed, not just for irrigation, but to tempt travelers into pulling over and staying awhile. There are many large recreational reservoirs, including **Ute Lake** – the second largest in the state – in this seemingly arid section of New Mexico. That may help to explain why one of the Southwest's most popular and unlikely scuba diving destinations is located here at **Blue Hole** in **Santa Rosa**.

Along the western border of this region, the Great Plains meet the mountains. The majestic **Sangre de Cristo Mountains** rise just west of Interstate 25 and parallel the highway from Las Vegas to Raton, where **Raton Pass** serves as New Mexico's primary portal into Colorado. These mountains provide some of the best camping and hiking opportunities in the region. Numerous mountain streams, which eventually flow into the **Pecos** and **Canadian Rivers**, facilitate some of the most fabulous fly-fishing in the state.

Northeast New Mexico

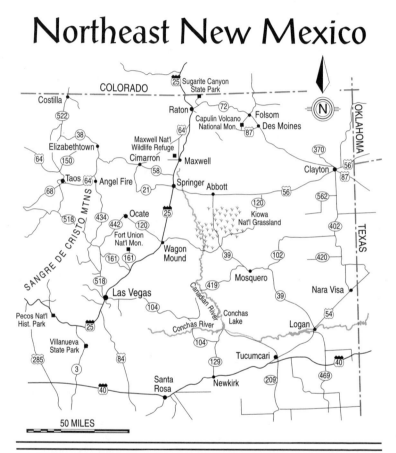

The areas described in this chapter range in elevation from 5,000 to more than 10,000 feet. If you live at lower elevations, expect to tire quickly during your first few days here. Exercise special caution when engaging in vigorous outdoor activities until your body adjusts to the decreased oxygen levels.

With the arid climate throughout New Mexico, dehydration is always a possibility. If you're planning activities such as hiking or backpacking, make sure to bring adequate water supplies. Winters here can be rough too, especially in the plains, where a "blue norther" can blow through, dropping the temperature by 40° in an hour. Heavy snows and cold weather necessitate thoughtful preparation and warm, layered clothing.

Touring

The suggested route to follow through this part of the state begins east of Santa Fe on Interstate 25. Continue north from Las Vegas to Raton, then east to Clayton, on US Highway 87. From there, parallel the Texas state line heading south on NM Highway 402 and US Highway 54 to Tucumcari, where Interstate 40 leads back west through Santa Rosa to Albuquerque.

Pecos National Historical Park

Actress Greer Garson and her husband, E.E. Fogelson, donated 365 acres of land about 26 miles southeast of Santa Fe to create **Pecos National Historical Park**, preserving one of the oldest and most visually engaging of New Mexico's pueblo ruins. Exit Interstate 25 near Rowe and continue north on NM 63 for about four miles to the entrance of the park. Mission ruins dating back to the 17th century and pueblo ruins from the 13th century can be seen today, but excavations of area pit dwellings suggest that Pecos' first inhabitants arrived as early as 800 A.D. By the 15th century, Pecos Pueblo stood five stories high and was home to more than 2,000 people. These people, thought to be descendants of the Anasazi, were not warriors like the plains Indians, but were corn and squash farmers. In 1540, Coronado was peacefully met west of Pecos and invited to visit. He sent Hernando de Alvarado and a small complement of soldiers to the pueblo, where they were told of riches in the plains to the east. A ploy to lure the Spaniards away from the Rio Grande pueblos, it worked and kept Coronado occupied searching for the so-called "lost cities of gold" until the summer of 1541 and his return to Mexico. Fifty years later, the Spanish returned, but this time they were met with rocks and arrows. Gaspar Castano de Sosa retaliated and, with only 37 soldiers, defeated the 500 Indians defending the pueblo.

The Spanish occupied Pecos for the next 100 years, building mission churches and carrying out farming and ranching in the area. In 1680 the Indians revolted, however, driving the Spaniards off and burning the mission. They tried to return to their pre-Conquest way of life, but 12 years later the Spanish were back to retake the pueblo – which was suffering from Comanche raids and from diseases introduced by the Europeans. In 1838, the pueblo was abandoned and the last 20 surviving Pecos Indians moved on to live at the Jemez Pueblo on the other side of Santa Fe.

Today a museum in the park's visitor center explains the pueblo's history in more detail and exhibits both Indian and Spanish artifacts found on site. The park is open 8 AM to 6 PM during the summer and 8 AM to 5 PM the rest of the year.

For information, contact **Pecos National Historic Park**, Drawer 11, Pecos, NM 87552, ☎ 505/757-6414.

Villanueva & Villanueva State Park

Exit Interstate 25 about halfway between Pecos and Las Vegas at NM 3 and follow it and the Pecos River 14 miles south to the village of **Villanueva**. Established in the 1790s as a walled outpost to protect settlers from raiding Comanches, but long bypassed by railroad and highway, this is one of the few New Mexican villages with at least part of its original walls remaining. Villanueva is not, however, a tourist trap. Visit the beautifully maintained mission church dating back to 1818 and stroll through the old plaza, taking in the remnants of Spanish Colonial charm.

From the Village, follow signs 1½ miles along the access road into a canyon studded with pinons and cottonwoods and the entrance to **Villanueva State Park**. To preserve some of the colonial atmosphere of the area, picnic shelters and other facilities in the park are done in brown adobe. A picturesque foot bridge crosses the Pecos River, which runs through the middle of the park. From that point, several hiking trails climb 400 feet to the top of the mesa overlooking the canyon. (See below, under Adventures on Foot.) The Pecos also provides excellent fishing, plus splendid wading and splashing to help cool off during hot summer days. (See below, under Adventures on Water.) Camping is available.

For information, contact **Villanueva State Park**, PO Box 40, Villanueva, NM 87583, ☎ 505/421-2957.

Las Vegas

Since its beginnings in 1821 as Nuestra Señora de Los Dolores des Las Vegas Grande (Our Lady of Sorrows of the Large Meadows), a Mexican land grant to some sheep ranchers, Las Vegas has grown to become the largest town in northeast New Mexico.

Situated in the eastern foothills of the Sangre de Cristo Mountains, its early days were beset with numerous Indian raids. This prompted the building of the town's historic Central Plaza in the 1830s to protect settlers against raiding tribes. Meanwhile, as travel increased on the Santa Fe Trail, the newly built plaza became a major trading center on the covered wagon superhighway. When General Kearny arrived in 1846 claiming the territory for the United States, Las Vegas served as a military headquarters until Fort Union was built five years later. It was the Atchison, Topeka, & Santa Fe Railroad, though, that brought true prosperity to town. By 1882, only three years after the arrival of the railroad, Las Vegas had become the region's most important commercial center. It had also earned the reputation as the "Wildest of the Wild West." With outlaws likes of Jesse James, Billy the Kid, Scarface Charlie, Stuttering Tom and Flapjack Bill making Las Vegas their hangout, it was commonplace for the *Daily Optic* to report 30 or more deaths by murder, self-defense or hanging in a one-month period. A local saloon owner even organized the Society of Bandits of New Mexico.

Today, of course, the Santa Fe Trail has given way to Interstate 25, and even though cars fly by at over 65 mph, things have slowed a bit in Las Vegas. Recreational and historical resources shape the current economy. The community has more than 900 buildings on the Federal Register of Historic Places and there are three specific self-guided walking tours through its Central Plaza area, Carnegie Park area and Old Railroad District (see below, under Adventures on Foot). The **Theodore Roosevelt Rough Riders Memorial and City Museum**, 727 Grand Ave. (in the same building as the Chamber of Commerce), is an interesting stop for any military buff. The memorial commemorates the Rough Riders' campaign in the Spanish-American War of 1898, as almost half of Teddy's Rough Riders were from New Mexico and many from Las Vegas. The museum is an oddball collection of Teddy's paraphernalia, as well as genuine historical pieces – military artifacts, pioneer and Indian weapons, domestic items and documents pertaining to local history. The museum is open daily, 8 AM to 4 PM. For information, ☎ 505/425-8726.

Montezuma Hot Springs, five miles north of the Central Plaza on Hot Springs Blvd./NM 65, is a good place to relax after a day of touring. According to legend, this series of public hot springs was visited by the Aztec chief Montezuma II in the 16th century to take advantage of believed healing properties of their waters. Some pools have shelters built around them, some are lined with concrete and others are as natural as they were when Montezuma soaked in them.

Right across the road from the hot springs is the historic **Montezuma Castle Hotel**. Built in 1882 by railroad owners to lure tourists from around the world to a lavish spa planned for construction around the hot springs, the hotel never fulfilled its potential. It was destroyed by fire and rebuilt twice, losing money from the start. The railroad owners finally gave up on it in 1903. Since then, the property has changed hands several times, the castle housing everything from a YMCA to a Jesuit Seminary. Today, it is home to the **Armand Hammer United World College of the American West**. Open since 1982, it is one of the most ambitious educational institutions in the world. Some 200 teenagers from 70 different countries gather here to undertake a demanding two-year curriculum, equivalent to the senior year of high school and the first year of college. Plus, there's the added bonus of multicultural workshops and special wilderness activities that take advantage of the college's proximity to the Santa Fe National Forest. Tours of the campus, including the beautifully restored Montezuma Castle, are available by appointment. For information, ☎ 505/454-1461.

The Las Vegas National Wildlife Refuge, on the southeast side of town, offers year-round opportunities for wildlife viewing. (See below, under Adventures On Foot.)

On the north edge of town, **Storrie Lake State Park**, supports numerous water-related activities. (See below, under Adventures On Water.) Camping is also available.

For information, contact the **Las Vegas/San Miguel Chamber of Commerce**, PO Box 148, Las Vegas, NM 87701, ☎ 505/425-8631 or 800/832-5947.

Fort Union National Monument

Fort Union was the headquarters for the Military Department of New Mexico from 1851 to 1891 and during its heyday was the most extensive military installation in the territory. Originally a collection of crude log buildings built near the intersection of the

Mountain and Cimarron Branches of the Santa Fe Trail, the fort served as a place for travelers to rest and refit at Sutler's Store before continuing their journey, and the troops' primary mission was to protect those travelers out on the trail. During the 1850s, several campaigns were launched from the fort against the Apache tribes of the southern Rockies, the Utes of southern Colorado, and the Kiowas and Comanches of the eastern plains, all of whom were disrupting traffic on the Santa Fe Trail.

During the Civil War most of the regular troops were withdrawn from Fort Union and replaced by volunteer regiments. Still dedicated to defending the Santa Fe Trail, which was now the main artery of supply for Federal forces, a second Fort Union, a star-shaped earthen fortification, was constructed to strengthen defenses. But Fort Union never saw any action during the war, as the only Confederate invasion of New Mexico was halted and turned back about 20 miles southeast of Santa Fe at the Battle of Glorieta Pass in 1862. The second Fort Union was soon thereafter abandoned.

In 1863, construction began on the third and (final) Fort Union which, when completed, was the largest installation in the territory. It included not only a military post, but a separate quartermaster depot with warehouses, corrals, shops, offices and quarters. Serving as the principal supply base for the Military Department of New Mexico, shipments of food, clothing, arms, ammunition, tools and building materials were unpacked and stored in warehouses here until assigned to other forts as needed. But, even though the supply function of Fort Union far overshadowed its military role, operations continued from the fort against hostile Indians who stepped up their raids during the chaos of the Civil War. Steady campaigns against the Apaches, Navajos, Cheyennes, Arapahos, Kiowas and Comanches finally brought an end to the Indian Wars in the spring of 1875. In the years after, the fort's company helped track down outlaws, quiet mob violence and mediate feuds, mostly in nearby Las Vegas. The supply depot continued to thrive until 1879, when the Santa Fe Railroad replaced the Santa Fe Trail, and by 1891 the fort had outlived its usefulness and was deserted.

It's the ruins of the third Fort Union Complex that you see when visiting the **Fort Union National Monument** today (see below, under Adventures On Foot). Exit Interstate 25 two miles north of Watrous and follow NM 161 for eight miles to its end and the park entrance. A small visitor center and museum greets guests at the monument. There are often costumed interpreters roaming the grounds to furnish a glimpse of the Old West and answer questions. No camping is allowed at the park, but there are picnic tables. The Monument is open daily, 8 AM to 5 PM. For information, contact **Fort Union National Monument**, Watrous, NM 87753, ☎ 505/425-8025.

Springer

The town of Springer popped up in 1879 with the arrival of the Santa Fe Railroad, and was the seat of Colfax County for almost 20 years until it moved up the road to Raton. Nowadays, there's not much going on in this sleepy little town at the intersection of Interstate 25 and US Highway 56. The old county courthouse is now home to the **Santa Fe Trail Museum**, Maxwell Street, Springer, ☎ 505/483-2341. This is not the most exciting museum in the state, but it does display the only electric chair ever used in New Mexico, complete with a convicted mannequin prepared to suffer its punishment. Perhaps more interesting than the museum, **The Livery Stable**, 220 Maxwell Street, Springer, ☎ 505/483-2269, is an antique shop in a century-old building occupying an entire city block. With over 10,000 pieces, an organizational system similar to grandma's attic and not one price tag in the place, the fun is in the finding – old Coca-Cola and Texaco signs, farm equipment, photographs, bottles, furniture, etc.

For information, contact the **Springer Chamber of Commerce**, PO Box 323, Springer, NM, 87747, ☎ 505/483-2998.

Kiowa National Grassland

One section of the three-state, 263,954-acre Kiowa National Grassland lies about 30 miles southeast of Springer. Take US 65 east to Abbott and then NM 39 south, which leads directly through the Canadian River Unit of this grassland – a project to reclaim prairie lands destroyed by over-farming and the resulting Great Plains Dust Bowl of the 1930s. Today, mule and pronghorn deer, bear, Barbary sheep (introduced from North Africa), mountain lion, wild turkeys, pheasant, ducks and geese abound near the 800-foot-deep Canadian River Canyon at the western border of the grassland. The river there also provides some good warm water fishing for bass, catfish and crappie, as does **Chicosa Lake State Park** in the southeast corner of the grassland. (See below, under Adventures On Water.)

For information, contact **Kiowa National Grassland**, 16 N. 2nd Street, Clayton, NM 88415, ☎ 505/374-9652.

Maxwell National Wildlife Refuge

Maxwell National Wildlife Refuge lies on 2,800 acres of grassland approximately 13 miles north of Springer. Take the Maxwell exit off of Interstate 25 and follow the signs via NM 445 and NM 505 to reach the refuge. Numerous unmarked dirt roads lead through and along the borders of the wildlife areas, which are used primarily by migratory waterfowl during fall and winter. Camping and fishing are available (see below under Adventures on Water).

For information, contact **Refuge Manager**, PO Box 276, Maxwell, NM 87728, ☎ 505/375-2331.

Raton

The small town of Raton (pop. 7,400) is probably most known by its location at the foot of Raton Pass, which was the most treacherous section of the Mountain Route of the Santa Fe Trail. But the actual town did not spring up until 1880 when the Atchison, Topeka & Santa Fe Railroad relocated its construction camp and station from Otero to the base of the pass. Within a year, a village of about 3,000 had grown around the railroad operation there. Soon the railroad, with the addition of coal mining in the area, was shaping a booming economy for the town.

Today, Raton Pass still serves as the primary gateway between Colorado and New Mexico and the Historic Santa Fe Depot continues to usher trains (including Amtrak passenger trains) in and out of town, but tourism is by far the mainstay of Raton's current economy.

The great outdoors is the main tourist draw in this area. New Mexico's newest state park, **Sugarite Canyon State Park** is just eight miles from town via NM 72 and NM 526, offering abundant hiking, fishing and camping (see below). Almost 30 miles east of town on US 64, **Capulin Volcano National Monument** is a natural wonder worth the drive to visit (see below).

The nation's largest and most comprehensive shooting facility lies 10 miles south of Raton on US 64. The **NRA Whittington Center** encompasses more than 33,000 acres offering hunting for deer, elk, turkey, bear and more. There are also 14 different shooting ranges, including high power, metallic silhouette, skeet, pistol, black powder, trap and sporting clays. National championships in many of these events are held here annually. Training in all shooting disciplines by nationally known instructors is also available.

For information, contact **NRA Whittington Center**, PO Box 30-06, Raton, NM 87740.

Whether or not shooting interests you, **The Vermejo Park Ranch** is a private resort and working cattle ranch on 588,000 acres 40 miles west of Raton. Guests are treated to hunting, fishing, horseback riding, skeet shooting and limitless opportunities for hiking and outdoor photography – all coupled with deluxe accommodations and gourmet meals. (See below, under Raton Accommodations.)

Brochures for a self-guided tour of the **Downtown Historic District** can be obtained at the Chamber of Commerce office, 100 Clayton Road/US 87/64, ☎ 505/445-3689. The tour is a kind of architectural timeline pointing out almost 30 buildings displaying different styles from the late 19th century through the early 20th. Two buildings on the route merit special mention. The first is the old Santa Fe Depot on First Street, which brought life to this town in the 1880s and still welcomes trains and passengers to town with its Mission Revival construction and colorful portals. The other is the **Shuler Theater** on Second Street. Undoubtedly Raton's architectural masterpiece, it was completed in 1915 and offers regular performances even today. The interior of the European-Rococo-style opera house boasts near-perfect acoustics and murals depicting local history. The murals, painted as a WPA project by Manville Chapman in the 1930s, decorate the lobby. For information and programming schedules, contact the **Historic Shuler Theater**, 131 N. Second Street, Raton, NM 87740, ☎ 505/445-5520.

The downtown district tour will also lead you by the **Raton Museum**, 218 South 1st Street, ☎ 505/445-8979. A storefront collection of Santa Fe Trail memorabilia, railroad artifacts and mining exhibits located in the old Coors Building, it is sure to interest any Old West buff.

The downs at **La Mesa Park**, on the south edge of town, are one of the most popular summer attractions in the area. Quarter horse racing on weekends and holidays from May to September tempts numerous guests to bet it all on their favorite mount. For information, contact La Mesa Park, Raton, NM 87740, ☎ 505/445-2301.

For further information, contact **Raton Chamber of Commerce**, PO Box 1211, Raton, NM 87740, ☎ 505/445-3689 or 800/638-6161.

Sugarite Canyon State Park

Established in 1985, Sugarite Canyon State Park is one of the newest and most beautiful parks in the state. The canyon was mined extensively between 1910 and 1941. A scenic hike through the old Sugarite Coal Camp ruins furnishes a glimpse of life in the canyon when more than 1,000 people lived and worked in the mines here.

Today, numerous hiking trails weave through the park which explodes with wildflowers each spring and summer. Two lakes, joined by a stream bisecting the park, make for great fishing. Their high mountain location and chilly waters, however, deter even the hardiest swimmers (see below, under Adventures on Water). Sugarite Canyon also experiences extremely cold winters, making it a popular destination for snowshoeing, cross-country skiing, sledding and ice fishing (see below, under Adventures on Snow).

A visitor center at the park's entrance contains a fine museum which documents the canyon's early mining history. Information on the park's geology and wildlife can also be obtained there. Camping is available.

For information, contact **Sugarite Canyon State Park**, HCR 63, Box 386, Raton, NM 87740, ☎ 505/445-5607.

Capulin Volcano National Monument

Capulin Mountain rises more than 1,000 feet above the plains of northeast New Mexico to a summit of 8,812 feet. This national monument, established in 1916, is visible for miles from the highway between Raton and Clayton and is about the only thing of interest between the two. The park entrance is 30 miles east of Raton on US 64/87 and then three miles north of Capulin on NM 325.

The visitor center at the base of this 10,000-year-old cinder cone shows a 10-minute film explaining volcanic activity and the history of the Capulin Volcano. Its last eruption was less than 25,000 years ago and scientists still consider it potentially active. A two-mile road spirals up the volcano to a parking lot near the summit. From here, and from hiking trails on the rim of the crater, there are spectacular 360-degree panoramic views of the surrounding countryside.

The visitor center at Capulin Volcano National Monument is open Labor Day through Memorial Day, 8 AM to 4:30 PM, and in summer 8 AM to 8 PM. There is small picnic area near the visitor center, but camping is not allowed in the park.

For information, contact **Capulin National Monument**, Capulin, NM 88414, ☎ 505/278-2201.

Folsom

In 1925, George McJunkin, foreman for the Crowfoot Ranch, discovered some large bones and a handful of flint spearheads in an arroyo near Folsom. Further findings led anthropologists to conclude that man had existed in this area more than 10,000 years earlier than previously believed. Despite its importance in the realm of scientific history, Folsom remains a tiny ranching community whose proximity to Capulin Volcano National Monument may serve as the only explanation for its tourist traffic.

If you do find yourself in Folsom, **the Folsom Museum**, displaying historical artifacts of the area as well as some 12,000-year-old spear points and fossils, is well worth a look since admission is free. The museum is on Main Street and is open daily 10 AM to 5 PM, Memorial Day through Labor Day. For information, ☎ 505/278-2122, or write Folsom Museum, Main Street, Folsom, NM 88419.

After visiting the museum, drive four miles north of town to **Folsom Falls**. This natural waterfall, fed by springs on the Dry Cimarron River, is a great spot for a picnic and some fishing.

Clayton

The town of Clayton lies 83 miles east of Raton, on US 87/64, in the heart of cowboy and dinosaur country. The last living dinosaurs roamed this area 100 million years ago, but several life-sized stone models occupy the little town. There are two on the lawn of the Clayton-Union County Chamber and Tourist Center at 1101 South First Street (Highway 87) and another in the Union County Historical Park on Wilson Street behind Union County General Hospital. Also, more than 500 dinosaur tracks are visible near the dam at **Clayton Lake State Park** 12 miles north of town (see below, under Adventures On Foot/Water).

Cowboys have more recently roamed these parts and Clayton has been a major cattle ranching and farming region since the coming of the railroad and the town's founding in 1888. The Cimarron Cut-Off of the Santa Fe Trail also crossed this territory following old Indian trails. But it was the 1901 public hanging (and inadvertent decapitation) of notorious outlaw Thomas "Black Jack" Ketchum, whose last words were "Let her rip," that made Clayton famous in cowboy lore.

The Herzstein Memorial Museum, at the corner of Second and Walnut in the restored 1920 United Methodist Church building, displays antiques and artifacts, photographs and documents, as well as fossils and footprints. Admission is free; for hours and information, ☎ 505/374-9508.

For information on Clayton, contact **Clayton-Union County Chamber and Tourist Information Center**, PO Box 476, Clayton, NM 88415, ☎ 505/374-9253.

Tucumcari

Tucumcari Tonight! is the slogan still visible on billboards for hundreds of miles in either direction from town on Interstate 40, a bit of memorabilia from Route 66 days. Back then, Tucumcari boasted more than 2,000 motel rooms for road-weary travelers requiring rest for another day of kicks on Old Route Six-Six. Judging from the neon overkill along the main drag, there have to be at least 2,000, if not more, motel rooms still available to those needing relief from their travels along Interstate 40.

If you find yourself in town with a little time to kill, swing by the **Tucumcari Historical Museum**, 416 S. Adam Street. A 19th-century windmill, military canons, a jet fighter, covered wagons and railroad cars occupy the grounds surrounding this three-story, red-brick monument to the typical small-town museum. Housed inside are copious collections of bottles, guns, barbed wire, minerals, petrified wood, saddles as well as several displays simply labeled, "more miscellaneous artifacts." But, for a chaotic collection of locally donated artifacts, many of the exhibits are put together quite nicely. Reproductions of a 1920s hospital room, an early Tucumcari sheriff's office, a one-room schoolhouse and an early post office lend a touch of credibility to this production of the Tucumcari Historical Research Institute. The Museum is open June 2 though September 2, Mon.-Sat. from 9 AM to 6 PM and Sunday 1 PM to 6 PM; during the rest of the year, from 9 AM to 5 PM

Tues.-Sat. and 1 PM to 5 PM on Sunday. For information, ☎ 505/461-4201.

The major tourist attractions in the area, however, are **Ute Lake** and **Conchas Lake State Parks**. Both are about 30 miles from town and both offer excellent fishing, swimming, sailing and water-skiing, as well as picnicking and camping. (See below, under Adventures on Water.)

During summer months, a popular area excursion is a trip to the **Caprock Amphitheater and Park**, roughly 30 miles southeast of town via Interstate 40 and NM 469. Various plays and musicals are performed there Thursday-Saturday. (See below, under "Eco-Tours & Cultural Excursions.")

For information, contact **Tucumcari/Quay County Chamber of Commerce**, PO Drawer E, Tucumcari, NM 88401, ☎ 505/461-1694.

Santa Rosa

Zipping along Interstate 40, uninformed travelers might glance at Santa Rosa thinking they'd just passed Tucumcari's twin sister. But, believe it or not, this town of 4,600 people on the eastern New Mexico prairie is one of the most visited scuba diving centers in the Southwest, billing itself as "The City of Natural Lakes." There are five lakes within a seven-mile radius of town. The most famous is **Blue Hole**, which is actually within the city limits. Divers from all over the country come here to explore the crystal-clear waters of this 81-foot-deep geological phenomenon. **Perch Lake**, on the south side of town, is also a popular dive spot. (See below, under Adventures on Water.)

About a block from Blue Hole, **Park Lake** is a favorite local swimming hole. Located in a public recreation area that sports picnic tables, tennis courts, a baseball diamond and a shower, this is a fine place to spend a relaxing day. No camping is allowed, however, as the park is only open from dawn 'til dusk.

Campers, fishermen and watersports enthusiasts should head for **Santa Rosa Lake State Park**, seven miles north of town. Camping and fishing are also available at **James Wallace Memorial Park and Power Dam** on the south edge of the city limits. (See below, under Adventures on Water.)

For information, contact **Santa Rosa Chamber of Commerce**, 486 Parker Ave., Santa Rosa, NM 88435, ☎ 505/472-3763.

Adventures

On Foot

The canyon at **Villanueva State Park** offers three hiking trails and three different experiences. Two trailheads are across the Pecos River footbridge from the main camping area. To the right, a long steep trail climbs 400 feet out of the canyon to a primitive camping area at the top of the mesa. Caves in the vertical cliffs along the way show signs of prehistoric Indian occupancy. Ruins of an old Spanish sheep farming community also can be visited on this hike. Left from the bridge, a more moderate trail edges the base of the canyon walls. A brochure describing the geology of the area, as evidenced by distinct layers visible in the cliff sides, is available from the park information center. A third trail, beginning from the El Cerro Upper Picnic Area, wanders out into the juniper, pinon, yucca and cactus at the higher (6,000 ft.) elevations of the park. This trail is a favorite among birdwatchers, who frequently spot cliff swallows, canyon wrens and pinon jays along the way. A birding list describing the 35 most common species in the park is also available at the information center. For information, contact **Villanueva State Park**, PO Box 40, Villanueva, NM 87583, ☎ 505/421-2957.

The Pecos Wilderness, located in the Santa Fe and Carson National Forests, contains 223,333 acres at the southern end of the majestic Sangre de Cristo Mountains. Magnificent scenery and quiet solitude attract many visitors to this area, and an extensive trail system provides numerous opportunities for both day hiking and extended backpacking trips. For information and maps, contact the **Las Vegas Ranger District**, 1926 N. 7th Street, Las Vegas, NM 87701, ☎ 505/425-3535 or 988-6995.

One of the most popular trails in the Pecos Wilderness is **Trail 223 to Hermit Peak**. About eight miles round trip with almost 3,000 feet in elevation gain, this hike to the summit of the most prominent peak in the southeastern arm of the Pecos Wilderness can be done as a strenuous day-trip or as a leisurely backpacking overnighter. Towering cliffs on this mountain's east face make Hermit Peak imposingly recognizable from miles around, while its summit affords spectacular views over the plains to the east where Santa Fe Trail wagon trains once roamed. If you camp near the summit, make sure to get up in time for sunrise.

A sign marking the trailhead is near the self-service pay station at El Porvenir Campground (see below, under Camping). The trail itself is well used and easy to follow. It does feature several stream crossings and gets steadily steeper as you go, until forced into seemingly endless switchbacks marking the hardest portion of the hike. The switchbacks end about half a mile from the summit, where the last remaining stretch of trail becomes pleasantly level and views become breathtaking. A sign marks the summit (10,212 feet). About 100 yards away, Hermit Peak's vertigo-inducing eastern cliff face falls to the floor of Gallinas Canyon leading on to the vast plains beyond. A short trail leads from the summit to the cave where a hermit supposedly lived for years, thus giving the peak its name. Backtrack on **Trail 223** to complete the eight-mile summit trek.

Continuing ahead on Trail 223 from the sign at the summit, turning left at each ensuing intersection and incorporating Trail 219/2477, creates a 14-mile loop which will bring you down El Porvenir Canyon and back to the trailhead at the campground. This loop is best attempted as an overnighter.

Water is available both at the trailhead and from a spring near the summit. Water from mountain streams along the way must be boiled or purified. A Pecos Wilderness, Santa Fe National Forest or El Porvenir 7.5-minute USGS quad map is needed for hiking in this area.

For information on guides or field trips in the Pecos Wilderness, contact: the **Randall Davey Audubon Center**, ☎ 505/983-4609, the **Santa Fe Group of the Sierra Club**, ☎ 505/983-2703, or the **New Mexico Mountain Club**, ☎ 505/831-0347.

If you would rather not tote a backpack, but would like to experience the beauty of the Pecos Wilderness from vantage points more pristine than the side of the road, look into llama trekking – an increasingly popular alternative these days. **Shining Star Ranch** offers a variety of trips into the back country, including a day trip with gourmet lunch to Hermit Peak. For information, contact PO Box 1341, Las Vegas, NM 87701, ☎ 505/425-1072 or 800/446-6914.

The **National Wildlife Refuge**, five miles south of Las Vegas via NM 104 and NM 281, provides year-round viewing of wildlife, including prairie falcons, mule deer, badgers and a variety of hawks. Migratory birds such as Canadian geese, snow geese, sandhill cranes, golden and bald eagles also frequent this refuge during late fall and early winter. Permits for access to a one-mile nature trail can be obtained at a visitor center in the park. A birding list containing the names of more than 240 species sighted in the area is also available. For information, contact the **Las Vegas National**

Wildlife Refuge Visitor Center, Route 1, PO Box 399, Las Vegas, NM 87701, ☎ 505/425-3581.

The Citizens Committee for Historic Preservation publishes several brochures and maps describing self-guided walking tours through historic Las Vegas. The most popular of these is the **Old Town Plaza and Bridge Street Walking Tour** which points out architecture dating from 1879 to 1930, painting a picture of Las Vegas in its heyday as a leading commercial center in the New Mexico Territory. The centerpiece is the 1881 Plaza Hotel, a beautifully restored example of Italianate architecture. Other Italianate and Neo-Classical brick buildings contrast with traditional southwestern adobe and sandstone buildings, illustrating what an interesting time the early 20th century was for local building design. Walking tour maps and brochures can be obtained through the **Las Vegas/San Miguel Chamber of Commerce**, PO Box 148, Las Vegas 87701, ☎ 505/425-8631 or 800/832-5947, or stop by 727 Grand Avenue between 9 AM and 4 PM, Mon.-Fri.

The self-guided walking trail at **Fort Union National Monument** leads tourists on a path through the melting adobe ruins that once were the most important 19th-century military installation in the New Mexico Territory. Today only foundations, walls and chimneys remain. The stone cell block of the military prison is the only building left with a ceiling, yet it is not difficult to look out over the plains and imagine this fort in its prime when trail-weary wagon trains stopped here to resupply and soldiers set out to war against raiding Indian tribes.

From the visitor center at **Sugarite Canyon State Park**, a well-maintained trail follows alongside a beautiful mountain stream, eventually crossing it and wandering through the ruins of the old Sugarite Canyon Coal Camp. In the early 1900s, this camp was the hub of mining activity in the canyon and home to more than 1,000 people. The old Coal Camp Trail leads from here up to one of the mines or you can continue on the River Walk Trail which loops back to the visitor center.

Two hiking trails leave from the Soda Pocket Campground at Sugarite Canyon State Park. The trailhead for the **Vista Grande Nature Trail** is at the southwest corner. A short loop trail weaves through ponderosa pines and oak groves bursting with wildflowers of every color during spring and summer. The **Ponderosa Ridge/Opportunity Trail** leaves from the north end of the campground. Allow most of the day to hike this long loop trail, which takes you to the highest point in the park at 8,400 ft. This vantage point affords some of the finest views of the canyon and the trail offers good opportunities for viewing park wildlife. Critters ranging from skunks to squirrels, plus deer, elk, mountain lions and bears, are sometimes encountered by hikers in Sugarite Canyon.

Capulin Volcano National Monument has three self-guided trails with plaques describing plants, volcanic phenomena and panoramic views along the way. The 200-foot trail behind the visitors center at the park entrance is a good place to occupy the kids while mom and dad pay entrance fees and check out the small visitor center. This trail also is accessible to handicapped persons. Drive a spiraling two-mile road to the summit parking area for access to the other two trails. One of them is only 0.2 miles long, leading down to the bottom of the crater and its vent. Even though there's no glowing lava to be seen nowadays, the bottom of this crater is a spooky place. Since Capulin's last eruption was only 10,000 years ago, scientists still consider it potentially active. The **Crater Rim Trail**, one mile long, traces the rim completely at the volcano's 8,182-foot summit. The spectacular views from the rim are the main reason people visit this national monument. Looking north and east on a clear day, Colorado, Kansas, Oklahoma and Texas are visible. To the south, look out over the grassy plains where, in the late 19th century, wagon trains traveled the Cimarron Cut-Off of the Santa Fe Trail bound for Fort Union. The most breathtaking view, however, lies to the west, where snowcapped peaks of the Sangre de Cristo Mountains rise majestically from the vast expanse of rangeland that separates them from Capulin.

There are several hiking trails around the lake at **Clayton Lake State Park**, 12 miles north of Clayton off NM Highway 370. The most rewarding one is on the southeast side of the lake. Drive to a small parking lot and look for a sign pointing out Dinosaur Tracks trail head. This half-mile trail leads across the dam to a small interpretive center and a boardwalk, which allows viewing of more than 500 dinosaur tracks. Best time to view the tracks is early in the morning or late in the afternoon, when longer shadows give the tracks more definition.

More than three miles of the **Dry Cimarron Cut-Off** route of the old Santa Fe Trail are set aside for hiking and horseback riding through the **Kiowa National Grasslands**, 13 miles north of Clayton on NM Highway 406.

On Wheels

The northeast section of New Mexico is really more suited to your RV or sedan rather than your road or mountain bike. There just aren't many mountains around, and towns are too few and far between for touring comfort.

If you have your bike with you, though, pedaling through the many state parks in the region will give you a chance to stretch your legs, take in some fresh air and enjoy the always beautiful (or at least interesting) scenery.

Santa Fe National Forest west of Las Vegas is the best bet for mountain bikers who want to ride in truly mountainous terrain. A forest service map of the area will reveal numerous dirt roads and accessible trails. Please remember, however, that bikes are not allowed in wilderness areas. Also, trails in the backcountry are usually steeper and more difficult than forest roads, and people on foot or horseback have the right of way.

For information, including tours and organized trips, contact **New Mexico Touring Society**, 4115 12th Street NW, Albuquerque, NM 87107, ☎ 505/344-1038.

On Water

The Pecos Wilderness, located in the Santa Fe and Carson National Forests at the southern end of the Sangre de Cristo Mountains, features the headwaters of the **Pecos River**. From its origin, 13½ miles of this river are designated as part of the nation's Wild and Scenic Rivers System and provide some of northeast New Mexico's finest fishing opportunities. NM 63 north, beyond the town of Pecos, parallels most of this wild and scenic section and several fishing access sites line the road. Stocked rainbows are everywhere, making this a popular stretch of water. Hike away from the road for a bit of solitude, better fishing and even the possibility of netting some wild browns. For information, contact the **Pecos Ranger District**, PO Drawer 429, Pecos 87552, ☎ 505/757-6121 or 988-6996.

Further down the Pecos, **Villanueva State Park**, 14 miles south of Interstate 25 via NM 3, offers some great fishing for cats and trout along the cottonwood-lined banks of the river. For information, contact **Villanueva State Park**, PO Box 40, Villanueva, NM 87583, ☎ 505/421-2957.

Storrie Lake State Park, four miles north of Las Vegas on NM 518, sits at the eastern foot of the Sangre de Cristo Mountains and the western edge of the Great Plains. This configuration of mountains, lake and plains provides for some of the most consistent winds around, which explains Storrie Lake State Park's reputation as one of the hottest windsurfing spots in the state. Mornings are notably calmer and better suited for beginners, while afternoon winds can really wail for more experienced surfers. On any given weekend, late spring to early fall, a veritable rainbow of sails criss-cross the surface of Storrie Lake. If you want to ride the wind yourself, it's BYOB (bring your own board), because there are no rental facilities at the park or in Las Vegas.

Water-skiing is also popular at Storrie Lake, along with year-round fishing for rainbow and German brown trout and crappie. Camping is available. For information, contact **Storrie Lake State Park**, PO Box 3157, Las Vegas, NM 87701, ☎ 505/425-7278.

Continue past Storrie Lake on NM 518 about 10 miles to the town of Sapello, then take NM 94 13 miles to Ledoux. From there, a rough three-mile 4WD road leads to **Morphy Lake State Park**. Difficult access helps keep this one of the most pristine parks in the state. Regularly stocked with trout, high-alpine Morphy Lake (7,840 feet elev.) offers some great fishing but, with less than 50 surface acres, only rowboats and canoes are allowed on the water. Camping is available.

Follow NM 518 to Mora, then take NM 434 north for 15 miles to the mountain scenery and wildflower-filled meadows that are the main draw at 80-acre **Coyote Creek State Park**. There's plenty of eye-soothing scenery and modest fly-fishing opportunities along the cottonwood-lined banks of Coyote Creek. Camping is available.

Take exit 404 off Interstate 25 about eight miles south of Springer and travel 14 miles down a gravel road (rough going for RVs) to find **Charette Lakes Fish and Wildlife Area**. This 410-acre lake is a great spot for fishing or birdwatching. Camping is available.

Boasting lunker-sized northern pike, **Springer Lake**, four miles northwest of Springer on NM Highway 468, is a favorite spot of area fishermen. Trout and catfish also swim this little fishing hole. Watch the weather, though, because the dirt road leading to the lake can get pretty soupy during a rain. Camping is available.

Chicosa Lake State Park, 55 miles southeast of Springer via US 56, NM 39 and NM 120, offers swimming, boating, fishing and camping. For information, contact **Chicosa Lake State Park**, General Delivery, Roy, NM 87743, ☎ 505/485-2424.

Two of the three small lakes at **Maxwell National Wildlife Refuge**, just north of Maxwell via NM 445 and NM 505, are open to sport fishing. Northern pike, trout and catfish are most likely to bend your pole on Lakes 13 and 14, where bank fishing is allowed during state regulated seasons. Lake 13 is also open to boats at trolling speeds only. Camping is available. For information, contact

Refuge Manager, PO Box 276, Maxwell, NM 87728, ☎ 505/375-2331.

Lake Maloya and Lake Alice, along with the stream that connects them, provide wonderful fishing for visitors to **Sugarite Canyon State Park**, eight miles northeast of Raton via NM 72 and NM 526. Camping is available near Lake Alice, the smaller of the two and a fine fly-fishing spot. Small boats at trolling speeds are allowed on the larger Lake Maloya, but only picnicking is permitted on its banks. Both lakes are popular ice fishing areas during the extremely cold winters in the canyon. For information, contact Sugarite Canyon State Park, HCR 63, Box 386, Raton, NM 87740, ☎ 505/445-5607.

Clayton Lake State Park, 12 miles north of Clayton off NM Highway 370, contains a 170-acre lake and one of the most extensive dinosaur trackways in North America (see above, Adventures On Foot). This little lake, the result of a dam built on Seneca Creek in 1955, is perfect for fishing. Anglers pull in trout, catfish, bass and walleye during a season that runs from April through October. Small sailboats, canoes, and fishing boats are allowed on the water, but anything with a motor is restricted to trolling speeds. Closed to fishing during the winter, Clayton Lake serves as a winter stopover for migratory waterfowl. Birdwatchers might see mallards, pintails, teals, Canadian geese and possibly a bald eagle or two. The lake's rocky shoreline is broken by a number of sandy beaches, making it great for swimming, and there are several sandstone cliffs to tempt daredevil divers. Camping and hiking are available. For information, contact **Clayton Lake State Park**, Star Route, Seneca, NM 88437, ☎ 505/374-8808.

The bountiful result of a dam built on the Canadian River in 1963, **Ute Lake State Park**, 25 miles northeast of Tucumcari via US 54, is home to the second largest lake in New Mexico. Ute Dam is not just any dam. Standing more than 120 feet tall and 2,000 feet wide with an 840-foot spillway, it is the largest labyrinth weir spillway facility in the entire world, capable of discharging 550,000 cubic feet of water per second.

Water sports are the big draw to the park, and several fishing tournaments are held here each year. Noted for its trophy-sized catfish, the lake is also stocked with a variety of bass, sunfish, bream, crappie, pike and perch.

Besides fishing, Ute Lake is a favorite destination for swimming, sailing, windsurfing, water skiing and scuba diving. A marina offers adequate docking facilities for boats of most sizes, as well as covered and uncovered long-term moorings. A store sells picnic and fishing supplies plus boat fuel and oil. Boat rentals are also available. Camping is available in three campgrounds on the lake, all with boat ramps. For information, contact **Logan-Ute Lake Chamber of Commerce**, Logan, NM 88426.

Conchas Lake State Park is 32 miles northwest of Tucumcari via NM 104. Watersports enthusiasts can enjoy sailing, boating, waterskiing, windsurfing, swimming and scuba diving on more than 15 square miles of water. The lake is also open to year-round fishing and is well stocked with walleye, catfish, bluegill, crappie and largemouth bass.

Most of the lake's shoreline, however, is privately owned, so public access is pretty much limited to three state park recreation areas. The **Central Recreation Area** is primarily for picnics and camping, with no facilities other than pit toilets. The **North** and **South Recreation Areas** both feature boat launching ramps, marinas, restrooms, boat and motor services, and stores to purchase fishing supplies and groceries. Camping is available in all three areas. Information may be obtained at a visitors center near the park entrance or by contacting **New Mexico State Park and Recreation Division**, PO Box 35, Conchas Dam, NM 88416, ☎ 505/868-2270.

Every year, the famous **Blue Hole** attracts thousands of scuba divers from all over the country to Santa Rosa – New Mexico's dive capital. Only 60 to 80 feet across at the surface, but expanding to as much as 130 feet across at the bottom, this 81-foot-deep natural artesian spring sometimes sees more than 200 divers a day. The novelty of Blue Hole, though, is not so much its shape or its location in the middle of the arid New Mexicodesert, but the clarity of its waters. A subterranean river flowing at a rate of 3,000 gallons per minute keeps Blue Hole's water so perfectly clear that divers at the bottom can see people 80 feet above at the surface and vice-versa. Plus, the spring's constant 64°F allows for year-round diving. Air and equipment are sometimes available at a small dive shop next to the hole. But divers first need to obtain permits from the Santa Rosa Police Department, located at City Hall on 5th Street.

If, however, you just want to cool off on a hot summer's day, jump right in – no permit needed. Blue Hole is open to swimmers of all abilities. One half of its banks have been paved, and steps allow even the most timid easy access into the water. The other half of the circular pool is lined with 15-foot-high cliffs for those who would rather jump or dive into its fresh clear depths. But be careful. There are no lifeguards, so you swim or dive at your own risk.

For information, contact **Santa Rosa Chamber of Commerce**, 486 Parker Ave., Santa Rosa, NM 88435, ☎ 505/472-3763.

Perch Lake, just a couple of miles southeast of town via NM 91, is another popular Santa Rosa scuba spot. Used primarily for advanced dive training, it contains a twin-engine plane submerged at 55 feet.

Area fishermen prefer to cast their lines from the banks of a petite spring-fed pond at **James Wallace Memorial Park and Power Dam**. To find this basin of bass, catfish and trout, follow 3rd Street south to the outskirts of Santa Rosa, where it becomes NM 91. The park is on the south side of the road. Camping is available.

Water-skiers, windsurfers and the like need to take 2nd Street north to Eddy Ave., and then follow the signs seven miles out of town to **Santa Rosa Lake State Park**. This, the largest lake in the area, is also popular for catfish, walleye, crappie and bass fishing. A small visitors center is located across the dam near the Corps of Engineers' office. Camping is available at two campgrounds in the park. For information, contact **Park Manager, Santa Rosa Lake**, Box 345, Santa Rosa, NM 88435, ☎ 505/472-3115.

On Snow

Even though this section of New Mexico is not particularly well known for its winter recreation, several trails in **Gallinas Canyon**, roughly 20 miles west of Las Vegas via NM 65, are popular with area cross-country skiers and snowshoers. One in particular is **Dispensas Trail**, which branches off from Trail 223 to Hermit Peak (see above, under Adventures on foot). **Sugarite Canyon State Park**, near Raton, is another good snowshoeing and cross-country skiing destination, especially along Opportunity Trail at Lake Maloya. Ice fishing on both Lake Maloya and Lake Alice is also possible during winter. The park is a favorite among Raton families for sledding and tubing. (See above, under Touring.)

Eco-Tours & Cultural Excursions

Rangers at the **Capulin Volcano National Monument** conduct periodic sunrise, sunset and astronomy programs from the crater rim. Contact Capulin Volcano National Monument, Capulin, NM 88414. ☎ 505/278-2201.

The New Mexico Outdoor Drama Association presents various plays and musicals each summer at the **Caprock Amphitheater**

and Park, located about 30 miles southeast of Tucumcari. Take Interstate 40 east to San Jon and then NM 469 south 10 miles to find this natural stone amphitheater perched atop the bluffs of the Llano Estacado (Caprock). The most popular production presented here is the historical musical drama *Billy the Kid*, which returns to this thousand-seat theater every summer. Shows are Thursday through Saturday, mid-June to late August. For information, contact **Billy the Kid**, Box 337, San Jon, NM 88434, ☎ 505/576-2455 or 505/576-2779.

Where to Stay & Eat

Travel began in this region along the Santa Fe Trail, which gave way to the railroad, then to Route 66, and now to Interstate Highways 25 and 40. That, of course, has prompted the proliferation of chain motels and restaurants grouped around interstate off-ramps. There is usually something better off the beaten path.

Accommodations

LAS VEGAS

A rich history and close proximity to Fort Union National Monument, Storrie Lake State Park and all the recreational opportunities of the Santa Fe National Forest make it worth spending a day or two in Las Vegas.

A stay at **The Plaza Hotel**, 230 Old Town Plaza, ☎ 505/425-3591, is hands down the best way to experience this town's Old West roots. Built in 1882 when Las Vegas was one of the West's leading commercial centers, the hotel once hosted railroad barons, prominent politicians, businessmen and film stars such as Romaine Fielding and Tom Mix, not to mention some of the most notorious outlaws and infamous characters of the times including Billy the Kid, Doc Holiday and Big Nose Kate. Carefully maintained and restored to their original splendor, rooms are decorated to perfection with Victorian antiques, but retain all the conveniences of a modern hotel (your television may be hidden inside an elegant wooden armoire). The Plaza Hotel is listed on both the State Register of Cultural Properties and the National Register of Historic Places but, for all of its history and luxury, the rooms are reasonably affordable. A beautifully refurbished 1893 Victorian home houses the **Carriage House Bed and Breakfast**, 925 6th Street, ☎ 505/454-1784. Elegant public areas complement six charming rooms and two suites. Situated just four blocks from downtown, it too is listed on the National Register of Historic Places.

The hacienda-style **Inn on the Santa Fe Trail**, 1133 Grand Avenue, ☎ 505/425-6791, is another appealing option. Set around a private courtyard, rooms feature handmade furnishings and paintings by southwestern artists.

Las Vegas also offers 12 other motels, so finding a place to stay is rarely a problem. Most of these are located on the north end of town, with **Comfort Inn**, 2500 North Grand, ☎ 505/425-1100, **Days Inn**, 2000 North Grande, ☎ 505/425-1967, and **Super 8 Motel**, 2029 N. Hwy 85, ☎ 505/425-5288, representing the national chains. Comfort Inn and Days Inn both have swimming pools.

RV travelers who want to stick close to town should check out **Las Vegas KOA**, five miles south of town, Interstate 25 (Exit 339) and US 84, ☎ 505/454-0180. Featuring a gift shop, heated pool and free morning coffee, it offers more than some of the town's motels. **Las Vegas RV Park**, NM 518, ☎ 505/425-5640, is another alternative.

SPRINGER

Since Interstate 25 skirts the western edge of Springer, most people bypass the town. Should you find yourself spending the night here, there are two locally owned motels and five restaurants. Go first to **The Brown Hotel & Café, Bed and Breakfast**, 308 Maxwell Street, ☎ 505/483-2269. Situated in one of Springer's older buildings, now renovated and furnished with antiques, this quaint little inn is really the only place to stay. And if you're staying, you might as well eat – huevos rancheros to French toast for breakfast, enchiladas to burgers for lunch, and steak or chicken for dinner.

RATON

Raton's close proximity to Raton Pass, making it the gateway city between Colorado and New Mexico is reflected in the considerable volume of traffic on Interstate 25 flanking the eastern edge of town. As a result, some 20 carbon-copy motels can be found near the interstate. National chain representatives are: **Motel 6**, 1600

Cedar Street/I-25 & US 87, ☎ 505/445-2777; **Best Western Sands Manor Motel**, 300 Clayton Road/US 87, ☎ 505/445-2737 or 800/528-1234; and **Super 8 Motel**, 610 Cedar/I-25 & US 87, ☎ 505/445-2355 or 800/800-8000.

The best choice for an extended stay in Raton, however, is **The Red Violet Inn**, 344 North Second Street, ☎ 505/445-9778. This turn-of-the-century red-brick Victorian bed & breakfast offers four rooms decorated with Hopi rugs and four-poster and brass beds stacked high with hand-made quilts.

RVs can pull into the **Summerlan RV Park**, 1900 S. Cedar/I-25 & US 87, ☎ 505/445-9536, or the **Raton KOA**, 1330 South Second Street, ☎ 505/445-3488. The latter offers free cable TV and a full tackle shop selling both hunting and fishing supplies and licenses.

Deluxe accommodations and gourmet meals are only part of the appeal at **Vermejo Park Ranch**, the premier resort in the Raton area. Located 40 miles west of town via NM 555, this working cattle ranch caters to a maximum of 80 guests who have plenty of room to roam across more than 588,000 acres, extending from the plains to well above timberline in the beautiful Sangre de Cristo Mountains. Hiking and photography opportunities abound and visitors are free to roam the ranch, with or without a guide, where you might discover a ghost town or an abandoned mine. Horseback riding is also available. The park's nearly 30 miles of streams and 21 well-stocked lakes are a dream-come-true for guest fishermen, who consistently yank trophy-sized rainbow trout, German brown trout, Coho salmon and rare cutthroat trout from these waters. The ranch is also known worldwide for its big game hunting. Most guests stay in Southwestern-style rooms at the striking main lodge built from native stone, but two exclusive lodges are also available for those who want greater privacy. Meals are served family-style in a rustic wooden central lodge.

For information, contact **Vermejo Park Ranch**, PO Drawer E, Raton, NM 87740, ☎ 505/445-3097 or 505/445-3474.

CLAYTON

None of the half-dozen motels here are worth getting excited about. So, your best bet for a good night's rest is probably the **Days Inn**, South Highway 87, in Clayton ☎ 505/374-8127. If that's booked, try **Holiday Motel**, North Highway 87, ☎ 505/374-2558, or **Kokopelli Lodge**, 702 South First Street, ☎ 505/374-2589 or 800/392-6691. **Meadowlark KOA Kampground**, 903 South Fifth Street, ☎ 505/374-9508, is the best choice for RVrs or campers. Open

March 1 through October 31, it offers full hookups, free morning coffee and muffins, a gift and supply shop, as well as a corral for your horses. **Mission Motel & RV Park**, 214 North First Street, ☎ 505/374-9890, also offers full RV hookups.

TUCUMCARI

With 30 motels, approximately 2,000 motel rooms and just as much neon as back in the Old Route 66 days, a traveler should have no trouble finding a place to bed down in Tucumcari. Unfortunately, there is hardly any attempt at individuality among the town's numerous motels. If you're out doing the Route 66 thing, the **Blue Swallow Motel**, 815 E. Tucumcari Blvd., ☎ 505/461-9849, is listed on both the State and National Historic Registers. Internationally known through books, magazines and television as a Route 66 landmark, its neon standard heralds 12 rooms with 100% refrigerated air, TV and budget prices. This is surely one of America's roadside treasures.

Adventure aside, the chain motels here are your best bet for a clean comfortable room. Best Western offers three branches in town: the **Aruba**, 700 E. Tucumcari Blvd., ☎ 505/461-3335, the **Discovery**, 200 E. Estrella Ave., ☎ 505/461-4884, and the **Pow Wow**, 801 E. Tucumcari Blvd., ☎ 505/461-0500. All three have swimming pools and adjacent restaurants. The Pow Wow features a lounge. **Comfort Inn**, 2800 E. Tucumcari Blvd., ☎ 505/461-4094, also features a pool and adjacent restaurant. So does **Motel 6**, 2900 E. Tucumcari Blvd., ☎ 505/461-4791, **Rodeway Inn East**, 1023 E. Tucumcari Blvd., ☎ 505/461-0360, **Rodeway Inn West**, 1302 W. Tucumcari Blvd., ☎ 505/461-3140 and **Super 8**, 4001 E. Tucumcari Blvd., ☎ 505/461-4444. **Holiday Inn**, 3716 E. Tucumcari Blvd., ☎ 505/461-3780, offers a restaurant, lounge and pool.

For RV travelers, full hookups, showers and cable TV are available at **Kiva Campground**, 1416 E. Tucumcari Blvd., ☎ 505/461-1561, **Cactus/Red Arrow Campground**, 1316 E. Tucumcari Blvd., ☎ 505/461-2501, and **Hunt's Trailer Park**, 501 W. Tucumcari Blvd., ☎ 505/461-3600. **Mountain Road RV Park**, 1700 Mountain Road, ☎ 505/461-9628, provides full hookups, showers, a laundry, a playground and a store/gift shop. Tucumcari's **KOA Campground**, South Frontage Road, Interstate 40 exit 335, ☎ 505/461-1841, has all of that, plus a heated pool.

SANTA ROSA

If you were asleep at the wheel traveling west on Interstate 40 and missed the exit for Tucumcari's magnificent motel mecca, don't panic. There are 16 more just like 'em one hour down the road in Santa Rosa. Again, the nationals will be your best bet for a good night's rest. Try the **Adobe Inn Best Western**, Will Rogers Drive, ☎ 505/472-3446; **Motel 6**, Interstate 40 East Exit 277 and Will Rogers Drive, ☎ 505/472-3266; or **Super 8**, 1201 Will Rogers Drive, ☎ 505/472-5388.

Santa Rosa's **KOA**, north of Interstate 40 between Exits 275 & 277, ☎ 505/472-3126, offers a heated pool, restaurant, cable TV and, of course, full hookups.

Restaurants

LAS VEGAS

The Plaza Hotel's **Landmark Grill**, 230 Old Town Plaza, ☎ 505/425-3591, is by far the most elegant of Las Vegas' 37 restaurants. Both Mexican and Continental variations of seafood, chicken and beef dishes round out the dinner menu. Breakfast and lunch are also served, as well as a popular Sunday brunch. They will even prepare packed lunches for travelers on the go. The adjoining **Byron T's Saloon** presents some of the best night life in the area, along with appetizer selections and, of course, a full bar.

Gilbert's Café, 1816 Old Town Plaza, ☎ 505/425-5569, is the place to go for inexpensive Mexican food. Homemade burritos, enchiladas and tacos are served for lunch and dinner; huevos rancheros and your basic bacon 'n egg combos are for breakfast.

Just off the plaza, **El Rialto Restaurant**, 141 Bridge Street, ☎ 505/454-0037, will make you pay a little more for their Mexican and American food, but great atmosphere and giant margaritas make up for the added cost.

A fun option for a late breakfast, especially if you're planning a morning walk trough the Plaza and Bridge Street Historic Districts (see above, under Adventures On Foot), **Bridge Street Books & Coffeehouse**, 131 Bridge Street, ☎ 505/454-8211, serves cappuccino/espresso and assorted pastries amid a wild collection of new and used books and magazines. With chess boards and dominoes available for patrons, this is a popular evening hangout among local collegians, and is a good after-dinner alternative to the usual movie or bar hopping.

If you're one to follow the creed, "when in Las Vegas eat as the Las Vegasites eat," try either the **Campus Drive-In**, 1125 National Avenue, ☎ 505/425-9988, or the **Spic 'n Span Bakery & Cafe**, 713 Douglas Avenue, ☎ 505/425-6481. Both serve basic small town fare as well as standard New Mexican dishes, and heads tend to turn when a stranger walks in.

But if you're simply blowing through town, stopping only long enough to appease your starving children, a quick drive down Grand Avenue/US 85 or Mills Avenue/ALT US 85 will more than meet your needs, leading you past all the standby fast food outlets from **McDonalds** to **Taco Bell**.

RATON

Taking any exit off the interstate will put you within sight of a number of fast food options – Kentucky Fried Chicken to Dairy Queen.

If a sit-down restaurant is preferred, head to **Pappas Sweet Shop Restaurant**, 1201 South Second Street, ☎ 505/445-9811. Opening as a candy store and soda fountain in 1923, this family-owned establishment has grown into a full-fledged restaurant with a menu offering Mexican, Italian and American dishes. Pappas is also popular for breakfast.

Morning coffee and various baked goods can also be found at **Eva's Bakery**, 134 North Second Street, ☎ 505/445-3781. Sandwiches on homemade buns are available for lunch as well.

CLAYTON

If you're entering New Mexico from the east on Highway 87, **La Palomita Restaurant**, 1022 South First Street, ☎ 505/374-2127, offers your first chance to wrap your taste buds around some authentic and very good Mexican food. This might be the best restaurant in town, and it definitely is the best breakfast spot, serving tasty breakfast burritos and huevos rancheros, as well as the standard bacon 'n eggs. Another candidate for best-food-in-town honors is the **Eklund Dining Room & Saloon**, 15 Main Street, ☎ 505/374-2551. This is Clayton's Main Street landmark. Built in 1892 as the Eklund Hotel, Dining Room and Saloon, this beautifully restored building has high ceilings, chandeliers and an unusual bar, complete with bullet holes in the original tin ceiling that really brings back the look and feel of the Old West. Historical significance aside, the food's quite good. The menu includes Union County-grown beef and potatoes, Mexican dishes, chicken and seafood. If you don't have time for a sit-down meal, there are, of course, a number of fast food restaurants huddled alongside Highway 87.

TUCUMCARI

Coincidentally, there is exactly one restaurant for each of Tucumcari's 30 motels and all but six of them are located right next door to their partner lodging establishments. There is nothing special here so you might as well stop in at **Del's**, 1202 E. Tucumcari Blvd., ☎ 505/461-1740. This classic Route 66 diner serves steaks, burgers, Mexican dishes and some seafood – all at reasonable prices. Not interested? Signs for **McDonalds**, **Pizza Hut**, **Subway**, **Sonic**, **Hardee's** and **Kentucky Fried Chicken** are all visible from Interstate 40.

SANTA ROSA

There's at least one good diner that has survived from Route 66 days in each little town along the old highway, and in Santa Rosa it is the **Comet Drive-In Restaurant**, 217 Parker Ave. Best known for its New Mexican blue-corn specialties and chile rellenos, there are burgers and other diner fare available as well. But whatever you decide on for an entrée, it has to be followed with a slice of one of the Comet's fabulous homemade pies.

For steaks, seafood and a salad bar, head over to **Joseph's Restaurant & Cantina**, 865 Will Rogers Drive, ☎ 505/472-3361. This is also the best place in town for a good margarita or for some two-stepping. Live country-and-western bands play here every Friday and Saturday night.

If you are looking for something fast or ordinary, the majority of Santa Rosa's restaurants are located on Will Rogers Drive – including **McDonalds** and **Dairy Queen**.

Camping

Huge cottonwood and pinon trees shade numerous campsites throughout the beautiful 1,584-acre **Villanueva State Park**, 14 miles south of Interstate 25 via NM 3. Most sites are situated along the banks of the Pecos River and have picnic tables with adobe shelters, grills and drinking water. There is also a separate picnic area, a playground and a modern restroom with hot showers.

El Porvenir Campground, about 17 miles west of Las Vegas, offers several campsites with picnic tables, grills, drinking water and pit toilets. Follow NM 65 west from Las Vegas through beautiful Gallinas Canyon until the road splits at about 14½ miles. Take the right fork and follow the signs to the campground in the Santa Fe National Forest. Primitive camping is also available in the surrounding forest. ☎ 505/425-3535 or 988-6995.

The campground at **Storrie Lake State Park**, four miles north of Las Vegas on NM 518, offers 11 sites with electricity and water, and 21 picnic tables with shelters and grills. There's a visitor center, comfort station with restrooms and hot showers, and a dump station. Primitive camping is also available. ☎ 505/425-7278.

One of the most secluded parks in the state, **Morphy Lake State Park**, reached via a three mile stretch of rough 4WD road west of Ledoux off NM 94, offers sites with picnic tables, fire rings and pit toilets. Primitive camping is also available.

Coyote Creek State Park, 15 miles north of Mora on NM 434, offers primitive camping, as well as sites with picnic tables, fire rings and pit toilets. Some sites have shelters, but no hookups. Exit 404 on Interstate 25, about eight miles south of Springer, leads 14 miles down a rough gravel road to **Charette Lakes Fish & Wildlife Area**. Camping is limited to 10 days at this isolated lake, but if you want solitude, this is a great spot. It's 22 miles from the nearest town, so it's quite possible to be the only person on the lake during the week. Stone picnic tables and pit toilets are situated around the lake, but there is no water or electricity.

Camping is allowed at **Springer Lake**, four miles northwest of Springer on NM 568, but there are no developed camp sites and fires are not permitted. So this makes a better picnic site than an overnighter. ☎ 505/483-2998.

The bank fishing areas around Lakes 13 and 14 at **Maxwell National Wildlife Refuge** are open for camping with a three-day limit during state regulated seasons. There are, however, no designated sights or facilities. ☎ 505/375-2331.

Sugarite Canyon State Park, eight miles northeast of Raton, offers two campgrounds with restrooms and RV hookups. Lake Alice Campground, on one of the best fly-fishing lakes in the park, has water at each site. Soda Pocket Campground presents the most spectacular panoramic views of the canyon and is equipped with a group camping area and campfire amphitheater, both of which can be reserved through the park headquarters. For information, contact Sugarite Canyon State Park, HCR 63, Box 386, Raton, NM 87740, ☎ 505/445-5607.

The don't-blink-you'll-miss-it town of Capulin, just south of Capulin Volcano National Monument, offers the only camping between Raton and Clayton at **Capulin Camp**, where there are RV sites with hookups, tent sites and hot showers. The Mt. Capulin General store and a gas station make up the remainder of the town.

Clayton Lake State Park, 12 miles north of Clayton off NM 370, offers 35 developed campsites with covered picnic tables, several pit toilets, a comfort station with showers, but no electrical hookups or other services. ☎ 505/374-8808.

There are three state-maintained campgrounds at **Ute Lake State Park**, 25 miles northeast of Tucumcari via US 54. All three have boat ramps, shelters and picnic tables, but only the **North Area** has hot showers and flush toilets. Showers and modern restrooms are also available at the main office/visitors center. RV hookups are located in several sites throughout the park. Contact the Ute Lake Chamber of Commerce at Logan, NM 88426 or at Tucumcari, ☎ 505/461-1694.

Conchas Lake State Park, 32 miles northeast of Tucumcari via NM 104, also has three campgrounds and more than 150 campsites. The **Central Recreation Area** has picnic tables, shelters and grills at roughly half of its campsites, but offers no other facilities aside from pit toilets. The **North** and **South Recreation Areas** provide sites with shelters, picnic tables, grills, water, restrooms and nearby stores where fishing supplies and groceries may be obtained. Boat launching ramps and boat and motor services are also located in the North and South areas. The North area features an RV park with hookups, but the trailer sanitation dump is curiously located in the South recreation area. ☎ 505/868-2270.

Free camping is available around a small fishing pond at **James Wallace Memorial Park and Power Dam**, at the south end of 3rd Street in Santa Rosa. There are, however, no developed sites or facilities. ☎ 505/472-3763.

Santa Rosa Lake State Park has two campgrounds. The smaller **Juniper Park** area, located near the boat launching ramps, has a modern restroom and sites with grills and picnic tables. The main campground, **Rocky Point**, provides more than 40 sites with shelters, full hookups, picnic tables and grills. A restroom there also has hot showers. Take 2nd Street in Santa Rosa north to Eddy Ave., then follow the signs seven miles to the park. ☎ 505/472-3115.

Southeast New Mexico

If only you could travel into space, you would instantly recognize the defining feature of southeastern New Mexico – contrast. The glowing gypsum of **White Sands National Monument** edging the black lava rock of the **Valley of Fires** form one of the few geographical contrasts that astronauts can discern from space. Looking up at the snow-capped peak of **Sierra Blanca** reminds us of the amazing range of climates and life zones between the mountains and desert plains of the **Tularosa Basin** and how that relationship brought development to both regions. While railroad ties cut from trees in the mountain forests helped bring the railroad and prosperity to the plains, so did the railroads and thriving basin community of **Alamogordo** breathe life into the small mining and lumbering towns of **Cloudcroft** and **Ruidoso**, giving them new direction as vacation escapes for heat-scorched residents of the valley below. East of the mountains, the town of **Carlsbad** and the **Pecos River** form an oasis in the middle of the **Chihuahuan Desert**. Farther south, a vast underground realm contrasts with the sunlight of the world above at **Carlsbad Caverns National Park**.

Areas covered in this chapter range in elevation from 4,200 to 12,003 feet. If you come from lower elevations, expect to tire quickly until you acclimatize to the area. Exercise care during the first few days at altitude, especially if you're participating in vigorous activities.

The arid climate, even in the mountains, makes dehydration a constant possibility. If you're planning outdoor activities, summer or winter, be sure to pack plenty of water. Winters are basically mild at lower elevations in southeastern New Mexico, often with average high temperatures in the 60s. But when a storm does come, temperatures can dip below freezing and, with nothing to block the gusts on the flat eastern plains, the wind-chill factor can reach well below zero. The mountains, on the other hand, generally experience much colder winters, with heavy snows and average daytime temperatures dipping into the 30s. Again, layered clothing is a must for any outdoor winter activity.

Southeast New Mexico

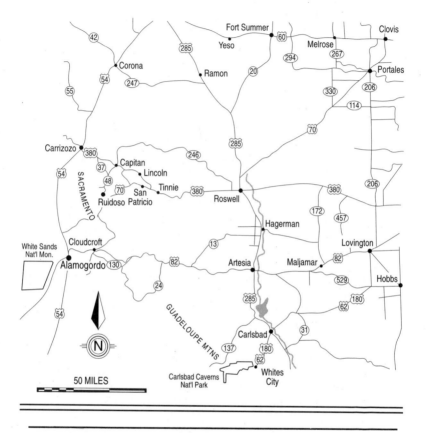

Fort Summer
Clovis
42
285
Yeso
60
Melrose
294
267
Corona
Ramon
20
Portales
54
247
330
206
55
114
70
Carrizozo
380
246
285
Capitan
37
Lincoln
48
San Patricio
206
54
70
Tinnie
380
380
Ruidoso
Roswell
172
457
Hagerman
SACRAMENTO
White Sands Nat'l Mon.
Cloudcroft
13
Lovington
Alamogordo
130
82
Artesia
Maljamar
82
24
529
Hobbs
54
285
180
62
GUADELOUPE MTNS
Carlsbad
31
N
137
180
62
50 MILES
Carlsbad Caverns Nat'l Park
Whites City

Touring

Most of the action is in the southern half of this region. But if you want to take in everything, the suggested route to follow begins east of Albuquerque, turning south from Interstate 40 in Santa Rosa to Fort Sumner via US 84. Continue east on US 84/60 to Clovis and then south to Portales via US 70. Roswell is the next stop, 91 miles southwest on US 70. This is where the interest begins to mount. Navigate US 285 south through Artesia to Carlsbad, then US 62/180 to Carlsbad Caverns National Monument. Do an about-face and backtrack to Artesia, turning west to Cloudcroft and

Alamogordo via US 82. US 70 south leads to White Sands National Monument, and US 70 north ushers you into the Ruidoso area, the touristic heart of Southeast New Mexico. Several day-trip opportunities unfold from here, including visits to the historic town of Lincoln, Smokey Bear State Park, Ski Apache and more.

Fort Sumner

The little town (1,500 pop.) of Fort Sumner is the remaining civilian settlement connected to the old Fort Sumner of military fame (or infamy, perhaps). In February, 1864, Colonel Kit Carson ended a two-year campaign against hostile Navajo Indians by chasing and eventually trapping them in Canyon de Chelly, Arizona. More than 3,000 Navajos were rounded up and marched on the infamous "Long Walk" – 300 miles from Fort Wingate, near Gallup – to Fort Sumner. There, in an attempt to promote self-sufficiency, the Navajos were forced into an experimental government concentration camp with a smaller group of captive Apaches from Bosque Redondo reservation. But by 1868, due to rampant disease and large numbers of deaths among the Indians, the army deemed the experiment a failure, an inevitable conclusion brought on by the harsh climate and infertile land around Fort Sumner. After concluding that the Navajo homelands were of no value to the white man anyway, the government allowed the few surviving Indians to walk back home and sold the fort to Lucien Maxwell in 1869.

With this addition, the Maxwell Ranch became the largest privately owned piece of property in the nation. But it's an event that happened on the ranch more than 10 years later that draws folks to Fort Sumner today. There, on July 14, 1881, in the home of Pete Maxwell, Sheriff Pat Garrett finally shot and killed the infamous Billy the Kid. And, even though most of the Kid's escapades took place more than 100 miles to the southwest during the bloody Lincoln County War, thousands of tourists each year visit the old Maxwell family cemetery, seven miles southeast of Fort Sumner via US 60 and Billy the Kid Road, just to see **Billy the Kid's Grave**. His tombstone, enclosed in an iron cage, is apparently as elusive as the outlaw himself once was – having been stolen numerous times and recovered from as far away as Southern California.

Adjacent to the cemetery, **The Old Fort Sumner Museum** displays letters written by Billy to the governor to negotiate a pardon, letters from Garrett to his wife detailing his search for the outlaw, a history of Billy the Kid impostors, a chronology of the

many movies about the Kid's violent life, as well as various artifacts and clues which suggest that Billy escaped again and lived
well into the 20th century, leading a life of seclusion in Texas and
Mexico. Artifacts and documents from the old fort are displayed,
as well as various pioneer tools, guns, historical photos and Native
American items. For the most part, this is a worthwhile museum,
but there is a bit of tourist-trapping. A two-headed calf converses
with itself in the corner, and there is, of course, a gift shop selling
Indian trinkets and reproductions of Billy the Kid wanted posters.
The museum is open daily, 9 AM to 5 PM. For information,
☎ 505/355-2942.

Not too far down the road from the museum (follow the signs),
Fort Sumner State Monument marks the location of the old fort.
Low adobe walls are all that remain, but displays at a small visitors
center relate the camp's history and a simple shrine of stones
brought from the Navajo Reservation stands as a memorial to those
who lived and died there. The monument is open Thursday
through Monday, 9 AM to 6 PM during the summer and 8AM to 5
PM the rest of the year. For information, ☎ 505/355-2573.

Back in town, the **Billy the Kid Museum**, 1601 East Fort Sumner Avenue, ☎ 505/355-2380, displays numerous ranch antiques,
firearms, carriages and Model Ts, as well as a jail cell in which Billy
the Kid is said to have been imprisoned. Open daily 9AM to 5 PM.

The other touring option in the area is **Sumner Lake State
Park**, 16 miles northwest of town via US 84 and NM 203.
☎ 505/355-2541. (See below, under Adventures on Water.)

Clovis

This town that saw its beginnings, in typical Southwest fashion, as a railroad division point, quite amazingly became a hotbed
of rock & roll discoveries in the 50s, 60s and 70s. In a simple
recording studio at 1313 West 7th Street, a sound engineer by the
name of Norman Petty made stars out of Roy Orbison, Buddy
Knox, Roger Williams and others by giving them their first breaks.
It all started when a little-known band drove across the border
from Lubbock, Texas, to try to hammer out a new sound. With
Petty's help, Buddy Holly and the Crickets produced and recorded
such influential songs as "Peggy Sue," "Maybe Baby" and "That'll
be the Day," thus redefining contemporary music in, of all places,
Clovis, NM.

Holly and Petty are gone now, but their contribution to the music world is remembered annually at the **Clovis Music Festival**. Each year thousands of fans of vintage rock & roll from around the country and the world descend on this little town to celebrate the sound that was born here and to tour the studios where it all began. For festival dates and information, contact the **Clovis/Curry County Chamber of Commerce**, 215 North Main, Clovis, NM, 88101, ☎ 505/763-3435.

The **Norman Petty Recording Studios** is still a working studio, but it has moved into a fancy building downtown, at 206 North Main. Call ☎ 505/763-7565 to ask about a tour.

Today, the music scene in town has slowed a bit, and Clovis has more or less resumed its old identity. The railroad continues to play an important role with its big switching yard, though Cannon Air Force Base, six miles west of town, is by far the largest employer. Almost 15% of the Clovis population is employed in some capacity at Cannon.

Other than that, farming and ranching are the driving forces of the local economy, and have been since the town's beginnings. In fact, Curry County brings in more than $160 million annually in agricultural revenue, and weekly livestock auctions have made Clovis the largest horse and mule market in the United States. The town also hosts the largest county fair in the state in late August. Unfortunately, if you find yourself in town when it's not fair or festival time and you aren't looking to buy a horse, there's not a lot to do here except go to the mall or the zoo. The mall is on Prince Street, but you can go to malls anywhere. So, you'd just as well head over to **Hillcrest Park Zoo** on Sycamore Street. More than 200 species of birds and animals are on display here in a well-kept 22-acre park. The zoo is open Tuesday-Sunday, 9AM to 6 PM. For information, ☎ 505/762-1101.

Portales

Sometimes referred to as Clovis' sister city, Portales also sprang up at the turn of the century with the railroad and is today an important agriculture center as well. But, while the town 20 miles north on US 70 was rock and rolling in the 50s, Portales was busy building **Eastern New Mexico University** into the largest and most influential educational/cultural center on this side of the state. Today nearly 4,000 students from the United States and abroad attend ENMU, earning degrees in business, education, technology, science and the arts.

One of the most exciting and long-standing projects of the university is the administration of **Blackwater Draw Archaeological Site**, located about five miles north of US 70, just east of Portales via NM 467. One of the best known and most significant sites in North American archaeology since its discovery in 1932, Blackwater Draw presents evidence of human presence in conjunction with fossils of Late Pleistocene era plant life, woolly mammoths and sabertooth tigers. All of this pinpoints man's existence in the area more than 9,000 years earlier than previously believed. The site has attracted numerous scientific investigations by such organizations as the Carnegie Institute, Smithsonian Institution, Academy of Natural Sciences, United States National Museum, and National Geographic Society. Blackwater Draw also was recently added to the National Register of Historic Places. The site is open to the public 10 AM to 5 PM, Monday through Saturday, and 12 noon to 5 PM on Sunday during summer months and on weekends, Labor Day to October and March to Memorial Day.

Also under ENMU direction, **The Blackwater Draw Museum** may be more interesting for tourists than the actual site. Located seven miles east of Portales via US 70, the facility is a combination laboratory and museum. On display are exhibits explaining current digs at the site as well as actual fossils and artifacts found since Blackwater's discovery in 1932. The museum is open daily (except Mondays, Labor Day to Memorial Day) from 10 AM to 5 PM; 12 noon to 5 PM on Sundays.

For information, contact Blackwater Draw Site and Museum, Station 9, Eastern New Mexico University, Portales, NM 88130, ☎ 505/356-5235 (Site) or 505/562-2202 (Museum).

After taking in the prehistoric exhibits relating to the Blackwater Draw, **Roosevelt County Historical Museum**, on ENMU's campus across from the administration building, will give you a better idea of what life was like in the area's more recent past. Exhibits include Kiowa and Comanche spear points and tools, pioneer game traps, branding irons, barbed wire, medical equipment, toys, saddles and handmade quilts. The museum also sponsors a lecture series each year and hosts numerous art shows and seminars. For hours and information, ☎ 505/562-2592.

If a little rest and recreation is all you want, head for **Oasis State Park**, seven miles north of town via NM 467. Complete with shade trees and a four-acre fishing lake, this 194-acre park is truly an oasis in the middle of southeast New Mexico's barren, windswept plains. Camping is available. For information, ☎ 505/356-5331.

Birdwatchers and nature enthusiasts may want to visit the **Grulla National Wildlife Refuge**, 20 miles east of Portales via NM 88. The least developed of New Mexico's five national wildlife refuges with no visitor center or other facilities on site, this is still a great spot for migratory waterfowl viewing (including sandhill cranes) during fall and winter months. For information, contact Grulla National Wildlife Refuge, PO Box 549, Muleshoe, TX 79347-0549, ☎ 806/946-3341.

For more information, contact **Portales/Roosevelt County Chamber of Commerce**, 7th & Abilene, Portales, NM 88130, ☎ 505/356-8541 or 800/635-8036.

Roswell

The largest city in southeast New Mexico with 50,000 people, Roswell is one of the few significant eastern plains communities that did not spring up beside a set of railroad tracks. Rather, it was cattle tracks that brought life into this area. The 1860s and '70s saw Roswell become a stopover for cowboys moving herds up the Chisholm and Goodnight-Loving trails. The railroad, connecting Amarillo and Carlsbad, did not arrive until several years later. By then, the discovery of a large aquifer which could be tapped for irrigation had already assured the town's future as an agricultural center. Today, even though it has become the commercial hub for southeastern New Mexico, Roswell remains more a crossroads than a destination. Tourists heading south to Carlsbad or east into the mountains rarely slow down enough to notice that there is quite a bit to see and do here.

Each summer Roswell hosts the **UFO Encounter Festival** to celebrate the alleged crash of a flying saucer near town in 1947. The crash or "Roswell Incident" has fascinated scientists and the public for decades due to tight military security surrounding the event and it recently achieved national television fame in the movie *Roswell*. Two museums in town dedicated to UFO phenomena and research cater to growing public interest on the subject. The **International UFO Museum and Research Center**, 400 North Main, ☎ 505/625-9495, offers a video introducing you to witnesses who participated in the retrieval of the alleged space aliens back in '47, as well as documents and statements from military personnel who were on duty at the time of the incident. Other flying saucer exhibits and a research library fill the rest of the museum. The **Outa Limits UFO Enigma Museum**, 6108 South Main, ☎ 505/347-2275, has a good collection of books, exhibits and videos on this fascinating field of study. For those who just don't buy it, Roswell offers three other conventional museums dealing with less controversial aspects of the city's history and culture. The **Roswell Museum and Art Center**, 100 11th, ☎ 505/624-6744, is the best and largest of the three. The museum houses a fantastic collection of artifacts, encompassing ancient history, Native Americans, experimental rockets and current technologies. The Robert H. Goddard Collection documents this famous area scientist's ground-breaking research leading to the launch of the world's first liquid-fueled rocket. There is an exact replica of the lab in which Goddard worked during his time in Roswell, complete with engine parts, rocket assemblies, nose cones and photos of early experiments. There's a planetarium, too, which presents a variety of astronomy programs.

Even more impressive, however, is the Art Center, where 17 galleries combine to make this one of the finest repositories of art in the state. The Southwest Collection includes works by such famous painters and sculptors as Georgia O'Keeffe, Stuart Davis and John Marin. There is a separate collection of works by the Roswell-born landscape and portrait painter, Peter Hurd, which concentrates on his landscapes of the southwest. A collection donated by Roger Aston consisting of more than 2,000 pieces documents the history of the southwest through its art with items as various as Native American quillwork and the artistic details on western firearms. The most interesting exhibit, however, may be the Native American and Hispanic Collection. Striking because it is so different from the typical southwestern exhibits of this kind, it features work by contemporary 20th-century artists rather than those of days gone by. The Art Center also supports the work of aspiring area artists and art students by providing studios and classrooms.

The **Chaves County Historical Museum**, 200 North Lea Avenue, ☎ 505/622-8333, is located in the 1910 home of James Phelps White, an early Roswell area farmer and civic leader. Each room in this two-story prairie-style house is so skillfully decorated with pioneer antiques and Victorian furniture that you'd think the owners had just stepped out for the afternoon.

Military buffs should head over to the campus of the New Mexico Military Institute. Graduates from this institute have participated in each United States military campaign since the Spanish-American War. It is also the alma mater of artist Peter Hurd and Dallas Cowboys' football quarterback, Roger Staubach. The **Gen-**

eral Douglas L. McBride Museum, located on campus at 101 West College Boulevard, ☎ 505/624-8220, has exhibits on the institute's more famous graduates but, more importantly, it has war memorabilia from every campaign to which its graduates have contributed. Grouped by war, this museum showcases some intriguing articles, including items recovered from the Bataan Death March and a Harley-Davidson motorcycle mounted with machine-guns that was used in General Pershing's 1916 assault on Pancho Villa.

If the sun's out and you'd rather not spend your day inside, there are plenty of outdoor activities to occupy your time in the Roswell area. For starters, try the **Spring River Park and Zoo**, at the corner of College Boulevard and Atkinson Avenue. The zoo displays a number of wild animals such as bobcats, bison and bears, and the adjoining park offers large lawns, picnic tables, a fishing pond (for youngsters only), a carousel and a miniature train ride. Both are open to the public daily from 10 AM to sunset.

From the park, a system of bike trails leads into town connecting most of the other city parks, where numerous outdoor tennis and basketball courts are located. (See below, under Adventures on Wheels.)

Cool off with a swim at **Bottomless Lakes State Park**, just 15 miles east of town via US 380 and NM 409. Hiking and camping are also available. ☎ 505/624-6058. (See below, under Adventures on Foot/Water.)

The **Bitter Lake National Wildlife Refuge** occupies nearly 25,000 acres northeast of Roswell. Hundreds of thousands of snow geese, sandhill cranes and various ducks find respite here each fall. An eight-mile self-guided auto tour route winds through the southern section of the refuge. A birding list can be obtained at the visitor center near the park entrance. Several wildlife viewing stations and picnic tables are scattered around the area, but no camping is allowed. Take Pine Lodge Road east off US 285 near the mall at the north end of town and follow the signs to the refuge headquarters, which is open daily year round. You may want to call ahead to make sure the birds are "in." For information, ☎ 505/622-6755 or contact Bitter Lake National Wildlife Refuge, PO Box 7, Roswell, NM 88202-0007. The **Roswell Airport**, at the Roswell Industrial Air Center, offers passenger service from Albuquerque and Dallas via **Mesa Air**, ☎ 800/MESA-AIR. Passenger service from Dallas and Ruidoso is also offered by Lone Star Air, ☎ 505/336-4893 or 800/877-3932. Rental cars are available at the airport from either **Hertz**, ☎ 800/654-3131, or **National**, ☎ 505/347-2323.

For information, contact the **Roswell Chamber of Commerce**, PO Box 70, Roswell, NM 88202-0070, ☎ 505/623-5695.

Artesia

Named for the huge underground water supply and the artesian wells drilled here in the early 1900s, Artesia was at one time the site of the deepest drilled water well in the world. But it's a well of a different sort that fuels this little town's current economy. In 1924, New Mexico's first oil well was drilled here, and today the oil industry is by far the area's largest employer.

Aside from that, Artesia is a simple farming and ranching community. You'll find far more alfalfa, cotton, cattle and pecans than fellow tourists here. Most people pass through on their way to Carlsbad Caverns and never even stop. When they do, it is usually to visit the **Historical Museum and Art Center**, 505 West Richardson, Artesia, NM 88211, ☎ 505/748-2390. The museum displays relate to local history connected with the oil industry and area agriculture. The art center showcases the work of local artists.

For information, contact the **Artesia Chamber of Commerce**, PO Box 99, Artesia, NM 88211, ☎ 505/746-2744 or 800/658-6251.

Carlsbad

Carlsbad Caverns are not in Carlsbad. They are actually about 27 miles south of town, but this is where most travelers come to gain access to America's best known subterranean national park. A veritable oasis in the desert, the Carlsbad area surprises most visitors with the number of other recreational options in addition to the world famous caverns.

The Pecos River should probably get credit for Carlsbad's current location. During the mid- to late 19th century, this was an important stop for cowboys working the cattle trails from Texas up to Colorado and Montana. Today the section of river that constitutes the city's eastern border has been dammed in several places, widening and deepening it to form **Lake Carlsbad** and **Lower Tansill Lake**. (See below, under Adventures on Water.) Both provide year-round recreation, and their western banks have been landscaped and developed to create the **Pecos Riverwalk** park. More than four miles of paved trails pass through lush picnic areas with tables and large shade trees. There is also a tennis and racquetball complex, complete with pro shop.

Two state parks are located near town. The first, **Brantley Lake State Park**, 12 miles north of Carlsbad via US 285, is a much larger body of water than the two located in the city. ☎ 505/457-2384. (See below, under Adventures on Water.)

The second, **Living Desert Zoological and Botanical State Park**, on the northwest edge of Carlsbad off US 285, is an essential stop for all travelers to the region. This complex offers fascinating exhibits dedicated to the interpretation of the Chihuahuan Desert life zone which extends from Mexico through Texas and covers much of southeastern New Mexico. Displays in the attractive visitor center and park headquarters explain area geology, archaeology, plant and animal life and history. A series of self-guided trails lead from the center through dunes, arroyos and canyons landscaped with various native plants, including cholla, cowtongue and prickly-pear cactus, yucca, acacia, agave, juniper and pinyon pine. Wild animals of the region such as rattlesnakes, javalinas, gray wolves, bison, elk and mountain lions also inhabit the walking trail area of the park. But don't fear – the animals are safely separated from park visitors by their partitioned natural habitats. The park is open daily, 8 AM to 7 PM May 15 through Labor Day and 9AM to 4 PM the rest of the year. For information, contact **Living Desert State Park**, Box 100, Carlsbad, NM 88220, ☎ 505/887-5516.

The **Carlsbad Museum and Art Center**, 418 West Fox, ☎ 505/887-0276, is another popular area attraction, especially during the heat of the day. Exhibits contain Indian and prehistoric artifacts including mammoth and new-world horse fossils. Antique saddles, guns, clothes and furniture fill out the rest of the collection. The art gallery features the McAdoo Collection, including pieces from the famous Taos Artist Society. The work of local artists is also showcased here.

Air service from Albuquerque is available through **Mesa Air**, ☎ 505/885-0245 or 800/MESA-AIR, to the **Cavern City Air Terminal**, five miles south of town on National Parks Highway. (See below, under Adventures in the Air.)

Rental cars may be obtained at the Cavern City Air Terminal through **Hertz**, ☎ 505/887-1500.

For more information, contact **Carlsbad Chamber of Commerce and Convention & Visitors' Bureau**, PO Box 910, Carlsbad, NM 88220, ☎ 505/887-6516 or 800/221-1224.

White's City

White's City is the tourist trap at the main gate to Carlsbad Caverns National Park. If you've been listening to your radio within 200 miles of the park, you've no doubt heard the fabulous tales of wonders to be found here. And, although it is the most convenient place to stay when visiting the caverns, prices are generally high and the services are no better than they are in Carlsbad proper.

If you do stop here and have some time, **The Million Dollar Museum**, Main Street, ☎ 505/785-2291, exhibits such curious Old West relics as a 6,000-year-old mummified Indian, the first car west of the Pecos, antique dolls, guns and other various artifacts. There's also a shooting gallery and arcade nearby.

Just up the hill from the White's City information center and gift shop, **Granny's Opera House** provides evening entertainment for area tourists. Crowds are encouraged to boo, hiss and throw popcorn at the villains in old-fashioned melodramas and vaudeville skits performed Thursday through Saturday, June to September. Reservations are preferred. For information, ☎ 505/785-2291.

Carlsbad Caverns National Park

One of the largest cave systems in the world and probably the most visited national park in New Mexico, Carlsbad Caverns National Park entertains more than 700,000 people a year and, since its official opening in 1923, close to 35 million tourists from all over the world have journeyed into its marvelous depths. Travel 27 miles south of Carlsbad on National Parks Highway/US 180 to reach the Park.

Faded pictographs and other artifacts found near the cave's natural entrance prove that early Native Americans knew of this natural wonder. Archaeologists, though, have found no signs of entry past the cave mouth. The huge drop-off immediately past the opening apparently kept would-be explorers out until the late 19th century. Stories about which cattle-herding cowboy was the first to lower himself via lasso into the cave still circulate around the area. Serious exploration was begun in 1903 by a mining company with plans to harvest the large deposits of bat guano found in the cave for fertilizer. Guano was the mining company's only real concern and, since the bats inhabited only the first few chambers, exploration was limited. One miner, though, fell in love with the cave and took it upon himself to conduct deeper probes on his own time. Armed with only a lantern, James White made it to some of the farthest reaches of the system, including the Big Room which is the primary chamber visited by tourists today. His stories, relating the wonders he'd seen there, convinced the commissioner of the General Land Office to send an examiner to consider the cave as a possible national monument. Carlsbad Caverns received that status shortly after its examination in 1923. Then, with the publication of a story and photos by *National Geographic* in 1924, interest in the caverns exploded world-wide. In 1930, President Herbert Hoover declared Carlsbad Caverns a national park.

Currently, the park includes about 46,700 acres and more than 80 caves. And, while its first tourists were lowered into the cave by a bucket designed to haul bat guano, thousands of contemporary tourists simply ride the elevator from the visitor center down to the Big Room. Today, two self-guided walking tours explore the main cave along well-lit and maintained trails, one via elevator access and the other following a trail from the natural entrance. There are also numerous opportunities for ranger-guided tours of the wilder caves in the park and for general hiking and backpacking through the park's Chihuahuan Desert landscapes up above. (See below, under Adventures on Foot.)

There is a great bookstore at the visitors center as well as a gift shop, restaurants, kennel service and various exhibits pertaining to the cave's history and geology.

Carlsbad Caverns is open daily year-round except for Christmas Day. Summer park hours are from 8AM to 7PM, with the final cave entry at 5PM. The rest of the year, the park is open from 8AM to 5:30PM, with the final cave entry at 3:30PM. For information, contact **Carlsbad Caverns National Park**, 3225 National Parks Highway, Carlsbad, NM 88220, ☎ 505/785-2232.

Cloudcroft

The small community of Cloudcroft, nestled in the pines of the Sacramento Mountains high above the barren Tularosa Basin, remains today the cool mountain resort retreat of its founders' original intention. In 1899, the Alamogordo and Sacramento Mountain Railway, which was conducting logging operations in the mountains above Alamogordo for railroad cross-ties, built a lodge retreat for its executives at the highest point along one of its log-bearing railways. The lodge, offering not only an escape from the blazing summer heat in the desert below but a hotel, restaurant, dance pavilion, tennis courts, golf links, bowling alley and children's playground, soon became a favorite summer destination of vacationers throughout New Mexico, Texas and even the Oklahoma Territory.

The Lodge at Cloudcroft, featuring one of the loftiest and most scenic golf courses in North America, remains the driving force behind the community's tourist economy. It is considered by many to be the only place to stay in the area – no matter what kind of mountain vacation is planned. (See below, under Cloudcroft Accommodations.) Surrounded by 215,000 acres of the Lincoln National Forest, the town is a natural springboard for adventure tourists seeking hiking, backpacking, mountain biking and other outdoor activities. (See below, under Adventures on Foot/Wheels.) Horseback riding in the Sacramento Mountains is one of the most popular summer tourist pastimes. Two horse stables near town offer guided tours of the Lincoln National Forest backcountry.

> **Chippeway Riding Stables**, 602 Cox Canyon Highway, Cloudcroft, NM 88317, ☎ 505/682-2565.
> **Cloudcroft Trolley Co.**, seven miles east of the Cloudcroft Chamber of Commerce on US 82, PO Box 813, Cloudcroft, NM 88317, ☎ 505/687-3921 or 800/349-4535.

Cloudcroft offers winter recreation as well. **Snow Canyon Ski Area** is located nearby and many of the forest's hiking trails are popular winter escapes for snowshoers and cross-country skiers alike. (See below, under Adventures on Snow.)

The town of Cloudcroft itself is a small collection of galleries, shops and restaurants, plus one of the best small-town museums in the state. The **Sacramento Mountains Historical Museum** is across the road from the Chamber of Commerce on US 82. It features such outdoor exhibits as a pioneer barn, granary and authentic hand-hewn log cabin. Inside, visitors will find one of the best private arrowhead collections in the state, as well as tools and household items of early settlers and railroad workers. For information, ☎ 505/682-2932.

About 20 miles south of Cloudcroft via NM 24 and Forest Service Road 64, the **National Solar Observatory – Sacramento Peak** (better known as "Sunspot") is a research center for monitoring solar activity and studying other stars in the galaxy. The stunning views of the Tularosa Basin, White Sands and the Valley of Fires, all about 6,000 feet below, are worth the drive to Sacramento Peak. But it is the opportunity to tour the facility that brings most tourists here. One of the telescopes rises from 20 stories underground to 13 stories above ground level. Although visitors can't handle any of the observatory's stellar scopes, they may view current solar activity on a video monitor in the lobby or watch scientists studying various galactic phenomenon on similar computer monitors. Guided tours of the observatory are held on Saturdays at 2 PM.

For information, contact the **Cloudcroft Chamber of Commerce**, US 82, PO Box 1290, Cloudcroft, NM 88317, ☎ 505/682-2733.

Alamogordo

Two ranchers named John and Charles Eddy knew that the Tularosa Basin, even with its agricultural possibilities and resources, could never support a town without transportation. So in 1897, they began construction of a railroad line north out of El Paso. In the following year, they purchased the Alamo Ranch for $5,000, including water rights, and began laying out the town of **Alamogordo** as the railroad neared the site. They basically built their own town, and they were right about the railroad bringing life to the area. Alamogordo grew to become the center of commerce for the region. The railroad also established the city as the gateway to area tourism by providing access to the beautiful mountains surrounding the basin.

But mountains are not the only tourist draw to this area. The largest gypsum dune field in the world, **White Sands National Monument**, is located about 15 miles southwest of town. People come from all over the world to view and explore one of the most beautiful and bizarre landscapes this side of the Sahara. (See below, under Touring White Sands National Monument.)

Scenic hiking and camping opportunities also are available at the historic **Oliver Lee State Park** near the mouth of Dog Canyon, 15 miles south of Alamogordo via US 54. Archaeological evidence suggests that this area has been a campground for more than 6,000 years. Early humans took advantage of the dependable water supplies in the nearby canyon and used the gap to access the mountains from the desert floor. From the 1840s to the 1880s, Mescalero Apaches used Dog Canyon as a hideout and ambush site during numerous skirmishes with the US Calvary. After that, area settlers moved in to set up ranching operations and use the canyon's water as a source for irrigation. One of the most prominent area ranchers, Oliver Lee, for whom the park is named, served on the state legislature in the early 1900s. Exhibits at the visitor center explain the park's colorful history. Camping is available. For information, ☎ 505/437-8284. (See below, under Adventures on Foot.)

The railroad still passes through town, but these days, Alamogordo is associated with transportation of a much speedier sort. The Tularosa Basin, home to White Sands Missile Range and Holloman Air Force Base, has long been a key testing sight for experimental rocketry in conjunction with the US space program. Here, in 1954, a Holloman colonel named John P. Stapp made his mark as the fastest man in the world at the time, blazing across the desert at 632 miles per hour strapped to the front of a rocket sled called the Sonic Wind I. Holloman continues to play a major role in US space and military programs, as home base for the futuristic stealth bomber and to provide contingency support for the Space Shuttle at White Sands Space Harbor.

This may explain why the **International Space Hall of Fame** is located at the **Space Center** in Alamogordo. Housed in a five-story golden "cube" on Indian Wells Road at Scenic Drive, the center's exhibits document the history of the world's space programs and they include models of the Apollo and Gemini Command Modules, actual moon rocks, satellites, early rockets and a mock-up of a futuristic space station. The grounds surrounding the center make up the John P. Stapp Memorial Space Park, which displays the famous Sonic Wind I Rocket Sled, as well as numerous rockets and rocket engines. But don't let the word "memorial" mislead you; Col. Stapp still lives in the area. He and other local scientists/space explorers often visit the center, bringing its exhibits to life with their first-hand accounts of famous events. The center also features the **Clyde W. Tombaugh Space Theater**, a planetarium that presents Omnimax movies and laser light shows, as well as astronomy programs. The center is open daily from 9AM to 6 PM. The theater also offers evening shows on Fridays and Saturdays.

For information, contact The Space Center, PO Box 533, Alamogordo, NM 88310, ☎ 505/437-2840 or 800/545-4021.

Also of interest in town, the **Toy Train Depot Museum & Ride**, 1991 White Sands Boulevard/US 54/70, ☎ 505/437-2855, celebrates America's love for little trains. More than 1,200 feet of operating model railways in all scales provide great entertainment for young and old. There are also many static displays and 2.2 miles of outdoor miniature railroad to ride.

Just down the road, the **Alameda Park Zoo**, 1321 White Sands Boulevard/US 54/70, ☎ 505/437-8430, displays more than 300 mammals and birds from all around the world. Visitors stroll through seven acres of native and exotic wildlife exhibits, including lions, endangered wolves and playful monkeys. The zoo is open daily from 9AM to 5 PM.

Mesa Air, ☎ 505/437-9111 or 800/MESA-AIR, provides passenger service to the **Alamogordo/White Sands Regional Airport**, Airport Road, ☎ 505/439-4110.

The **Alamo/El Paso Shuttle**, ☎ 505/437-1472 or 800/872-2701, provides scheduled van service between the Holiday Inn Alamogordo and the El Paso International Airport.

Rental cars are available at the Holiday Inn through **Avis**, 1401 South White Sands Boulevard, ☎ 505/437-3140 or 800/831-2847, and at the Alamogordo/White Sands Regional airport through **Hertz**, Airport Road, ☎ 505/437-7760 or 800/654-3131.

For information, contact the **Alamogordo Chamber of Commerce**, 1310 White Sands Boulevard/US 54/70, PO Box 518, Alamogordo, NM 88310, ☎ 505/437-6120 or 800/545-4021.

White Sands National Monument

At the end of the last Ice Age, some 24 to 12 thousand years ago, rain and snowmelt from the surrounding mountains began depositing dissolved gypsum, salt and other soluble minerals in one of the lowest points of the Tularosa Basin, Lake Otero. Once covering more than 1,600 square miles, this lake completely evaporated about 4,000 years ago, leaving a large dry lake bed. Subsequently, the prevailing winds removed most of the silt and clay from the bottom of the lake bed, revealing large deposits of crystalline gypsum. Through time, the forces of nature – heat, cold and wind, broke down the crystals into sand-sized particles, blew them northeast of the lake bed and created the largest gypsum dune field in the world.

White Sands National Monument encompasses more than 300 acres of snow-white sands about 15 miles southwest of Alamogordo via US 70. This stunning landscape is the leading tourist attraction in the Alamogordo area. The sandy sanctuary is situated only 60 minutes from popular resorts in the surrounding mountains, so visitors can ski in the morning, drive down for a late lunch in Alamogordo and stroll the afternoon away in their shorts, since winter temperatures on this vast oceanless beach average 65 to 75°. But it's not just the mild winter climate that draws folks here. Year-round, these seemingly endless soft white dunes astound visitors with their simple austere beauty.

A road leads into Heart of the Dunes, where numerous picnic areas with shaded tables have been scooped out of the sands. Be sure to bring along a good sized piece of cardboard, as many of the dunes are tall enough for sledding or surfing. Hiking opportunities range from free exploration to trekking along designated trails. Primitive camping is allowed. (See below, under Adventures on Foot.)

A visitor center at the park entrance offers wonderful exhibits detailing dune formation and park history as well as sharing information on area wildlife and vegetation. A gift shop, bookstore and restrooms are located there, too. Information centers and markers are also scattered throughout the park.

White Sands offers a wide variety of informative talks and presentations led by park rangers. (See below, under "Eco-Tours & Cultural Excursions.")

The monument is open daily from 7AM to 10AM during the summer and 7AM to sunset the rest of the year. For information, contact **White Sands National Monument**, PO Box 458, Alamogordo, NM 88311, ☎ 505/479-6124.

Ruidoso

Ruidoso is considered the jewel of southeastern New Mexico, offering visitors a delightful combination of forests, rippling brooks and majestic mountains. The name Ruidoso is Spanish for "noisy water" and it fits the town that grew up around **Dowlin's Mill**, built in 1853 on the river rushing through this picturesque valley. The mill has survived, serving as a post office, then a roadhouse, accommodating such notables as Billy the Kid and General "Black Jack" Pershing. Nowadays, the mill is operated as a curio shop on Sudderth Drive, where tourists can still buy stone ground corn meal.

Ruidoso's attraction as a tourist destination got a boost in the 1930s with the introduction of horse racing on a simple cleared strip along the Rio Ruidoso. Neighborly contests turned into nationally known, big-money affairs with the 1947 opening of Hollywood Park, which changed its name five years later to **Ruidoso Downs Racetrack**, ☎ 505/378-4140 or 800/622-6023. Designed for quarter horse racing, though thoroughbreds run here too, the Downs is home of the All American Futurity – the Kentucky Derby of quarter horse racing. In 1972, the All American became the first horse race in history to have a gross purse reach the $1 million mark and, with nearly $2 million at stake today, it remains the richest quarter horse race in the country. Ruidoso's population of only 7,000 permanent residents nearly doubles on opening day at the track in early May and more than triples during the Labor Day weekend running of the All American.

Not coincidentally, the **Anne C. Stradling Museum of the Horse, ☎** 505/378-4142 or 800/263-5929, is located right next door to the racetrack. Built in 1992 by Ruidoso Downs Racetrack owner, R.D. Hubbard, this spacious museum houses a fabulous collection of equine-related art and artifacts, much of it once belonging to the late, renowned horsewoman Anne C. Stradling. It has become a destination for horse-loving tourists from the world over. Exhibits include a Conestoga wagon, various buggies and sleighs and an 1866 12-passenger stagecoach, as well as saddles of Tibetan, Cossack, Charro, European and American design. There's also an impressive collection of equine-related art, with pieces by Remington and Russell. The museum's most striking piece of art, however, was just completed in 1995, and stands as the largest equine sculpture in the world. **"Free Spirits at Noisy Water,"** designed by internationally known local artist Dave McGary, is positioned in front of the museum on US 70 so as to be seen by virtually every passerby. It is a monument in bronze to seven standard breeds. A thoroughbred, quarter horse, appaloosa, paint mare and colt, Arabian, Morgan and standardbred – all at 1½ times life-size – dash across a 255-foot-long landscaped hillside, garnering doubletakes from unsuspecting motorists. The Museum is open daily from 9AM to 5:30 PM in the summer and 10AM to 5 PM the rest of the year.

The monument is outstanding. You can visit the artist's studio and gallery in downtown Ruidoso. One of 18 art galleries and working studios in the area, **McGary Studios – Expressions in Bronze,** 2002 Sudderth Drive, ☎ 505/257-1000 or 800/687-3424, is a testament to the fact that Ruidoso is fast becoming one of the leading quality art communities in the state. McGary actually specializes in sculpting Native Americans rather than horses, and several larger-than-life works majestically guard the grounds of his studio. In addition to studios and galleries, Ruidoso's two main streets, Sudderth Drive and Mechem Boulevard, are lined with shops, boutiques and restaurants aimed at the tide of tourists visiting the area year-round. They come in the summer for the horse races and in winter for **Ski Apache**, the nation's southernmost major ski area. Truth is, there may be more ski rental stores in town than art galleries. (See below under Adventures on Snow.)

During the in-between times and even during busy horse racing and ski seasons people come to Ruidoso to relax and play golf in the cool mountain air. Hiking, backpacking, camping, fishing and mountain biking are popular pursuits as well in the surrounding **Lincoln National Forest**. (See below, under Adventures on Foot/Wheels/Water.)

Lone Star Air, ☎ 505/336-4893 or 800/877-3932, offers regular service from Dallas to Sierra Blanca Regional Airport.

Car rentals are available through **Sierra Blanca Motor Company**, both at the airport, ☎ 505/336-7933, and in town at 300 West US 70, ☎ 505/257-4081.

For information, contact the **Ruidoso Valley Chamber of Commerce**, PO Box 698, Ruidoso, NM 88345, ☎ 505/257-7395 or 800/253-2255.

Carrizozo Area

Carrizozo may be the seat of Lincoln County, but there isn't much to see or do within the town itself. But you will pass through it to reach three interesting touring destinations that can be visited as part of a fun day-trip from Ruidoso. Stop here to gas up the car and grab some snacks, but don't waste too much time because there's lots to see not far down the road.

About 35 miles south of town off US 54, **Three Rivers Petroglyph National Recreation Site** provides a glimpse into the lives of the area's earliest human inhabitants. More than 5,000 petroglyphs have been counted in a large boulder field near the western base of Sierra Blanca, the highest peak in southern New Mexico. These images of animals, people and celestial figures are believed to have been chiseled into the rocks by the Mimbres people, a Native American culture centuries older than the Anasazi of northwestern New Mexico. A short trail weaves through the boulder field from a picnic area near the site. Another short trail leaves from the picnic area toward a stream where a partially reconstructed Mimbres village reveals the tribe's progression in home construction from pit houses to adobe huts and then to multi-room adobe structures. With the petroglyphs and ruins in the foreground and Sierra Blanca's snow-capped peak in the background, this area offers some great photographic opportunities, especially late in the afternoon.

The **Valley of Fires Recreation Area**, a strikingly harsh landscape five miles west of Carrizozo on US 380, is a remnant of the most recent lava flow in the continental United States. Somewhere between 1,500 and 2,000 years ago, the Tularosa Valley was suddenly ablaze with molten rock. Today, the jagged black lava dominates a 44-mile north-south stretch of the valley floor, covering 125 square miles. Spanish explorers named the area the Malpais or Badlands because the rough and broken lava rendered the region impassable except on foot. Despite its foreboding nature, there is abundant life in the Malpais. Mule deer, coyote, fox and bobcat inhabit the lava flow, and during late spring to early summer, wildflowers and cactus blooms produce splashes of color across the landscape. The Valley of Fires Recreation area is maintained by the Bureau of Land Management. A visitor information station provides literature about the area and a map to guide you along a short nature trail. Camping is available. For information, contact the **Bureau of Land Management**, PO Drawer 1857, Roswell, NM 88202-1857, ☎ 505/624-1790.

In the 1890s, **White Oaks**, 12 miles northeast of Carrizozo via NM 349, was a thriving mining community of 1,500 people. Today it is the area's most interesting ghost town. Crumbling buildings and rusting mine equipment dot the northwestern face of the Capitan mountain range, reminding visitors of boom-days long ago. A fading cemetery remains as a monument to folks who almost made it big here, and a small museum in the old school-house preserves the last of their belongings.

For information, contact the **Carrizozo Chamber of Commerce**, PO Box 567, Carrizozo, NM 88301.

Capitan

In the spring of 1950, a small bear cub was rescued from a raging forest fire in the mountains northeast of Capitan. Firefighters flew the injured cub to Santa Fe for treatment. During recovery he picked up the name "Smokey." Later returned to Capitan for release into the wild, Smokey chose not to leave his newfound human friends and later that year he was given a home at the Washington, DC Zoo. From that point on, Smokey became the most famous spokesbear in history. Research indicates that the ad campaign ("Smokey says, 'Only you can prevent forest fires.'") has saved the country close to $30 billion, cutting the number of forest fires almost in half.

Smokey died peacefully of natural causes in 1976 and the townspeople of Capitan, without any outside funding, built a park and memorial museum in his honor. The bear was flown back to his hometown for funeral services and is now buried at **Smokey Bear Historical State Park**. This little park, right in the middle of Capitan on US 380, features a visitor center that shows films about

Smokey's life as well as forest fire prevention. Outside, an interpretive nature trail takes you through a landscaped park designed to represent the various life zones found in the surrounding region. Smokey's grave lies at the end of the trail. The Park is open daily from 9AM to 5 PM. For information, ☎ 505/354-2748.

Aside from a couple of small antique and crafts shops, there's not much else in Capitan – save one of the best restaurants in the state. (See below, under Where to Stay & Eat.)

The foothills around Capitan are mostly public lands administered by the Bureau of Land Management and they offer plenty of opportunities for outdoor enthusiasts. The most unsung of such possibilities is **Fort Stanton Cave** – the third largest in New Mexico. (See below, under Adventures on Foot.)

History buffs passing through the area might enjoy a stop at **Fort Stanton**. Built in 1855, the fort played a major role in protecting settlers from the White Mountain and Mescalero Apaches. Little known, too, is that it was the setting for a Civil War battle in 1861 that completely destroyed the complex. Fort Stanton was rebuilt at its present site in 1868 and continued to serve the military until 1896. Although empty today, the fort's facilities were utilized as both a medical and mental treatment center through the years. As a result, most of the buildings are surprisingly well preserved. You can look around the place and the fort's parade grounds are a great spot for a picnic. Fort Stanton is located on NM 214 three miles south of US 380 between Capitan and Lincoln.

For information, contact the **Capitan Chamber of Commerce**, PO Box 268, Capitan, NM 88316, ☎ 505/354-2273.

Lincoln

While several towns across the state claim to have been visited by New Mexico's most notorious outlaw, **Lincoln** is home to the true legend of Billy the Kid, for it was here that all the trouble started. The erection of nearby Fort Stanton in 1855 sparked an economic boom in the little cowtown of Lincoln and an intense rivalry developed between local merchants over supply contracts with the fort. John Tunstall and L.G. Murphy were leading competitors for the contracts during the 1870s. In 1878, a number of Murphy's men, expecting to end the rivalry in typical wild-west fashion, ambushed and killed Tunstall. But William Bonney (Billy the Kid), a loyal ranch hand of the fallen merchant, witnessed the murder and vowed to avenge the death of his boss by killing every last man involved with the attack. He was among the leaders of a small army formed by Tunstall supporters. Ensuing events produced one of the bloodiest chapters in New Mexico's history. Dubbed the Lincoln County War, this old-fashioned gang fight raged on for almost a year, climaxing in a five-day shootout on the streets of Lincoln. After the dust and smoke settled, The Kid submitted to arrest in order to testify, under the promise that the governor would grant pardons to all parties involved. But, after testifying, he learned that the US attorney intended to prosecute and had arranged a hanging – disregarding the governor's pardon. Shooting his way out of the Lincoln County Courthouse and killing two deputies, Billy escaped, only to be relentlessly pursued by newly elected sheriff, Pat Garrett. Three months later, Garrett tracked Billy down in Fort Sumner. That's where the Kid's luck ran out when the sheriff shot and killed the wily 21-year-old outlaw in the bedroom of an area ranch house.

Nothing of great importance has happened in Lincoln since its glory days and the town remains much the same as it was in 1878. Now protected as the **Lincoln State Monument and National Landmark**, the town of only 70 residents thrives as a kind of living museum, remarkably devoid of the tacky trappings of tourism that most old-west towns are known for. There are no stagecoach tours or flashy saloons decked out in red velvet. The town's 40-odd original buildings have been carefully maintained by the Lincoln Historical Trust, the State of New Mexico and private benefactors so as to retain the town's historic integrity.

A visitor center offers maps for a self-guided walking tour of the town, a slide show and exhibits relating the history of the area before and after the Lincoln County War. The walking tour pinpoints the historically important structures in town, including John Tunstall's store, now preserved as a museum, the courthouse, the doctor's house, the Wortley Hotel, and El Torreon, a rock fortress built to protect early settlers from the Apaches. During the summer, costumed interpreters walk the streets giving insight into Lincoln's colorful past. Each August, the town hosts **Old Lincoln Days** with a parade, folk pageant, living history demonstrations and a reenactment of Billy the Kid's famous gun-blazing jail-break.

For information, contact the **Lincoln State Monument and National Landmark**, PO Box 36, Lincoln, NM 88338, ☎ 505/653-4372.

San Patricio/Tinnie

About 20 miles east of Ruidoso, nestled among the farms and ranches of the Hondo River Valley, the **Hurd-La Rinconada Gallery** houses one of the most important art collections in New Mexico. The gallery, located on the late Peter Hurd's Sentinel Ranch, features originals by Hurd, his wife Henriette Wyeth and their son Michael Hurd – three of the best known painters in the Southwest. Peter Hurd's most famous painting, his official portrait of President Lyndon B. Johnson, which was described by the subject as being "the ugliest thing (he) ever saw," is not displayed here but at the National Portrait Gallery in Washington D.C. What you will see here, though, are major works by the trio, including floral still lifes and beautiful southwestern landscapes, as well as Peter's whimsical political sketches of President Richard Nixon and other notables from the Watergate era. Also on display are works by Henriette's distinguished father, N.C. Wyeth, who became famous through his illustrations in such classic books as Robert Louis Stevenson's *Treasure Island* and James Fenimore Cooper's *The Last of the Mohicans* and *The Deerslayer*. The gallery, just south of US 70 at mile marker 281 near San Patricio, is open daily from 9 AM to 5 PM, Sundays 10 AM to 4 PM. For information, ☎ 505/653-4331.

Adventures

On Foot

Mirror Lake and **Lake in the Making Trail** at Bottomless Lakes State Park, 15 miles east of Roswell via US 380 and NM 409, begins at the visitor center near Cottonwood Lake. From there, the half-mile trail leads through a dry sinkhole that will someday become another "bottomless" lake and up to an overlook above the beautiful red cliff-lined Mirror Lake.

Exit US 285 about 10 miles north of Carlsbad and follow the signs for 25 miles southwest on NM 137 and then eight miles on Forest Road 276 to find the trailhead to **Sitting Bull Falls**. At 130 feet, these falls in the Guadalupe Mountain District of the Lincoln National Forest are the tallest in New Mexico and are a favorite summer picnic destination for Carlsbad area residents. From the picnic area at the parking lot, a trail heads south a few hundred yards to the base of the falls. A dip in the pools and streams here provides sure relief from the heat of the surrounding desert. Another trail (#68), heading out from the north end of the parking area, ascends 200 feet to the top of the plateau and reaches Sitting Bull Stream after about half a mile. A trek to the top of the falls is well worth the view, but be careful; a number of hikers have been killed or injured falling from this site. The trail continues up the stream about three more miles to the continuation of NM 137 and passes Sitting Bull Spring along the way. The Forest Service does not allow camping at the falls or picnic area but does allow it along Trail #68. Maps of the Lincoln National Forest (Guadalupe District), Red Bluff Draw and Queen 7.5 USGS quads will come in handy while hiking in this area.

Visitors to **Carlsbad Caverns National Park**, 27 miles south of Carlsbad via National Parks Highway/US 180, may choose from several self-guided and ranger-led caving adventures. Of the self-guided routes, the **Big Room Tour** is by far the most popular and the least strenuous. Access to the Big Room is afforded via elevator from the visitor center, taking participants 755 feet below the surface to the Underground Lunchroom. From there, a one-mile stroll around the perimeter of the cave's largest room (1,800 feet long and 255 feet tall) takes about one hour, passing such famous formations as the Bottomless Pit, Giant Dome, Rock of Ages and Painted Grotto. This relatively level trail is paved and well lit the entire way and is accessible to wheelchairs. Visitors on all tours of Carlsbad Cave return to the surface via the elevators.

The **Natural Entrance Route** is the longer and more rewarding of self-guided tours. It follows the traditional explorer's route into the cave, passing through Bat Cave and past unique formations with names like the Whale's Mouth, Witch's Finger and the Boneyard. This tour ends at the Underground Lunchroom, where participants may choose to return to the surface or continue on the Big Room Tour. The path to this point is also paved and well lit but is much steeper and more strenuous than the one through Big Room. Allow one hour to navigate the Natural Entrance Route and 2½ hours for the combined tours.

For more adventurous souls, a few extra dollars on top of the standard caverns entry fee reserves a spot in one of the exciting ranger-guided tours through the wilder sections of the caverns. These tours offer participants a thrilling but safe glimpse into the world of true spelunking. Reservations are recommended. For information, ☎ 505/785-2232, ext. 429.

The **King's Palace Tour** follows paved trails into four highly decorated chambers 830 feet below the surface. Rangers often conduct "black-out" programs during this tour, turning off all lights and allowing participants to experience the absolute blackness of a natural cavern environment. This tour begins and ends at the Underground Lunchroom and, while it is considered less strenuous than the Natural Entrance Route, it involves descending, and later climbing, an 80-foot hill. The 1½-hour tour is offered four times daily and is limited to 75 visitors.

The easiest of the "off-trail" tours is the **Left Hand Tunnel Tour**. In the tradition of early Carlsbad touring, the ranger's lantern provides the only light while tramping this half-mile stretch of earth-packed trail. Crystal clear pools and ancient reef fossils are highlighted along the way. Limited to 20 people, this tour lasts about two hours and is offered at 1 PM on Tuesday and Thursday only.

The **Lower Cave Tour** is a moderately strenuous "wild" cave tour. Accessing these highly decorated passages 90 feet below the Big Room involves climbing up and down 50-foot ladders. But this is one of the few areas where visitors can view rare cave pearl formations. A helmet with headlamp is provided to each participant, but you must bring your own gloves and four AA batteries. A maximum of 12 people may join this three-hour tour, offered at 1 PM on Monday, Wednesday and Friday.

A much more difficult and challenging adventure escorts cavers into the beautiful **Hall of the White Giant**. But to reach this remote chamber in Carlsbad Cavern, tour members must crawl long distances, squeeze through tight passages and chimney up slippery flowstone-lined sections of the route. This tour, which lasts three to four hours, is best for those interested in true spelunking. Helmets with headlamps are provided, but participants need to bring gloves, kneepads and four AA batteries. Offered only at 1 PM on Saturday, this tour is limited to 10 people.

Rangers also lead tours through two of the park's backcountry caves. Tours of **Spider Cave** are considered very strenuous. Visitors crawl through tight spaces and navigate difficult canyon passages to gain access to unusually decorated chambers in a complex maze cavern system. The tour begins with a 30-minute hike from the visitor center across desert terrain to the mouth of the cave. From there, the tour takes three to four hours. Again, helmets with headlamps are provided; participants supply gloves, kneepads and four AA batteries. This tour is limited to eight people and departs on Sunday at 1 PM. Tours of **Slaughter Canyon Cave** are not nearly as difficult as those through Spider Cave, but its location at the other end of the park from the Carlsbad Caverns Visitor Center is not very convenient for travelers who have scheduled only one day in the area. Beginning from the Slaughter Canyon

Parking Lot, located 23 miles southwest of the visitor center via US 180/62 and NM 418, a half-mile hike gaining 500 feet in elevation to the cave entrance is the most strenuous part of the tour. From the cave's mouth, tours usually last about two hours, and participants see the 89-foot-tall Monarch Column – one of the world's tallest – the crystal-decorated Christmas Tree Column and the Chinese Wall, a delicate ankle-high rimstone dam. On this tour, the ranger's lantern is the only source of light, but tour members are allowed to carry flashlights if they wish. Reservations are required for this tour, with a maximum of 25 people per outing. It is offered daily at 10 AM and 1 PM during the summer but only on Saturday and Sunday the rest of the year.

Wild caving is also allowed in 10 of the park's 80 undeveloped caves. A special permit from the Resource Office is required. For information, ☎ 505/785-2104.

More than 50 miles of trails through Carlsbad Caverns National Park's 46,000 acres of desert and mountain wilderness provide numerous opportunities for day hikes and backcountry camping. Check out the **Yucca Canyon** and **North Slaughter Canyon Trails** in the southwest section of the park or the **Rattlesnake Canyon Trail** near the Carlsbad Caverns Visitor Center. Rangers at the visitor center can provide permits and give trail recommendations and advice. Topo maps of the area are available at the Cavern Bookstore in the visitor center.

Hundreds of hiking and backpacking opportunities abound in the **Sacramento Mountains** of **Lincoln National Forest** surrounding Cloudcroft. Before extended treks in this area, obtain a Lincoln National Forest map, the USGS 15-minute quads for Cloudcroft and Alamogordo or the specific USGS 7.5-minute quads for the areas in which you intend to hike. For information, contact the **Cloudcroft Ranger Station,** ☎ 505/682-2551.

Driving US 82 between Cloudcroft and Alamogordo, Mexican Trestle is sure to catch your eye. From the highway, a pull-off and overlook allow you to view this massive turn-of-the-century railroad bridge, but **Rail Trail** lets you inspect it up close. An access road just east of mile marker 16 on US 82 in Cloudcroft leads to the trailhead at a parking and picnic area. From there, the trestle is about one mile down a well-maintained section of old railroad grade.

A parking area across the highway from the Mexican Trestle Overlook marks the trailhead for **Osha Trail**. A quarter-mile access trail leads up from the highway to join a 2.6-mile loop trail through oak brush, pine and fir trees. Alternate access is via Pines Campground, one mile north of Cloudcroft on NM 24.

Rim Trail, or Trail #105, is the most popular in the area. It follows the western rim of the Sacramento Mountains for 14 miles through lush forests that open at several points along the way to afford spectacular views of Tularosa Basin and White Sands 6,000 feet below. Drive two miles south from Cloudcroft on NM 130 and take the Sunspot Highway exit. The trailhead is just 0.1 mile down the road near the Slide Campground. Primitive camping is allowed all along the trail, which ends at Atkinson Field, a large grassy meadow and popular undeveloped campsite. Trail 105 more or less parallels Sunspot Highway and a number of Forest Service spurs cross the trail, allowing the option to shorten the trail with a car shuttle back to Slide Campground. There is no water available on the trail, but the Forest Service access roads make it easy to stash supplies at strategic points along the trail. To Atkinson Field and back, Rim Trail is an easy two- or three-day, 28-mile backpacking trek. Split into sections, it offers several good day-hiking opportunities. Be alert, because horses, mountain bikes and even motorcycles are also allowed here.

About 15 miles south of Cloudcroft, via Sunspot Highway and Forest Road 164, **Willie White Trail**, or Trail #112/113, is a very rewarding day-hike, especially in fall when the mountains are ablaze with color. From the parking lot at Bluff Springs, 4.4 miles down Forest Road 164, Trail #112 follows an old railroad grade east about a half-mile, where it meets Trail #113 heading southwest 1½ miles into a grassy canyon bottom. It then departs the railroad grade and continues up the canyon to Water Canyon Road. Follow the road north to Forest Road 164 and back to Bluff Spring. Round-trip, Willie White Trail is about four miles and climbs from 8,000 feet to 9,350 feet. Bluff Springs itself is a favorite picnicking and camping area. The spring flows across a grassy meadow and drops into a small, picturesque waterfall on the other side.

The trail through **Dog Canyon**, leaving from **Oliver Lee State Park** 15 miles south of Alamogordo, is popular not only for its rugged mountain scenery but for its historic reflections as well. This trail has been used for thousands of years as a route away from the heat of the barren Tularosa Basin to the cool breezes of the Sacramento Mountains. In the 1800s, it was a safe haven for the Mescalero Apaches during their many skirmishes with the US Cavalry. One particular battle in 1880 proved the canyon's strategic value, when 60 soldiers chased a group of Indians high into the canyon. As they reached a steep section of trail called the "Eyebrow," they were ambushed. The Apaches sent huge boulders rolling down the canyon, killing and injuring many of the troopers before they could escape.

The trail leaves from the visitor center at the state park and climbs more than 3,000 feet in only 4.2 miles. It is a strenuous hike, but the views from the ridge are worth the effort, especially at sunset. Water is available at the trailhead and about half-way up the trail at Dog Canyon Stream. Boil or treat any water taken from the stream. On the ridge, the trail ends at Forest Road 90, making this a good option for a day-hike with a pre-arranged car shuttle – although a high clearance vehicle is recommended. Primitive camping is allowed in the canyon, so you can make the trek an over-nighter if you wish.

White Sands National Monument, 15 miles southwest of Alamogordo via US 70, offers several hiking opportunities across its spectacular shimmering white dunes. When hiking the dunes, be sure to wear sunglasses and plenty of sunscreen. The sand is extremely bright and reflects the sun's rays from every angle.

The **Big Dune Trail** is the first you will pass as you drive into the Heart of the Sands from the visitor center. A trail guide obtained at the visitor center or trailhead explains dune formation and vegetation. Numbered markers along the way correspond with entries in the guide. Allow one or two hours to fully enjoy this short loop trail.

The next trailhead you'll come to is the **Back Country Camp-site Trail**. Marked only by posts, since winds can erase footprints and trails in less than an hour, this 0.3-mile trail leads to the only campsite in the park. Be sure to obtain a permit from the visitor center and camp if you have time. On full-moon nights, the snow-white sands amplify the light, making the dunes bright enough for hiking without flashlights. Be careful, though, not to stray too far from camp. Once your tent is out of sight, the dunes all begin to look very much alike and it is easy to get lost. Also, since the monument doesn't open until after sunrise, camping is the only way to experience the park at this magical golden hour. The dunes are periodically closed to overnight camping due to testing at the White Sands Missile Range. You may want to call the visitor center prior to your visit to see if any testing is planned. ☎ 505/479-6124.

The trailhead for the longest marked trail in the park is found at the extreme end of the Dunes Drive in the Heart of the Sands. The **Alkali Flat Trail** crosses 2½ miles of sand to reach the prehis-toric dry lake bed that is the origin of most of the gypsum sand comprising the present dunes. While most of the new sand blowing into the dunes is forming 10 miles south of this trail's end, at dry Lake Lucero, a visit to Alkali Flat is still interesting due to the large number of fossilized footprints left by prehistoric mammoths, cam-els and bison. The trail itself passes through one of the most pristine dune formations in the park. Allow most of the day for this hike.

Even though it is only five miles round-trip, walking in the sand is much slower than trekking across hard-packed trails. Be sure to carry plenty of water, since there is none available along the way. A flashlight will come in handy, too, if you're planning to be out after sunset. As mentioned before, wind can erase footprints and trails in less than an hour. This trail is marked by white posts with orange reflectors, visible from one to the next; but, even on full moon nights, they are hard to see without a flashlight.

Hiking in the Lincoln National Forest surrounding Ruidoso reveals some of the most dramatic scenery in the Southeast. The most striking natural feature has to be 12,003-foot **Sierra Blanca Peak** – the highest mountain in Southern New Mexico. The trailhead for a five-mile summit trail is found at a small parking area atop Ski Area Road just before the entrance to Ski Apache. Take marked **Trail #15** from the parking area along a small stream and across a grassy meadow to the junction with **Trail #25**. Go left on 25. About a half-mile from the junction, the trail enters a gently sloping valley with many possible campsites. Across the valley, the trail continues into a dense forest that often holds snow well into the summer. Climbing steadily, you will join **Trail #78** about 2½ miles after leaving the trailhead. Again, take the left fork and continue climbing to the crest of the range. The trail follows the crest to the summit of Lookout Mountain at 11,580 feet, where the national forest trail officially ends. The remaining 1¼ miles to the summit is actually on Mescalero Apache Reservation land but, as long as you don't hunt, build fires or camp, hiking the peak is permitted. Follow a well-worn path across a saddle and then up to the summit. Try to stay on the established route; the tundra, covered with flowers during the summer, is very fragile. From the top, you'll enjoy some of the best views in the state. To the south, White Sands National Monument sparkles in the sun. Northward, the Sangre de Cristos rise around Santa Fe. Looking far to the west, you may see the vast Gila Wilderness, and to the east, on a clear day, you can see the Guadalupe Mountains stretching into West Texas. Return to the parking area the same way you came or descend one of the numerous ski area runs, although they are much steeper. The area above the timberline can be very cold and windy even in summer, so take adequate clothing. Also, summer thunderstorms build very quickly on the peak. Plan to finish your hike in the early afternoon, by the time most summer storms begin. Water is available on the trail at Ice Spring near the junction of Trails 25 and 78. White Mountain Wilderness, Lincoln National Forest and Sierra Blanca 15-minute USGS quad maps will come in handy during this hike.

The trail to **Monjeau Lookout** shares the same trailhead as the Sierra Blanca summit trail. Instead of taking the left fork at the juncture of 15 and 25, go right and follow 25 for 5½ miles to Monjeau. The trail passes junctions with several other trails and crosses one Forest Service road, but most if it follows a fairly level ridge between the ski area and the lookout. With a pre-arranged car shuttle, you can finish your hike at Monjeau; if not, return the way you came. Either way, make sure to climb the lookout tower at the peak. There are spectacular 360° views from atop rugged granite cliffs. No easily accessible water is found along this trail, and since it follows a ridge, it is susceptible to lightning, so keep a sharp eye on the weather. In addition to the maps used for the Sierra Blanca hike, an Angus 7.5-minute USGS quad will help guide you from the ski area to Monjeau Lookout.

Trail #25 can be done in its entirety as an extended two- or three-day backpacking trip, starting from Monjeau Lookout or Nogal Peak. A well-marked dirt road off Ski Area Road accesses the Monjeau trailhead near the Lookout. To find Nogal Peak trailhead, take NM 48 north out of Ruidoso to NM 37 and turn left. After about 1½ miles, exit left onto Forest Road 107, marked Bonito Lake and Southfork Campground. Follow 107 to its end, passing the lake, the campground and Runnels' Horse Stables near the end of the road. A small parking area and the trailhead are at the road's end. Water is available at various springs along the way. Add the Nogal Peak 15-minute USGS quad to your maps for this trail.

For information, contact the **Lincoln National Forest – Smokey Bear Ranger Station**, Mechem Drive, Ruidoso, NM 88345, ☎ 505/257-4095.

Ruidoso Tour Services, 2415 Sudderth Drive, ☎ 505/257-4000 or 800/687-3501, will lead you on guided hikes in the Lincoln National Forest, using llamas to tote backpacks and lunch.

Fort Stanton Recreation Area covers 24,715 acres of public land between Capitan and Lincoln and is administered by the Bureau of Land Management. Picnicking, hiking, mountain biking, cross-country skiing, horseback riding, fishing, and camping are popular pursuits in this area.

The area's most interesting feature is the **Fort Stanton Cave**. Soldiers from nearby Fort Stanton were probably the first white men to see the cave in about 1855, but archaeological evidence indicates that Native Americans knew of and used the cave as early as 1500 AD. With more than eight miles of mapped chambers and passages and at least 12 more miles of uncharted territory, this is the third largest cave in New Mexico. Recreational caving is allowed in Fort Stanton Cave only with a permit issued by the BLM.

Normally, the cave entrance is gated and locked. Make sure some-one in your party is familiar with caving techniques and safety, or arrange for a volunteer BLM guide to accompany you. For infor-mation, contact the **Bureau of Land Management**, PO Drawer 1857, Roswell, NM 88201, ☎ 505/624-1790. Permit requests are taken by mail or in person through the Bureau of Land Manage-ment, 1717 West 2nd, PO Box 1397, Roswell, NM 88201.

SOUTHEASTERN NEW MEXICO
BACKPACKING & CAMPING OUTFITTERS

Faith Mountain Sports, 2313 Sudderth Drive, ☎ 505/257-2769, in Ruidoso. Rental equipment available.
Outdoor Adventures, 1516 East 10th, ☎ 505/434-1920, in Alamo-gordo.

On Horseback

RUIDOSO

Several area outfitters provide horseback riding into the beau-tiful mountain backcountry on the outskirts of town:

Buddie's Stables, 707 Gavilan Canyon Road, ☎ 505/258-4027.
Cowboy Stables, 1764 West US 70, ☎ 505/378-8217.
Grindstone Stables, 200 Grindstone Resort Dr., ☎ 505/257-2241.
Inn of the Mountain Gods, Carrizo Canyon Road, ☎ 505/257-5141.
Runnel's Stables, end of Forest Road 107 past Bonito Lake, ☎ 505/258-3495.
And one offers llama trekking: **Shiloh Ranch**, PO Box 1558, ☎ 505/336-4334

On Wheels

More than five miles of paved trails suitable for jogging, biking, skating and roller blading meander through the city of **Roswell**. The trails connect Cahoon Park on the west edge of town and Spring River Park on the east side, while weaving through historic neighborhoods as well as other city parks.

Walnut Canyon Drive is a one-hour, self-guided tour through the scenic Chihuahuan Desert near Carlsbad Cavern. This 9½-mile gravel road is suitable for most vehicles except RVs and trailers, but is quite bumpy. If you have your mountain bikes with you, the rugged desert scenery may be better enjoyed on two wheels rather than four. An informative guidebook is available at the Carlsbad Caverns Visitor Center.

The Sacramento Mountains surrounding Cloudcroft offer numerous opportunities for fabulous mountain bike rides. **Osha** and **Rim Trails** are two of the most popular in the area. Osha is an easy 2.6-mile single-track loop and is fun for most beginning and intermediate riders. Rim Trail is more difficult and much longer – 14 miles one-way. This trail's steep sections of single-track are crisscrossed with roots and scattered with rocks and stumps, making it a technical and exciting ride for intermediate to advanced bikers. Rim Trail can be ridden as a long day's adventure or split into shorter sections by using one of the Forest Service access roads that cross the route to escape onto Sunspot Highway. (See above, under Adventures on Foot.)

Pumphouse Canyon is a seven-mile loop near Cloudcroft, combining single-track, double-track and paved roads to make for a fun ride. Pedal or drive two miles southeast of town to the Sleepygrass Campground via NM 24 and Forest Road 24. About 200 yards before the campground, a trail leads to the right up Pumphouse Canyon. The trail climbs gradually for more than two miles until it reaches the ski area. From there, you can ride out to US 82, go left 1½ miles to Forest Road 24B, which heads down Apache Canyon and back to Sleepygrass Campground. Beginning and intermediate riders will find this ride somewhat challenging, as the trail climbs 750 feet, topping out at 9,000 feet. It is short enough, however, to require only a moderate level of fitness.

A longer but easier circuit, **Silver Springs Loop** originates right from town. Park at the Cloudcroft Ranger Station and ride 4½ miles northeast on NM 24 to Forest Road 162 and take a left up Silver Springs Canyon. About four miles up the canyon, the road joins Forest Road 206. Bear left at the fork and it's downhill all the way back to US 82. A left here takes you back to Cloudcroft. This ride gains 960 feet in elevation but, stretched out over 12 miles of paved roads and hard-packed double-track, it will seem easy even to novice and intermediate riders in good shape.

The **Lincoln National Forest** in and around Ruidoso offers some of the best mountain biking in southeastern New Mexico. Riders unsure of their ability at altitude should head for **Trail 588**. Take US 70 east through Ruidoso Downs and, just past Conlee's Nursery, turn right onto Forest Road 420. The trailhead will be on your left at about seven miles. The first four miles of Trail 588 wind through a scenic valley that's generally flat-to-downhill double-track. Then the trail forks. If you're already breathing hard, take 588B to the right about one more mile to the trail's end and double back to your car. If you feel good and are really ready to challenge yourself, continue on 588 for some expert-caliber terrain that gets steeper and rockier as you go. After 2½ miles, the trail rejoins Forest Road 420. At this point you can double back and enjoy the steep technical section you just suffered up, or turn right and take a leisurely spin on 420 back to your car.

A section of trails known to Ruidoso residents as the **Spaghetti Bowl** provides more than 10 miles of exciting intermediate-level riding. Just past the Smokey Bear Ranger Station on Mechem Drive, turn onto Cedar Creek Road and park at the first campground on your right. From the sheltered picnic tables, a trail leads into the hills, becoming a virtual maze of single-track generally void of obstacles. One particularly intense section features steep down-hills, tight banking corners, frame-bending dips and body-jarring jumps. It's called the Race Course and you'll know it when you see it.

Expert riders may opt to continue past the Spaghetti Bowl on Cedar Creek Road to Spring Canyon. Turn right and go 0.8 miles up the canyon to find the trailhead for **T-13** marked by a sign on your right. This trail is only 1.7 miles long, but its steep grades and difficult obstacles make it seem 10 times longer to those unpre-pared for its challenges. At the trail's end, it intersects Ski Run Road, where you can double back to your car.

Road bikers and mountain bikers alike may appreciate the challenge that **Ski Run Road** has to offer, but only the very well conditioned rider should attempt this route. Turn onto Ski Run Road, park at the softball fields on your left about 0.2 miles down the road, take a long drag from your oxygen tank and begin to ride. The first four miles or so are misleadingly tame, winding peace-fully through the canyon. Enjoy it while it lasts, because from there the road gains nearly 3,000 feet in a seven-mile series of lung- and leg-testing switchbacks. The air thins, and the views become in-creasingly spectacular as you reach the apex of the climb at Windy Point Overlook. Get off your bike, stretch your legs and take a long look at the marvelous views from this high mountain vantage point. But you'd better not be looking at anything other than the road during the ride down. No matter how long the pump to the summit took you – three, five, seven hours – the coast down will take less than 30 minutes. It's an exhilarating ride at break-neck speeds: worth it if you're careful, worth a trip to the hospital if you're not. Do not attempt this ride during ski season because traffic on the road is too heavy for safe riding.

SOUTHEASTERN NEW MEXICO BIKE OUTFITTERS

Ruidoso's two full-service bike shops offer the only rental equipment in southeastern New Mexico.
Rocky Mountain Sports, 1103 Mechem, ☎ 505/258-3224.
Faith Mountain Sports, 2313 Sudderth Drive, ☎ 505/257-2769.

Quality sales and service may also be found at these area retailers.
Outdoor Adventures, 1516 East 10th, ☎ 505/434-1920, in Alamogordo.
Bikes Unlimited, 1405 West 2nd, ☎ 800/585-4245, in Roswell.

Ruidoso Tour Services, 2415 Sudderth Drive, ☎ 505/257-4000 or 800/687-3501, runs jeep tours into the White Mountain Wilderness and Lincoln National Forest near Ruidoso. Tours, ranging from one to four hours, are designed for those interested in wildlife viewing, natural and cultural history, archaeology and geology.

On Water

Occupying 11,000 acres, 16 miles northwest of Fort Sumner via US 84 and NM 3203, **Sumner Lake State Park** is the fourth largest state park in New Mexico. Popular for boating, waterskiing, and swimming, the lake is stocked with bluegill, pike, catfish, bass and crappie. Developed areas below the dam also provide fishing and general recreation on both banks of the Pecos River. Plus, there are tennis courts and a playground in the park. Camping is available. For information, ☎ 505/355-2541.

Cowboys moving cattle along the Goodnight-Loving Trail once stopped near Roswell at what is today **Bottomless Lakes State Park** to water their animals and, in a romp, dare each other to reach the bottom and bring up mud. Their attempts always failed, thus the park's misleading name. The depths of the seven lakes in the park actually range from 17 to 90 feet deep and they are the result of collapsed salt caves. With surface areas ranging from a few hundred square feet at Devil's Inkwell to more than 13 acres at Lea Lake, this park caters to watersports enthusiasts of the non-boating variety. Two of the lakes are too alkaline to support fish, but four others are regularly stocked with rainbow trout. **Lea Lake**, the largest, is the only one where swimming is allowed. Scuba diving and windsurfing are popular here, too. Lea Lake also features a public beach, rowboat rentals, a small store and restaurant. A visitor center, located near Cottonwood Lake, just past the park entrance, has literature as well as exhibits explaining area geology. The park is about 15 miles east of Roswell via US 380 and NM 409. Camping is available. For information, ☎ 505/624-6058.

Scuba equipment sales, service and rentals can be obtained through **Divers II Dive Centers**, 633 West US 70, in Roswell, ☎ 505/622-8131, or 701 East First, suite #712, in Alamogordo, ☎ 505/437-5610.

Three dams across the Pecos River in the Carlsbad vicinity provide multiple opportunities for watersports enthusiasts year-round, thanks to winter temperatures averaging near 60°. **Lake Carlsbad** is a long, narrow body of water forming the eastern border of the city. Boating, sailing, water skiing and jet skiing are allowed on the lake. Its waters are also regularly stocked with trout, bass, perch and catfish. Just south of the main boat ramp, more than 1,000 feet of beach is available for swimming, complete with slides, diving boards and a diving tower.

Lower Tansill Lake begins just south of Lake Carlsbad. This calm reservoir is reserved for fishing, canoeing and sailing. Motor boats are restricted to trolling speeds. Like its neighbor upstream, Tansill is well-stocked with trout, bass, perch and catfish. **Brantley Lake State Park**, 15 miles north of Carlsbad via US 285 and NM 30, is the largest of the area's lakes. Fairly consistent desert winds make this a popular windsurfing destination. Two boat ramps provide surface access to boaters, sailors, water-skiers and fisher-men. Lurking in the depths are largemouth and white bass, wall-eye, catfish, bluegill and crappie. A visitor center is stationed near the main entrance to the park, and a day-use picnic area with sheltered tables and grills is located near the water. Camping is available. For information, contact Brantley Lake State Park, PO Box 2288, Carlsbad, NM 88221, ☎ 505/457-2384.

Several mountain streams flow into **Bonito Lake**, approximately 15 miles north of Ruidoso. Take NM 48 north to NM 37, then go 1½ miles to Forest Road 107, marked Bonito Lake. Only bank fishing is allowed on this pristine little mountain lake, but that's sufficient most days to catch your limit of edible-sized trout. Fishing season on the lake runs from April 1 to November 30 and is further restricted to the hours between 5 AM and 10 PM. Camping is available.

Rio Bonito runs east from the dam at Bonito Lake and into the Fort Stanton Recreation Area, where it affords year-round fishing opportunities.

On Snow

Owned and operated by The Lodge at Cloudcroft, **Snow Canyon Ski Area** offers downhill skiing and a variety of winter activities for the whole family. Located just east of Cloudcroft on US 82, the area features 21 runs serviced by one chairlift and two surface lifts, providing 700 feet of vertical drop over 68 skiable acres. There is also a halfpipe for snowboarders, and six 500-foot-long individual tubing chutes, making this one of the safest tubing spots in the area. A maze of trails for snowmobiling and cross-country skiing also emanates from the ski area. Equipment for all activities is available through the rental shop. Instruction in alpine and nordic skiing as well as snowboarding is available through the Snow Canyon Ski School, ☎ 505/682-2333.

The season at Snow Canyon runs from mid-December to mid-March, weather permitting. The area is open daily from opening day to January 8 and is closed on Tuesdays and Thursdays the rest of the season. Hours are from 9AM to 4 PM, with full-day and half-day lift tickets available.

For information, contact Snow Canyon, PO Box 498, Cloudcroft, NM 88317, ☎ 505/682-2333 or 800/333-7542. **Osha** and **Willie White Trails** are also popular with area snowshoers and cross-country skiers. (See above, under Adventures on Foot.)

With 54 runs and 1,900 feet of vertical drop, **Ski Apache**, just 15 miles from Ruidoso, is the southernmost major ski area in the United States. It also offers the largest lift capacity in the state, scooting more than 15,000 skiers up the hill every hour via two surface lifts, two double chairs, five triple chairs, one quad chair and the only gondola in New Mexico. Owned by the Mescalero Apache Indians, Native American lift operators and trail names like Geronimo and Screaming Eagle make their influence one of the defining qualities of the area. With an average annual snowfall of 15 feet, the area rarely needs to use its extensive snow-making equipment, but it is available on more than a third of the mountain if conditions demand. Most people love to ski here. The beginner and intermediate terrain is perfectly groomed, the steeps and deep powder on the black diamond runs are exhilarating and the views out across the desert from this high-mountain paradise are sensational. On a clear day, visibility from the chairlifts, ridges and peaks can extend to 200 miles. Both alpine and nordic skiing are available, as is snowboarding.

A variety of services are available at Ski Apache. Both the Main Lodge and Elk Lodge, at the chair-eight complex, offer cafeteria-style restaurants, and the Main Lodge features a bar called the "Broken Ski Saloon." Two snack bars are also located on the mountain as well as two open-air burger stands. A full-service rental/repair shop for both skis and snowboards is available along with an ATM machine and a number of first aid stations. PSIA-certified ski and snowboard instruction is also available and first-timers receive a free lift ticket with the purchase of a lesson.

RUIDOSO SKI SHOPS

Rental equipment can also be obtained through any of the following Ruidoso ski shops.

Mountain Ski Shop, 2716 Sudderth Drive, ☎ 505/257-4695.

Pro Ski Sports, 2000 Sudderth Drive, ☎ 505/257-5096.

Rocky Mountain Sports, 1103 Mechem Drive, ☎ 505/258-3224.

Steed's Ski Sports, 1017 Mechem Drive, ☎ 505/258-5562. Also rents nordic equipment.

Wild West Ski Shop, 1408 Mechem Drive, ☎ 505/258-3131.

For information, contact Ski Apache, PO Box 220, Ruidoso, NM 88345, ☎ 505/336-4356 or 505/257-9001 for the snow report.

The 12½-mile road to the ski area can be treacherous during heavy snowfalls, as it climbs nearly 3,000 feet in a seven-mile stretch of hair-raising switchbacks. Chains are often required on two-wheel drive vehicles and should always be carried to the area whatever the prevailing conditions.

In the Air

Sunshine Soaring Activities offers glider rides as well as FAA-certified glider instruction at the Cavern City Air Terminal, five miles south of Carlsbad on National Parks Highway. This is one of the most exhilarating, yet peaceful ways to take in all of the area's sights – and the only affordable way to do it from on high. FAA regulations limit passengers to a maximum of 220 pounds. If you top that figure, start your diet today because this is something you don't want to miss. For information, ☎ 505/370-2720.

Eco-Tours & Cultural Excursions

Each evening during the summer and early fall at **Carlsbad Caverns National Park**, thousands of Mexican free-tail bats rush from the mouth of the cave. An undulating whirlwind of wings, they head for the Pecos and Black River Valleys to gorge on night-flying insects until dawn. Rangers present "**Bat Flight Talks**" each evening at the stone amphitheater near the natural cave entrance. The talk culminates with the exciting fluttering exodus of bats from the cave. Bat flights last anywhere from 20 minutes to 2½ hours. Admission is free, but times vary nightly. For information, ☎ 505/785-2232.

White Sands Missile Range dominates the Tularosa Basin west of US 54. Here on July 16, 1945, the world's first nuclear bomb was exploded. Radiation levels at **Trinity Site** have since dropped low enough for brief visitation. Once every April and October, military police conduct tours to "Ground Zero" and base facilities where the bomb was assembled. For information, contact the Alamogordo Chamber of Commerce, PO Box 518, Alamogordo, NM 88310, ☎ 505/437-6120 or 800/545-4021.

Rangers at **White Sands National Monument** offer informative talks and presentations on a number of subjects at the park. White Sands extends its hours on full moon nights from May through October and rangers or special guest speakers present programs in a natural sand amphitheater at the Heart of the Sands. Entertaining one-hour programs also are presented at the amphitheater nightly during the summer, dealing with historical or natural aspects of the park. Friday night programs have astronomical themes and may feature star talks, telescope sessions or slide shows. Daily during May, June and July and sometimes during August and September, rangers lead sunset strolls through the dunes pointing out interesting features, giving tips to photographers and commenting on wildlife and vegetation. Each Saturday and Sunday at 10 AM and 2 PM, rangers lead a one-hour driving safari along Dunes Drive with stops for short nature walks. Once each month, rangers and military police conduct a trip through part of the White Sands Missile range to dry Lake Lucero. This is the dunes' present source of gypsum sand. The tour lasts three hours and includes a 35-mile drive round-trip and a one-mile hike to the dry lake bed. Reservations are required. For information, contact White Sands National Monument, PO Box 458, Alamogordo, NM 88311, ☎ 505/479-6124.

Where to Stay & Eat

Most tourist travel in this section takes place in the Ruidoso and Carlsbad areas. So the best accommodations and restaurants are concentrated there. But nearly every town in Southeast New Mexico makes some attempt at hospitality.

Accommodations

FORT SUMNER

Should you find yourself in Fort Sumner at nightfall and you don't feel like driving 60 miles to Clovis, don't fret. There is a brand new **Super 8 Motel** at 1707 East Sumner offering some of the nicest and cleanest rooms in the area. For reservations, ☎ 505/355-7888 or 800/800-8000. The **Oasis Motel**, 1704 East Sumner, ☎ 505/355-7414, or the **Coronado Motel**, 309 West Sumner, ☎ 505/355-2466, are the only other lodgings in town, but they're okay if Super 8 is full.

CLOVIS

Three US highways run through Clovis and most of the town's lodging is located along a stretch of road shared by all three, called Mabry Drive.

The nicest rooms in town are at the **Holiday Inn**, 2700 Mabry, ☎ 505/762-4491, which also provides the most amenities, including a lounge, dining room, racquetball courts, sauna and indoor/outdoor pools.

Just next door, **Motel 6**, 2620 Mabry, ☎ 505/762-2995, is the best bet for the traveler on a budget. Farther down the road, the **Best Western**, 1516 Mabry, ☎ 505/762-3808, falls somewhere in between.

PORTALES

Portales has plenty of lodging, thanks primarily to Eastern New Mexico University. The newest rooms are to be found at the **Super 8 Motel**, 1805 West 2nd Street/US 70, ☎ 505/356-8518 or

800/800-8000. The most historic and interesting accommodations are downtown at the old **Portales Inn**, 218 West 3rd Street, ☎ 505/359-1208.

The best choice for lodging, though, is probably the **Morning Star Inn**, 620 West 2nd Street/US 70, ☎ 505/356-2994. This is a cute little bed & breakfast with three rooms and shared baths. A continental breakfast for two people is included in the rate.

ROSWELL

There are more than plenty of lodging possibilities in the crossroads community of Roswell. Most of the newer, nicer hotels and motels, featuring restaurants, lounges and room service, are found on North Main/US 285. The less expensive motels tend to be distributed along 2nd Street/US 70-380.

Two inns in town battle for top honors. **Best Western Sally Port Inn**, 2000 North Main, ☎ 505/622-6430, offers a restaurant, tropical atrium and full spa facilities. Spacious, comfortable rooms feature large picture windows and some are equipped with mini-bars. **Roswell Inn**, 1815 North Main, ☎ 505/623-4920, has attractive landscaped grounds, a swimming pool, a restaurant and a fireplace lounge that makes a fine place for evening relaxation. Rooms feature contemporary Southwestern decor, comfortable sitting areas, oak furniture and king- and queen-sized beds. If you're looking to go easy on the pocketbook, try **Comfort Inn**, 2803 West 2nd Street, ☎ 505/623-9440 or 800/221-2222, **Budget Inn**, 2101 North Main, ☎ 505/623-6050, or **Days Inn**, 1310 North Main, ☎ 505/623-4021.

ARTESIA

Most travelers who stay here are oil industry executives. Consequently, the few local lodging establishments are actually pretty nice. In fact, one of the nicest bed & breakfasts in this part of the state is found in Artesia. The **Heritage Inn**, 209 West Main, ☎ 505/748-2552 or 800/594-7392, located in a beautifully restored downtown building dating back to 1905, offers eight spacious rooms – each individually and elegantly furnished in Colonial American decor. All rooms feature queen beds, computer modem hookups, television and private baths. There is also an outside patio and deck area for relaxation, as well as a parlor with a modest library, television and VCR. A continental breakfast is served every morning.

The **Best Western Pecos Inn**, 2209 West Main Street, ☎ 505/748-3324, offers large double rooms, a bar/lounge and a restaurant serving breakfast, lunch and dinner.

CARLSBAD

There are 17 motels from which to base your explorations of the Carlsbad area. All of them are on the city's main thoroughfare, Canal Street, which turns into National Parks Highway on the south side of town.

For those wishing to stay downtown, try the **Holiday Inn-Carlsbad**, 601 Canal Street, ☎ 505/885-8500 or 800/742-9586. Rooms are large and comfortable and there's a pair of restaurants, a lounge, heated swimming pool and spa. Another option is the **Best Western Motel Stevens**, 1829 Canal Street, ☎ 505/887-2851 or 800/730-2851, featuring a restaurant, lounge and pool, along with Best Western's usual high-standard rooms.

If you plan only to visit the Caves, a motel on the southern edge of town will start you off a little closer. **Quality Inn**, 3706 National Parks Highway, ☎ 505/887-2861 or 800/321-2861, features a restaurant, lounge, pool and spa. It offers a free full breakfast with each night's stay. **Days Inn**, 3910 National Parks Highway, ☎ 505/887-7800, touts a free continental breakfast and has an indoor pool and spa.

The budget traveler will always find a clean comfortable room at **Motel 6**, 3824 National Parks Highway, ☎ 505/885-0011. They also have a pool.

WHITE'S CITY

It's an unabashed tourist trap, but White's City's accommodations are the most convenient for those visiting the caverns. Operated by Best Western and upholding high standards for nice clean rooms, the **Cavern Inn** and **Guadalupe Inn**, Main Street, ☎ 505/785-2291 or 800/CAVERNS, will put you as close to the park entrance as you can get without sleeping in your car. Both feature restaurants, lounges, heated pools and spas.

White's City RV Park, Main Street, ☎ 505/785-2291 or 800/CAVERNS, has numerous pull-through sites with full hookups and sheltered picnic tables. There is also a large grassy tent area as well as a swimming pool.

CLOUDCROFT

If it weren't for **The Lodge**, Cloudcroft might not even exist. Built in 1899 as a mountain retreat for railroad executives, the resort immediately turned Cloudcroft into the favorite summer escape of sun-scorched vacationers from Arizona to Texas. Since its origins, it has undergone numerous renovations, but the original appearance remains almost unchanged. In fact, inscriptions from some of its earliest guests, including Pancho Villa, Judy Garland and Clark Gable, are still visible on the walls of The Lodge's four-story, copper-domed observatory. In the lobby, elegant wood moldings, early 1900s furniture, antique fixtures and mounted game hint of old money, and each of its 47 individually decorated rooms features antique furniture, high beds draped with down quilts and the original radiators that lull you to sleep, hissing softly as they warm crisp mountain evenings.

Perched more than 9,000 feet atop the Sacramento Mountains, the Lodge is home to one of the highest and most scenic golf links in North America. In the winter, it operates a small, easy-going ski area, perfect for family recreation. The Lodge offers several different "Stay and Ski" or "Stay and Golf" packages that make vacations here quite affordable. Guests may also enjoy swimming in the outdoor pool, soaking in the hot tub or relaxing in the dry sauna. If that doesn't help you unwind, an appointment with the inn's certified massage therapist surely will. One of the state's better restaurants, a gift shop, a jewelry store and a pro shop for the golfers round out the rest of The Lodge's amenities.

The Lodge also offers bed and breakfast-style accommodations at **The Pavilion** nearby. In a beautifully restored historic structure, 11 delightfully decorated rooms feature knotted-pine walls, rustic stone fireplaces and large beds with down comforters.

Larger groups may choose to rent **The Retreat**. This large four-bedroom mountain home was built adjacent to The Lodge with hand-hewn railroad beams and provides a complete kitchen, comfortable dining room and spacious family room.

Guests at both The Retreat and The Pavilion benefit from full use of all Lodge facilities.

For information, contact The Lodge, #1 Corona Place, PO Box 497, Cloudcroft, NM 88317, ☎ 505/682-2566 or 800/395-6343.

There are also several condos and cabins for rent in the Cloudcroft area. For information, contact the Cloudcroft Chamber of Commerce, PO Box 1290, Cloudcroft, NM 88317, ☎ 505/682-2733.

ALAMOGORDO

Most visitors to the area choose the nearby mountain towns of Cloudcroft and Ruidoso for lodging. But if you're here and want to spend the night, **Holiday Inn Alamogordo**, 1401 South White Sands Boulevard, ☎ 505/437-7100, or **Super 8 Motel**, 3204 North White Sands Boulevard, ☎ 505/434-4205 or 800/800-8000, will meet your needs. Both offer clean, comfortable rooms with king-sized beds. Both have adjacent restaurants, and Holiday Inn has a heated outdoor swimming pool.

RV travellers should pull into the **Alamogordo/White Sands KOA**, 412 24th Street, ☎ 505/437-3003 or 800/424-8227. Sites feature large trees, privacy walls and, of course, full hookups. There is also a heated pool, a grassy tent area and a gift and supply shop.

RUIDOSO

Being the most popular tourist spot in the southern mountains, Ruidoso has a large number and variety of lodging options. But don't expect to buzz into town and get the room of your choice without a reservation. During horse racing and ski seasons, hotels, motels and cabins are heavily booked. Call ahead to get what you want.

Inn of the Mountain Gods, Carrizo Canyon Road, ☎ 505/257-5141, is the finest resort in all of New Mexico. Owned and operated by the Mescalero Apaches and located on their reservation just south of Ruidoso, this huge complex is also one of the most picturesque resorts in the Southwest. Nestled on a lake under the shadow of Sierra Blanca Peak, the Inn offers a full slate of activities, including fishing, canoeing, swimming, tennis and horseback riding. The Inn also features one of the most beautiful and difficult golf courses in the state. In the lobby, a bold, three-story, copper-chimneyed circular fireplace introduces the Inn's rich, rustic design. Large rooms and spacious suites are decorated with a Southwest/Native American flair and most of them feature private balconies overlooking the lake. A night's stay here is expensive but, even if you can't afford to stay, you're still welcome to dine at one of the award-winning restaurants, enjoy live entertainment in the lounge or try your luck at the only gambling casino in this part of the state.

Although a step or two down from the Mescaleros' grand palace, **Best Western Swiss Chalet Inn**, 1451 Mechem Drive, ☎ 505/258-3333, or **Enchantment Inn**, 307 US 70 West, ☎ 505/378-4051 or 800/435-0280, both offer comfortably appointed deluxe rooms with king or queen beds, indoor swimming pools, spas, restaurants and lounges. The Swiss Chalet is on the North side of town, providing easy access to the ski area and Lincoln National Forest. The Enchantment is on the southeast side of town nearer the racetrack.

Shadow Mountain Lodge, 107 Main Road, ☎ 505/257-2165, offers a tranquil retreat in the pines of Ruidoso's upper canyon. Pleasantly warmed in winter by cozy fireplaces, 19 rooms feature kitchenettes and king beds. The Lodge also affords direct fishing access to Rio Ruidoso.

The best and most traditional way to experience Ruidoso is by staying in an intimate log cabin tucked away in the forest. **Dan Dee Cabins**, 310 Main Road, ☎ 505/257-2165, offers just that sort of experience. Spread across five landscaped acres dotted with picnic tables and barbecue grills, 14 pine log cabins with kitchenettes, fireplaces and rustic wooden furniture are just steps away from the fishing waters of the Rio Ruidoso and year-round resort activities.

Those seeking clean, convenient no-frills lodging should try **Super 8 Motel**, junction of US 70 and NM 48, ☎ 505/378-8180. The place actually offers a frill or two, such as a hot tub and sauna.

As bed & breakfasts become increasingly popular, Ruidoso is keeping up with the trend. **Monjeau Shadows Bed & Breakfast**, NM 37, ☎ 505/336-4191, is a handsome four-story Victorian home offering seven large comfortable rooms. Each is charmingly decorated with antiques and family heirlooms and features a private bath. The proprietors will even schedule tours, horseback rides or tee-times and then arrange for a massage therapist to greet you at days end.

Closer to town, **Scandia Chalet Bed & Breakfast**, NM 48, ☎ 505/336-7741, has three rooms in the main house and one fully equipped one-bedroom cottage out back. The main house features a glass atrium with fireplace, vaulted ceilings and European decor. A room on the second floor has a private double jacuzzi. The cottage has a dining room, sitting room, kitchen and bath.

RV travelers should head for **Twin Spruce Campground**, US 70 West, ☎ 505/257-4310. Offering 100 campsites, 74 of which feature full hookups, this may be one of the most complete campgrounds in the state. It boasts a heated pool and Jacuzzi, game room, gift and supply shop, charcoal grills and tables, laundry, playgrounds, satellite TV, restrooms and showers.

If you don't need all that hoopla, try **Tall Pines RV Park**, 1800 Sudderth Drive, ☎ 505/257-5233. Even though it is situated right on Ruidoso's main drag, campsites are nestled back in the trees and it is actually quite peaceful.

Also near the center of town, **Blue Spruce RV Park**, NM 48, ☎ 505/257-7993, features a number of sites with full hookups.

Local realtors, such as **Gary Lynch Realty**, 419 Mechem Drive, ☎ 505/257-4011, represent hundreds of condos and private vacation rentals. For information, contact **Ruidoso Valley Chamber of Commerce**, PO Box 698, Ruidoso, NM 88345, ☎ 505/257-7395 or 800/253-2255.

CARRIZOZO

You should really go elsewhere for lodging, but if you're stuck here and must find a place to stay, **Four Winds Motel**, at the junction of US 380 and US 54, ☎ 505/648-2356, has rooms with beds, sheets and pillows at budget prices.

Better yet, head for nearby Nogal (take US 380 east to NM 37 and turn right) and the tranquil environs of **Paz de Nogal**, NM 37, Nogal, ☎ 505/354-2826. This country B&B occupies a restored 1856 adobe ranch house, complete with a walled courtyard. There are six guest rooms, all with private baths and three with fireplaces. A hearty ranch breakfast is included and is served family-style indoors or in the courtyard. Bonus features include a hot tub, tennis courts and stables. Yes, you can bring your horses or pets. Paz de Nogal is Santa Fe-style – minus the high cost and crowds.

LINCOLN

Two bed and breakfasts in Lincoln offer deluxe lodging in beautifully restored historic buildings. Billy the Kid himself is said to have spent a night or two at **Casa de Patron**, US 380, ☎ 505/653-4676, when it was the home of his good friend, Juan Patron, a prominent local leader and Speaker of the House in the Territorial Legislature. Three spacious rooms in the main house are immaculately decorated with historic photos, lace curtains and antique quilts on beds with carved wooden headboards. Two casitas (small houses) are also available. Casita Bonita, a handmade adobe perfect for romantic getaways, features beamed cathedral ceilings and a circular staircase leading from the living area to a loft with an antique queen-sized bed. Casita de Paz is a larger adobe, better suited for families, with its two-bedroom suite, living area and large yard.

The **Ellis Store Bed & Breakfast**, US 380, ☎ 800/653-6460, occupies the oldest building in Lincoln. This charmingly restored

Territorial-period adobe offers private rooms and baths, lovely gardens and a perfect porch for relaxing on a quite afternoon.

SAN PATRICIO/TINNIE

Three attractive guest homes are available at the beautiful **Hurd Ranch**, mile marker 281 just south of US 70 near San Patricio. It is a gallery and home to one of America's leading artist trios – Henriette Wyeth, Michael Hurd and the late Peter Hurd. Apple House and Orchard House are one-bedroom adobes, beautifully restored from original ranch buildings and decorated with a blend of traditional Southwestern and contemporary furniture, saltillo tile and Native American rugs. Each features a full kitchen, large bath, living area with fireplace and charming patio. La Helenita is a newly constructed two-bedroom home designed by Michael Hurd. It provides two full baths, a Jacuzzi tub, large living area and kitchen. Soft colors and textures accentuate a lovely array of antique and contemporary furnishings and enchanting fireplaces. Just 20 miles east of Ruidoso, these units are ideally situated for extended exploration of the area. For information, contact **Hurd Ranch Guest Homes**, PO Box 100, San Patricio, NM 88348, ☎ 505/653-4331 or 800/658-6912.

Restaurants

CLOVIS

With nearly 35,000 residents, Clovis is a good-sized town by New Mexico standards and so there are a number of good restaurants. In keeping with area economics, it seems fitting that **Ranchers' and Farmers' Steakhouse**, 816 Lexington Road (just off Prince Street near the mall), ☎ 505/763-6335, is the best place in town for T-bones, rib-eyes and filets. They also serve a spicy Cajun prime rib and several Mexican specialties.

For a full-blown Mexican restaurant, try **Juanito's**, 1608 Mabry, ☎ 505/762-7822.

The most surprising restaurant, however, has to be the **Shogun**, 600 Pile Street, ☎ 505/762-8577. You'll find a knife-wielding chef preparing tasty steak, chicken and seafood in the traditional Japanese style right at your table.

If you're short on time, a trip down Mabry Drive or Prince Street will lead you to McDonalds, Burger King, Dairy Queen, Kentucky Fried Chicken and all the rest of your fast food favorites.

PORTALES

The **Cattle Baron Steak and Seafood Grill**, 1600 South Avenue D, ☎ 505/356-5587, offers one of the best salad bars around. Entrées are pretty savory as well. You can't go wrong ordering steak teriyaki, filet Oscar or chicken Alfredo.

A little less fancy, the **Wagon Wheel**, 521 West 17th, ☎ 505/356-5036, serves standard down-home favorites – chicken fried steak and all-you-can-eat fried catfish on Friday, plus daily Mexican specials.

A full Mexican menu is found at **La Hacienda**, 909 North Ave K, ☎ 505/359-0280. All the standards are excellent, but if you've never tried stuffed sopaipillos, go out on a limb here – you won't regret it.

Numerous fast food joints have been keeping the ENMU students alive for years. A drive down 2nd Street/US 70 will put you in touch with McDonalds, Burger King, Sonic, Subway, Pizza Hut and the rest.

ROSWELL

Dining rooms at both the **Roswell Inn** and the **Sally Port Inn** are worth trying, but the best motel restaurant by far is **The Claim Restaurant and Saloon** located underground at the **Days Inn**, 1310 North Main, ☎ 505/623-6042. Its menu of steaks, chicken and seafood represents some of the city's finest dining in a casual come-as-you-are atmosphere.

The dining room at **Mario's**, 200 East 2nd Street, ☎ 505/623-1740, is another good choice for filet mignon, flautas de pollo or the catch of the day. They also have a superb salad bar. The **Cattle Baron Steak and Seafood Grill**, 1113 North Main, ☎ 505/622-2465, however, retains the top salad bar title and is also a fine choice for prime rib, chicken Alfredo or mahi mahi. **Peppers Bar & Grill**, 500 North Main in the Sunwest Bank Building, ☎ 505/623-4021, may be the area's best new restaurant, serving fajitas, ribs, sandwiches and burgers. Its lively atmosphere makes Peppers a very popular place among Roswellites.

Junk food lovers, rejoice! Roswell is jokingly regarded as having more fast food restaurants per square block than anyplace in the world. Although this has never been proven by scientific study, you'll be hard pressed to name a franchise not represented here; some have as many as three or four different locations around town. Drive down 2nd Street/US 70-380 or Main Street/US 285 to realize your wildest fast food fantasies.

ARTESIA

La Fonda, 210 West Main, ☎ 505/746-9411, is by far the best restaurant in town, specializing in traditional Mexican food with an atmosphere to match. Folks from both Roswell and Carlsbad often drive over just to eat here.

CARLSBAD

Ventana's Restaurant at the Holiday Inn, 601 South Canal Street, ☎ 505/885-8500, and the restaurant at the Best Western Motel Stevens, 1829 South Canal Street, ☎ 505/887-2851, both have extensive menus featuring a variety of steak, chicken and seafood entrées. The Phoenix Bar & Grill, also at the Holiday Inn, features lighter fare, including burgers and fries in a casual atmosphere. The Bar here also offers music and dancing nightly.

Fans of good homemade Mexican food should try the Cortez Café, 506 South Canal Street, ☎ 505/885-4747. Great food and low prices have made this a local favorite for more than 50 years.

All of the standard fast food restaurants are located on US 285 as it weaves through town under the guise of Pierce or Canal Streets.

CARLSBAD CAVERNS/WHITE'S CITY

There are only two restaurants in White's City and they're both in the same building on Main Street. The Velvet Garter Restaurant & Saloon is the nicer of the two, serving steaks, fajitas, seafood and cocktails. The other, Fast Jacks, serves standard roadside fare – chicken fried steak, burgers and sandwiches.

There are also two restaurants in the Carlsbad Caverns National Park. The Underground Lunchroom and Restaurant, deep inside the caverns near the elevators, is by far the most popular, but unfortunately it has the worst food. Served cafeteria-style, boxed ham and cheese sandwiches and microwave-warmed pizzas and chicken fingers fill out the menu. If you think you can survive the elevator ride to the surface without fainting from hunger, the restaurant in the visitor center serves burgers, chicken and hotdogs cooked on a real grill.

CLOUDCROFT

Rebecca's, at The Lodge in Cloudcroft, ☎ 505/682-3131, offers the remarkable combination of fine dining, good service and fabulous views. Watching the sunset over White Sands, nearly 6,000 feet below, makes dining here a special event. White linen, wicker furniture and music floating from a grand piano heighten the elegant atmosphere. Southwestern cuisine and classic continental dishes, expertly prepared by one of New Mexico's top chefs, are a perfect complement to the views and pleasant surroundings. Rebecca's is open daily for breakfast, lunch and dinner. Be sure to ask about The Lodge's resident ghost, after whom the restaurant is named.

Kokopelli's Restaurant, 306 Burro Avenue, ☎ 505/682-2009, offers American and Mexican food in a unique setting in Cloudcroft's historic downtown.

Those with less time should try **Texas Pit Barbecue**, US 82, ☎ 505/682-2307. Quality mesquite-smoked beef and various other barbecued meats are served cafeteria-style at budget prices.

FORT SUMNER

Dining in Fort Sumner is somewhat limited. One bright spot is **Meagan's Daylight Donuts and Pizza House**, 315 Sumner Avenue, ☎ 505/355-9399. This is the only pizza parlor for 60 or more miles in any direction. It's always packed and the pizza is very good. As you might have guessed from the name, Meagan's also serves fresh donuts in the mornings.

If you aren't in the mood for Italian, **Fred's Restaurant**, 1408 East Sumner, ☎ 505/355-7500, **Frontier Restaurant**, 309 East Sumner, ☎ 505/355-7220, and **Sprout's Café**, 1701 East Sumner, ☎ 505/355-7278, all serve the basic roadside fare. **Dariland**, also on East Sumner, will fulfill any fast food needs.

ALAMOGORDO

US 54 and US 70 join at both the north and south edges of Alamogordo for a run through town as White Sands Boulevard. Most any fast food restaurant known to man can be found along this stretch of blacktop. For a sit-down meal, **Ramona's Restaurant**,

2913 White Sands Boulevard, ☎ 505/437-7616, serves the best Mexican food in town and some of the best chimichangas anywhere. Try **Angelina's**, 415 White Sands Boulevard, ☎ 505/434-1166, if you're in the mood for Italian. Start with the chicken cacciatore or the veal parmigiana and finish with a large bowl of spumoni (ice cream). If all you want is a good ol' steak, head to **Cattleman's Steak House**, 2904 North White Sands, ☎ 505/434-5252. Seafood, chicken and a salad bar are also featured.

RUIDOSO

Ruidoso is crawling with hungry visitors summer and winter, so the market is ripe for a host of good year-round restaurants. And Ruidoso has a bunch of them.

Farley's, 1200 Mechem Drive, ☎ 505/258-5676, probably is the most popular restaurant in town these days. The parking lot is packed almost every evening, but don't let that discourage you – it's a big place and they usually have room for everyone. The bar features billiard tables, buckets of free peanuts and TV monitors broadcasting various sporting events. The restaurant side of the establishment also features TV sports but is much quieter. A full menu is available on either side and features such entrées as green-chili cheeseburgers, fajitas, barbecued pizza and Caesar salads. Weather permitting, you can also dine and drink in Farley's outdoor beer garden.

A bit fancier, **InnCredible**, NM 48 North at Alto, ☎ 505/336-4312, has become famous through the years for its Wednesday night lobster special. Other standard entrées include prime rib, fettucini Alfredo and chicken Oscar, supplemented with an excellent wine list. The bar features local musicians on weekends.

Authentic international cuisine is a rare find in rural New Mexico (save Mexican, of course) but Ruidoso boasts two fine European eateries. **Che Bella**, Sudderth & Mechem, ☎ 505/257-7540, features northern Italian cuisine prepared to perfection by a real Italian chef and served in a slick contemporary setting on white linen tablecloths. Fresh salmon, rosemary pork loin and assorted pasta dishes are always superb. The French answer to Che Bella is **La Lorraine**, 2523 Sudderth Drive, ☎ 505/257-2954. Here's a touch of real Gallic charm, cleverly captured in a small New Mexican adobe. Dishes here are so beautifully prepared by the French owners that it almost seems a sacrilege to devour them. But, after the first bite, it seems a sin not to.

The Deck House, 200 Mechem, is a New Mexican adobe that doesn't pretend to be anything but a fabulous New Mexican food restaurant. Hearty burritos, enchiladas and chimichangas are served with chips and salsa on simple patio furniture.

At **Café Rio**, 2547 Sudderth Drive, ☎ 505/257-7746, the area's best pizzas and calzones are served in tandem with a brief gourmet menu consisting of quahog clams, spanakopita, Portuguese kale soup, scallops Galacian-style and a few other hard-to-spell items. The dessert menu is equally intriguing.

Homesick Texans should make a beeline for **Southern Accent**, 1028 Mechem, ☎ 505/258-3856, where they can feast on down-home-style barbecued brisket, sausage and ribs. Add a big heap of potato salad and a bowl of cobbler, and you'll be ready for another day or two in the mountains. Sack lunches are also available for skiers and picnickers.

At **In-Espresso-Ble Caffe House**, 2103 Sudderth, ☎ 505/420-0634, homemade pastries and coffee are available for breakfast and into the afternoon for weary shoppers working Ruidoso's main drag. On Friday and Saturday evenings, In-Espresso-Ble serves up live acoustic music, chess, checkers and dominoes along with its lattes, cappuccinos and espressos. It's a nice alternative to the standard bar-hopping scene.

Pony rides and staged gunfights precede the dinner bell at the **Flying J Ranch**, NM 48 north of Alto, ☎ 505/336-4330, where they herd you through a chuckwagon chow line loaded down with western sliced beef or chicken, beans, baked potatoes, buttermilk biscuits and applesauce. Whoa pardner! After dinner, the barn-sized mess hall becomes the scene of a country-western show of surprising merit. The Flying J Wranglers, featuring both a national champion fiddler and yodeler, perform original songs as well as western favorites. The Flying J chuckwagon dinner and show is offered nightly from May to September. Reservations are recommended.

CARRIZOZO

If you happen to be a connoisseur of funky out-of-the-way eateries, the **Outpost Bar & Grill**, 415 Central/US 54, ☎ 505/648-9994, is a joint that's sure to make you smile. The walls are littered with mounted critters from all over the world, including moose, ibex, lion and the elusive jackalope. Sporting events and country-western videos play on several TVs and about the only light in the room is over the pool tables. Steer clear of any posted specials, and go straight for one of the greasy-but-great green chili cheeseburgers. If you're really hungry, a basket of French fries can feed two or three folks.

CAPITAN

The *El Paso Times* gives **Hotel Chango**, 103 South Lincoln Avenue, ☎ 505/354-4213, its highest rating – four stars – placing it among the best restaurants in the region. High praise for a tiny restaurant in a town of 800 people, but the raves are justified and patrons drive for hours to sample the wonders produced in Jerrold Flores' and Manuel Salgado's kitchen. The chefs use their extensive training in Hawaiian, Oriental, classical European, and Southwestern cuisine to prepare a different four-entrée menu each night. Complemented by succulent soups, outstanding appetizers and tempting desserts, main courses may range from filet of mahi mahi swimming in a spicy New Mexican relish to beef bourguignon medallions doused with a dark French wine/basil/garlic sauce. Artistically decorated with mementos (constantly changing) from the owners' far-flung journeys, Hotel Chango is as much a cultural experience as it is a dining revelation. Open only for dinner Wednesday through Saturday and with just 26 seats available at eight tables, reservations are a must and should be made three or four days in advance. Prices are moderate considering the unbelievable fare. Hotel Chango is not really a hotel so, regrettably, you will have to leave after your dessert and coffee.

Just around the corner, **Spanky's Café**, 101 East Smokey Bear Boulevard, ☎ 505/354-2234, is equally impressive – so far as pizza is concerned. Here, the pizzas, calzones and other baked Italian specialties are prepared to perfection. Our favorite pizza comes topped with chicken, artichoke and green chili.

For those who prefer a basic roadside diner, **Smokey Bear Restaurant**, 310 West US 380, ☎ 505/354-2257, serves the standard burgers and sandwiches as well as Mexican specialties.

SAN PATRICIO/TINNIE

Tinnie Silver Dollar Restaurant and Lounge, located in the historic Tinnie Mercantile building, 25 miles east of Ruidoso via US 70, provides some of the finest dining in the area. An airy veranda looks out over the Hondo River Valley, offering a sublime spot for summer afternoon cocktails. On select Sundays, area musicians add their melodious musings to the soft summer breezes. Resembling a Victorian parlor, the intimate, candlelit main dining room features original paintings by local as well as nationally known artists. One small dining room is devoted to the work of Tinnie's artist neighbors, the internationally famous Hurd-Wyeth family.

Menu selections range from rosemary pork loin to prime rib or lobster. Open Wednesday through Friday, 5 PM to 10 PM, and Saturday and Sunday, 11:30 AM to 10 PM, ☎ 505/653-4425.

Camping

Several remote sites at **Sumner Lake State Park**, 16 miles northwest of Fort Sumner via US 84 and NM 203, allow primitive camping and picnicking. There is also a main campground with RV hookups, picnic tables, shelters, grills, tennis courts, a playground, restrooms and showers.

The campground at **Oasis State Park**, seven miles north of Portales via NM 467, offers just what its name suggests. Cedar, locust, and chinaberry trees shade most of the campsites scattered around a four-acre fishing lake, providing a welcome alternative to the windswept plains of Southeastern New Mexico. RV hookups are available at 10 sites and there is a comfort station with restrooms and hot showers.

Primitive camping is permitted throughout **Bottomless Lakes State Park**, 15 miles east of Roswell via US 380 and NM 409. You should, however, check with the visitor center for seasonal restrictions. The park also offers a developed campground with hookups near Lea Lake. (See above, under Adventures on Water.)

Primitive camping is permitted at **Brantley Lake State Park** on the southwest side of the lake. Access is off US 285 about 12 miles north of Carlsbad. Developed sites are available at the **Limestone Campground** in the main section of the park. Exit US 285 12 miles north of Carlsbad and follow County Road 30 to the east side of the Lake and the park's entrance. Here, 50 sites with electricity, water, shelters, tables and grills are situated on a butte high above the lake. Various trails and a road to the boat ramp afford access to the water. There is also a playground, sand volleyball courts and a comfort station with toilets and hot showers.

Numerous backcountry camping opportunities abound in the 215,000 acres of the **Lincoln National Forest** surrounding the town of Cloudcroft. There are also several Forest Service campgrounds. Nearest to Cloudcroft is **Pines Campground**. Take US 82 east and then NM 24 north to this 44-site campground with pit toilets, drinking water and picnic tables nestled beneath the pines. Similar camping is found at the **Slide**, **Deerhead** and **Sleepygrass Campgrounds** located south of town via NM 130 and the Sunspot Highway. Campers looking for sites with RV hookups should try **Silver**

Springs Recreational Campgrounds, five miles northeast of Cloudcroft via US 82 and NM 24. Facilities include 22 RV sites, a trout pond and a tackle shop which rents fishing gear. In town, the **Sugar Pines RV Park**, US 82, ☎ 505/682-3298, offers sites available by the day, week or month.

The campground at **Oliver Lee State Park**, 15 miles south of Alamogordo via US 54, is noted for the beautiful views it offers of sunset over the Tularosa Basin. Most of the 40-plus sites feature RV hookups, shelters, picnic tables and grills. There is also a modern restroom with showers and a visitor center. For information, ☎ 505/437-8284.

Primitive camping (no charge) is available at several National Forest sites along the road up to **Monjeau Lookout**, just off of Ski Area Road in Ruidoso. Restrooms and scattered picnic tables are found near the lookout tower.

Farther down Ski Area Road, **Oak Grove Campground** is another free national forest facility. The campground itself is delightfully tucked under the tall pines and oaks of the forest and each individual site is nicely secluded. Pit toilets only. ☎ 505/257-4095.

The area around **Bonito Lake**, about 15 miles north of Ruidoso via NM 37/48 and Bonito Lake Road, offers hundreds of primitive campsites in a beautiful canyon extending east and west from the lake. There are also several developed campgrounds with picnic tables, grills, water and restrooms. Most of these, however, are closed during winter.

Valley of Fires Recreation Area, five miles west of Carrizozo via US 380, has 19 campsites with shelters, grills and water. RV hookups are available at 14 of the sites. There is a visitor information station and a restroom but no showers. ☎ 505/624-1790.

Southwest New Mexico

Southwest New Mexico is the most rugged section of the state. Dominated by the 3.3 million acres of the **Gila National Forest**, the region is dotted with numerous ghost towns left over from the mining boom days of the early 1900s. **Silver City** remains as the one shining example of what could have been as it continues to bring in more than $90 million a year from its mining industries. It is also the gateway into the heart of the Gilas and to **Gila Cliff Dwellings National Monument**, where pueblo cave ruins from a thousand-year-old culture give us a glimpse into our human past. More than 750,000 acres of the national forest around the monument are designated wilderness. In fact, the **Gila Wilderness** was the first area in the nation to be granted that status. The mountains and streams, trails and lakes here are some of the most pristine in the country.

The **Rio Grande River Valley** is the other predominant geographic feature of the region, serving as its eastern boundary. It is home to one of the nation's best known wildlife refuges, **Bosque del Apache**, where more than 40,000 Canadian geese, 16,000 ducks and 14,000 sandhill cranes winter every year. South of the Bosque, man-made Elephant Butte Lake is the largest body of water in the state, and around it, **Elephant Butte Lake State Park** is the largest and most popular state park as well. **Las Cruces**, at the southern end of the valley, has recently grown to more than 67,000 people, eclipsing Santa Fe as the state's second-largest city.

There is, obviously, much to see and do in this region. Fortunately, the majority of touring takes place at relatively low altitude, ranging from 3,500 to 5,000 feet. The danger here comes during summer, when temperatures average 90° and often break the century mark. Because of the arid climate, dehydration, heat exhaustion and heat stroke are real concerns for those engaging in outdoor activity. Always carry adequate water supplies when touring the area. Altitudes reach nearly 11,000 feet in the mountainous national forest districts. Expect to tire quickly when visiting these areas and exercise caution when participating in vigorous outdoor activities. During winter, snow is common even at the southernmost latitudes. And, while at lower elevation it may melt within hours from the time the sun breaks, you will need warm layered clothing for both comfort and safety.

Southwest New Mexico

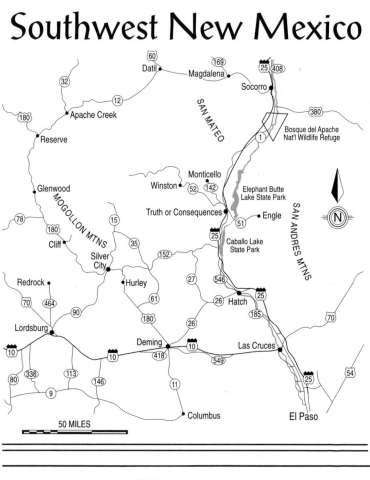

Touring

For touring in Southwest New Mexico, the suggested route begins in Albuquerque on Interstate 25, driving south through Socorro and Truth or Consequences to Las Cruces. Deming lies 60 miles to the west on Interstate 10. From there, a short excursion down NM 11 finds Columbus, NM, and the Mexican border. Or, continue west on I-10 to Lordsburg, Shakespeare Ghost Town and

Stein's Ghost Town. Silver City and the Gila Cliff Dwellings National Monument are north of Lordsburg via NM 90 and NM 15. From Silver City, US 180, NM 12 and US 60 takes you on a long scenic drive through the small towns of Glenwood, Datil and Magdalena, terminating back at Socorro where you began this loop.

Socorro

One of the oldest towns in New Mexico, Socorro was established in 1615 when two Franciscan priests began building Nuestra Senora del Socorro mission. Translated as "Our Lady of Help," the mission's purpose was to convert the peaceful Piro Pueblo Indians to Catholicism and to introduce European farming methods. Like most southern New Mexico settlements, however, Socorro was beset by raiding Apaches. By 1680, the mission and pueblo were abandoned, and the Piro people fled south to El Paso.

Socorro lay deserted for more than 100 years until an 1816 Spanish land grant deeded the area to a group of 21 families. Persevering against continued Apache raids, the families restored the mission, renaming it San Miguel Mission, and Socorro was reborn. In the 1880s, the railroad, bringing more people and soldiers into the area, helped end the Indian raids on the town and, with the discovery of silver in the nearby mountains, the town's population quickly climbed to more than 5,000.

Today, even though area mining operations have slowed almost to a halt, Socorro remains the home of the **New Mexico Institute of Mining and Technology**, offering degrees up to the doctoral level in the mining disciplines of geoscience, metallurgy, engineering, physics and computer sciences. The **Mineral Museum** on campus displays the largest (more than 10,000 specimens) mineral collection in the state, as well as local history and mining artifacts, fossils and photographs. The museum is open weekdays from 8 AM to 5 PM. For information, ☎ 505/835-5420.

The **San Miguel Mission**, still in use as a church, is one of 60 buildings deemed historically significant by the **Socorro County Historical Society**. Some of the more interesting buildings include a 1919 railroad hotel, an 1888 opera house and an 1880 brewery. Free maps of historic Socorro are available at the Chamber of Commerce, or write the Socorro County Historical Society, Box 923, Socorro, NM 87801.

Other touring opportunities in the area include hiking, biking, and rock climbing in the mountains west of town (see below, under Adventures on Foot/Wheels), as well as exploring the many ghost towns in the hills around **Magdalena**, 25 miles west via US 60. Continuing past Magdalena on US 60, the **Very Large Array Radio Telescope** site, about 50 miles from Socorro, is a must-see for every science or astronomy buff. There are also a number of wildlife viewing opportunities, especially at **Bosque del Apache National Wildlife Refuge**, 25 miles south on Interstate 25. (See below.)

For information, contact **Socorro County Chamber of Commerce**, 103 Francisco de Avondo, PO Box 743, Socorro, NM 87801, ☎ 505/835-0424.

Magdalena

Named for a rock-formation profile of Mary Magdalene, said to be visible in the mountains above town, **Magdalena** is the typical Old West town whose glory days have long since passed. The area boomed as a center for mining operations from 1886 to 1945, producing nearly $60 million in lead, zinc and silver ore during that period. But barely 1,000 people live here today, and the town sees few visitors. Tourists are usually just passing through on their way to explore numerous abandoned mines and ghost towns in the hills outside town.

The most interesting of them is **Kelly Mine** and ghost town, located three miles south of Magdalena via County Road 114 and Forest Road 101. At one time, Kelly was a bustling town of 3,000 people and the largest mining operation in the area. A little white church is all that remains recognizable among the numerous shops, saloons, hotels and houses that once comprised Kelly. Structures at the mine, however, have stood up much better. The refractory, boiler and assay, as well as several shafts with headframes and towers, hint at the formerly massive operations here. A number of mineral stockpiles scattered around the grounds still yield malachite, pyrite, quartz, smithsonite and fossils to eager rockhounds, but be careful when exploring, as crumbling mine shafts and decaying equipment are dangerous. The ghost town may be visited any time, but Kelly Mine is only open May 15 to October 15, Friday through Sunday, 10 AM to 4 PM. A required visitor's pass may be obtained at various locations in Magdalena. For information, ☎ 505/854-2415.

West of Magdalena, about 25 miles via US 60, the National Radio Astronomy Observatory's **Very Large Array Radio Telescope** is quite an astonishing sight for the unsuspecting motorist. Located on the high desert plains, 27 82-foot dish-shaped radio antennas arranged in a large "Y" stand collecting celestial data like something out of the latest *Star Wars* movie. One might think that a $78 million complex such as this would be restricted to authorized personnel. Quite to the contrary, a visitors center is located on the grounds near the center of the "Y," offering detailed exhibits explaining the intricacies of radio astronomy. You can even take a self-guided walking tour out among the antennas as well as through the computer room and control buildings, where further displays are arranged for visitors. Public access is also permitted into the large maintenance building, the site of all service and assembly for the 235-ton antennas. The VLA antennas are visible from US 60 approximately 25 miles west of Magdalena. To reach the visitors center, take the well-marked exit onto NM 52 and follow it for two miles to the VLA access road. The visitors center is open daily from 8:30 AM to sunset. For information, contact the Public Education Officer, National Radio Astronomy Observatory, Box 0, Socorro, NM 87801, ☎ 505/772-4255.

For information on Magdalena, contact **Magdalena Chamber of Commerce**, PO Box 281, Magdalena, NM 87825, ☎ 505/854-2261.

Bosque del Apache

Bosque del Apache National Wildlife Refuge was established in 1936 as a refuge and breeding ground for migratory waterfowl and other wildlife, but particularly for the endangered greater sandhill crane. During the first few years, fewer than 20 sandhills were spotted in the refuge, but today more than 14,000 spend their winters here. Current preservation efforts concentrate on rare and endangered whooping cranes. Conservation experiments have introduced whooping crane eggs into the nests of sandhill crane populations in Idaho, and each year 10 to 15 of the endangered birds arrive with the sandhills at the Bosque. This reserve is the most accessible spot in the United States to view this rare endangered species. Aside from the cranes, the refuge provides a habitat for more than 325 different bird species and some 135 different mammals, reptiles and amphibians. In addition to the rare cranes, more than 40,000 Canadian geese and 16,000 ducks winter here.

Of New Mexico's five national wildlife refuges, the 57,191-acre Bosque del Apache is by far the most popular with both tourists and wildlife. A visitor center at the park headquarters offers informative literature and exhibits on refuge conservation efforts and wildlife. A 15-mile self-guided auto tour route and several walking trails provide access to the actual wildlife areas where numerous viewing stands overlook pond, marsh and field habitats in the refuge. The Bosque is a nature photographer's and bird watcher's dream come true.

From Socorro, drive nine miles south on Interstate 25 and exit US 380 at San Antonio. At the caution light in town, turn right onto NM 1 and follow it eight miles to the Bosque. The refuge opens one hour before sunrise and closes one hour after sunset. The visitor center is open weekdays from 7:30 AM to 4 PM and weekends from 8 AM to 4:30 PM. For information, contact **Bosque del Apache National Wildlife Refuge**, PO Box 1246, Socorro, NM 87801-1246, ☎ 505/835-1828.

Truth or Consequences

Originally named Palomas Hot Springs for the large dove populations and natural hot springs in the area, it was later called just Hot Springs. This small resort town changed its name to Truth or Consequences in order to win a national radio show contest. In 1950, Ralph Edwards, host of the popular show, *Truth or Consequences*, offered to do the show's 10th anniversary broadcast on-location in the first town to change its name to that of his show. The community voted affirmatively and Hot Springs was in the national spotlight. Every year since, T or C (as it's referred to by locals) hosts Fiesta Days to commemorate the event and Edwards sometimes returns to oversee the festivities, which are held, appropriately, in Ralph Edwards Park.

During the 1972 Fiesta Days, T or C dedicated its **Geronimo Springs Museum**, 325 Main Street. One entire wing exhibits artifacts and mementos from Edwards' life and his show. The rest of the museum is actually quite interesting, displaying ancient Mimbres pottery, large arrowhead collections, early settler artifacts and mining tools. The museum is open Monday through Saturday from 9 AM to 5 PM and Sundays from 1 PM to 5 PM. For information, ☎ 505/894-6600.

The museum also offers interesting historical displays dealing with the town's recent past as a hot springs resort. T or C sits atop an apparently inexhaustible supply of hot mineral water. Between 1880 and 1930, several bath houses and resort spas were built around eight natural hot springs which surface in the city limits. Waters range from 98 to 115°. Although most of the spas are now somewhat run-down, they still attract a number of loyal bathers each year. **Sierra Grande Lodge and Health Spa**, 501 McAdoo, ☎ 505/894-6976, is perhaps the nicest spring still open to the public. The T or C Chamber of Commerce can provide a list of other springs in the area.

Although the popularity of T or C as a hot springs resort has long faded, nearby **Elephant Butte Lake State Park** continues to draw thousands of tourists as New Mexico's largest and most visited state park. (See below, under Adventures on Water.)

For information, contact **T or C/Sierra County Chamber of Commerce**, PO Box 31, Truth or Consequences, NM 87901, ☎ 505/894-3536 or 800/831-9487.

Hatch

The little town of Hatch deserves mention not because of any museum, restaurant or hotel or even fishing hole, hiking trail or camping site, but because it is the "Chili Capital of the World." Chilies harvested from these Rio Grande-irrigated fields make the best, salsas and sauces on the planet and are the spice behind the increasing popularity of Mexican food everywhere. Crops begin to ripen in late summer and through the fall hundreds of roadside vendors sell fresh-roasted green chilies and red chili ristras straight from the fields. New Mexican chefs, both amateur and professional, come from miles around to stock their pantries with the best chilies the state has to offer. Stop in if you're passing by on Interstate 25. If you miss harvest, you can still buy into the area's chili-mania as a number of shops in town sell chilies dried, canned, powdered and even emblazoned on T-shirts.

Las Cruces

The fertile Mesilla Valley on the Rio Grande has long been a hub of human activity. Inhabiting crude riverside villages, ancient desert dwellers of the Mogollon culture hunted and fished in the area and used native mesquite beans to make flour. Their civilization thrived for hundreds of years until they mysteriously disappeared not long after the time of Christ. Petroglyphs in the nearby mountains remain as the only distinct testimony to their culture. Centuries later, another group of Native Americans, perhaps related to the Mescalero Apache, moved into the area. When the first Spanish explorers, Alvar Nuñez Cabeza de Vaca and Juan de Onate, passed through the region, these people were there to greet them. The Spaniards named the people "Mansos" and built a mission in 1630 to concentrate the natives in the valley. Unfortunately, exposure to smallpox and other diseases killed many of the indigenous people, and in no time at all intermarriage between the surviving natives and the Spanish had so blurred identity lines that the tribe completely disappeared.

The settlement in the valley continued to thrive, however, becoming a major resting point and watering hole along the Camino Real or "Royal Road" between Mexico City and Santa Fe. In the 1700s and 1800s, Mescalero Apache raids along the route increased, and the Spanish custom of erecting small crosses at the site of fallen travelers soon earned the settlement the name La Placita de Las Cruces or "Little Place of the Crosses." When the Gadsden Purchase of 1853 annexed the lands west of the Rio Grande to the United States, the name was shortened to Las Cruces.

More than 67,000 people live in this the second largest city in New Mexico, and the area offers bountiful touring opportunities. Dating back to 1598, the community of **Mesilla**, three miles from the center of Las Cruces via NM 28, is the heart of Colonial Spanish influence in the valley. Its central plaza, protected as the **La Mesilla State Monument**, is one of the best preserved historic districts in the state. **San Albino Church**, built in 1851, stands at one end of the plaza – the oldest remaining mission church in the valley. In 1853, the Gadsden Purchase was signed in the center of Mesilla Plaza making it and all of the surrounding valley property of the United States. After that, it became an official stop on the Butterfield Stage Route and the old stage station now houses one of the area's most popular restaurants. Many other buildings house colorful shops and galleries. Most visitors, however, want to see the Mesilla Courthouse – site of Billy the Kid's famous 1880 murder trial in which he was convicted and sentenced to hang. True to his reputation, he escaped before they could tie the noose around his neck. Also on the plaza, the **Gadsden Museum**, NM 28 & Barker Road, holds numerous artifacts representing the Anglo, Spanish and Native American cultures in the valley. The museum is open daily from 9 AM to 5 PM. For information, ☎ 505/526-6293.

Fort Selden State Monument, 15 miles north of Las Cruces via Interstate 25 or NM 185, is another area attraction that lends insight into 19th-century life in the Mesilla Valley. Established in 1865 to protect Las Cruces and Mesilla against Apache raids, Fort Selden also played an important role guarding travelers and supply wagons on the Camino Real. The fort was decommissioned in 1891. A self-guided trail leads visitors through the ruins of the adobe complex. On weekends during the summer, costumed interpreters stroll the grounds giving demonstrations on the weapons, equipment and protocol of the early US Army. A visitor center at the monument displays uniforms, weapons, photographs and models of the fort to further illustrate its contributions to life in the valley. The monument is open daily from 9:30 AM to 5:30 PM, May 1 through September 15 and from 8:30 AM to 4:30 PM, September 16 through April 30. For information, ☎ 505/526-8911.

The **New Mexico Museum of Natural History**, located in the Mesilla Valley Mall on Lohman Street, presents a variety of exhibits on subjects ranging from dinosaurs to the planet Jupiter. Also featured are excellent traveling collections loaned from national museums, including the Smithsonian Institution. For information, ☎ 505/522-3120.

While Las Cruces prides itself on preservation of its cultural past, it has a keen eye on the future as well. The city is home to **New Mexico State University,** well-known for its agricultural college and for one of the country's largest planetary observatories. It is on the cutting edge of computer communications technologies as well. The **University Museum**, in Kent Hall on University Drive, features rotating cultural, historical and scientific exhibits. The museum is open Tuesday through Saturday from 10 AM to 4 PM and Sunday 1 PM to 4 PM. For information, ☎ 505/646-3739.

Summertime temperatures in Las Cruces can soar to above 100°, but the **Organ** and **Franklin Mountains** on the eastern outskirts of town provide year-round respite from the heat, offering recreation areas more than 2,000 feet above the sweltering valley floor. Mountain biking, hiking and four-wheeling opportunities abound. (See below, under Adventures on Foot/Wheels.) Camping is available. **Mesa Airlines,** ☎ 800/MESA-AIR, provides service into Las Cruces Municipal Airport.

Rental Cars are available through **Avis,** ☎ 505/522-1400, or **Hertz,** ☎ 505/521-4807.

For information, contact **Las Cruces Chamber of Commerce**, PO Drawer 519, Las Cruces, NM 88004, ☎ 505/524-1968.

Deming

Deming is a typical New Mexico prairie town, established in 1881 at the junction of the Southern Pacific and Atchison, Topeka & Santa Fe Railroads. Its only real claims to fame are 99.9%-pure drinking water from the underground Mimbres River and a comical duck race held every August.

If you're passing through and need a break from the monotony of the seamless desert scenery, Deming does feature a fine historical museum. The **Deming-Luna-Mimbres Museum**, 301 South Silver Street, displays early ranch memorabilia, including a chuckwagon, country kitchen, saddles and handmade quilts. There are also excellent collections of minerals, Mimbres pottery and more than 500 antique dolls. The museum is open daily from 9AM to 4 PM, Sunday from 1:30 PM to 4 PM. For information, contact **Luna County Historical Society, Inc.**, PO Box 1617, Deming, NM 88031, ☎ 505/546-2382.

Rock Hound State Park, 15 miles southeast of Deming via NM 11 and NM 141, may be the only park in the state where the standard etiquette of "take only pictures; leave only footprints" does not apply. In fact, rangers encourage visitors to take up to 15 pounds of souvenir rock per person. Agate, opal and onyx are just some of the many different stones routinely found at the 240-acre park in the western foothills of the Little Florida Mountains. Camping is available. For information, ☎ 505/546-1212.

For information, contact **Deming Chamber of Commerce**, PO Box 8, 800 East Pine Street, Deming, NM 88031, ☎ 505/546-2674.

Columbus

A sleepy village on the Mexican border, Columbus marks the site of the only attack on the US mainland by a foreign power. On March 9, 1916, Mexican revolutionary Pancho Villa led some 1,000 soldiers in an assault on the 13th Calvary at nearby Camp Furlong in response to President Wilson's recognition of Villa rival Venuestiano Carranzo as Mexico's president. Although outnumbered three to one, US troops successfully repelled the incursion, pushing Villa's forces back across the border. Not, however, before rebels mercilessly pillaged the town of Columbus, killing 16 people. President Wilson ordered General John "Blackjack" Pershing to carry out a retaliatory strike against Villa in an attempt to disband his army. Pershing pursued the rebels almost 500 miles into Mexico, killing more than 250, but never capturing Villa – who continued his battles against the Mexican government until he was assassinated in 1920.

Verging on ghost town status, Columbus maintains a rag-tag **Historical Museum** in the old Southern Pacific Railroad Depot. Exhibits include early weapons, furniture and clothing from the area. The museum is open Friday through Tuesday from 1 PM to 4 PM. For information, ☎ 505/531-2620.

Pancho Villa State Park, on the other hand, offers much better insight into the Villa raid. One of the small hills that was used as a US Cavalry lookout post has been beautifully landscaped as a desert botanical garden. Historical markers give details on the area and the battles with Mexican rebels. There are also ruins of old Camp Furlong headquarters and a visitor center with a small museum. Camping is available. For information, contact **Pancho Villa State Park**, PO Box 450, Columbus, NM 88029, ☎ 505/531-2711.

If you're not a history buff the only other reason to visit Columbus is **Palomas, Mexico**. Unlike El Paso/Juarez or San Diego/Tijuana, you don't have to wait in long lines to cross the border. You need to stop and buy Mexican car insurance if driving in but, if you park at the US Customs office, you can walk right over with no hassle at all. There's not a whole lot to do here, but your US dollars go twice as far in the little curio shops and restaurants. Plus, it's fun to visit another country, even if only for a few hours.

For information, contact **Columbus Chamber of Commerce**, PO Box 365, Columbus, NM 88029, ☎ 505/531-2236.

Lordsburg

The seat of New Mexico's "Boot-heel" Hidalgo County, Lordsburg, like many other towns in the area, was founded as a Southern Pacific Railroad project in the 1880s. The town is nationally known for its geothermal resources, with 246° temperatures having been recorded in many of the area's wells.

Tourists, however, enter the region to explore two well-preserved, privately owned ghost towns. **Shakespeare** has nothing to do with England's most lyrical bard. Instead, it once was home to more than 3,000 rowdy miners. Hotels, saloons, shops and brothels lined streets that were frequented by notorious outlaws, including the likes of Russian Bill, Sandy King and even Billy the Kid. Every other weekend, costumed interpreters lead guided tours of the historic buildings and relate true stories and popular legends to interested visitors. Four times a year, reenactments of western gunfights, hangings and dancehall performances are presented. Call ahead to see if tours are scheduled during your visit to the area. If you happen to miss one of the scheduled tours, you can still browse through the streets on your own. Shakespeare is located just south of Lordsburg. Take the Main Street exit (#22) off Interstate 10 and follow the signs south 2½ miles. For information, contact **Shakespeare Ghost Town**, Box 253, Lordsburg, NM 88045, ☎ 505/542-9034.

Originally a Butterfield Stage Station, **Steins Railroad Ghost Town** peaked in the early 1900s with the arrival of the Southern Pacific Railroad. More than 1,000 people once lived in the Old West town that supported two saloons, one dance hall, a constable and a justice of the peace. Visitors can stroll through 10 buildings that have been restored with authentic artifacts and furniture dating to the 1800s. Steins is 19 miles southwest of Lordsburg via Interstate 10. For information, contact **Steins Railroad Ghost Town**, Box 2185, Road Forks, NM 88045, ☎ 505/542-9791.

Silver City

Silver City was established in 1870 after – you guessed it – silver was discovered in the nearby mountains. By 1875, it had become the official seat of Grant County, serving as the commercial hub for all mining activity in the area.

About the same time Silver City was growing up, so was New Mexico's most infamous outlaw. Henry Antrim McCarty, alias William Bonney, alias Billy the Kid, spent his childhood causing mischief in the unsuspecting streets of Silver City. In fact, it was a prank robbery of a Chinese laundry here that led to his first arrest and the birth of his legend. The skinny 15-year-old made his first escape by climbing out the chimney of the Silver City jail. He lived the next six years on the run, getting caught and escaping numerous lockups along the way. But his luck eventually ran out at Fort Sumner in 1881, where he died at the hand of Sheriff Pat Garrett in a ranch house far from home.

Even though Silver City's most famous son didn't survive to see a ripe old age, Silver City has. It's the area's only 19th-century boom town to prosper and continue to show profit in the industry of its origin. Currently, Silver City produces more than $90 million a year worth of copper ore through its various mining enterprises.

Tourism too, is a big part of the town's economy, and much of it is related to mining history. **Tyrone** and **Pinos Altos** are two of the most popular ghost towns in the area. Tyrone, 10 miles west of town via NM 90, was home to more than 5,000 people in 1915. It was the largest operation at the time of the giant Phelps-Dodge Mining Company and featured a business complex and plaza that was constructed at a cost of more than one million dollars. Only the post office and a small mining office remain active.

Pinos Altos, seven miles north of Silver City via NM 15, was actually the first settlement in the area, arriving 10 years before its more prosperous southern neighbor. During its heyday, it had about 1,000 residents, several saloons and a Victorian opera house. A few people still cling to Pinos Altos and the finest restaurant in the area is located there. (See below, under Where to Stay & Eat.)

There are a number of historically interesting spots in Silver City itself. The most sought-out, but disappointing, of them is **Billy the Kid's Childhood Cabin**. Signs downtown entice you toward it, leading to a parking lot with another sign that reads, "Billy the Kid Cabin Site... the cabin was torn down in 1894." Much more interesting is **Big Ditch Park**, the result of an 1895 flood that, in one day, dropped Silver City's Main Street 50 feet below most of its businesses' front doorsteps. It is quite a sight to stroll the park with its high walls topped by the original storefronts of a prosperous business district. It is also fun to walk down Hudson Street, knowing that every entrance was actually designed as the back door.

Silver City Museum, 312 Broadway, offers wonderful insight into the early history of the town and area. Located in a historic Victorian home, the museum blends 19th-century antique furnishings, artifacts from ancient native cultures and mining tools from the surrounding ghost towns to paint a comprehensive picture of not only the town but the entire area. Hours are 9 AM to 4:30 PM, Tuesday through Friday and 10 AM to 4 PM, Saturday and Sunday. For information, ☎ 505/538-5921.

Western New Mexico University Museum, 10th Street on campus, represents Silver City's small liberal arts college rather proudly, featuring the largest collection of ancient Mimbres pottery in the country. Mimbres people lived 700 to 1,000 years ago and details in designs on their pottery suggests that they possessed advanced knowledge of astronomy. The collection has been displayed in prestigious museums the world over, including Paris, Copenhagen and Washington DC. For information, ☎ 505/538-6386.

Gila Cliff Dwellings National Monument, 45 miles north of Silver City, is another area attraction that offers a glimpse into the lives of our ancient ancestors. During the 1200s, a group of about 15 Mogollon families inhabited seven natural caves in what is now the Gila National Forest. They constructed 40 pueblo-style rooms and led prosperous lives farming and hunting in the nearby river valley – but mysteriously disappeared sometime in the early 1300s. A one-mile loop-trail affords access to the well-preserved ruins and a small visitor center at the trailhead provides exhibits detailing what is known about the Mogollon culture. Allow 2½ hours to drive the 45 miles from Silver City to the national monument as the road is extremely steep and has numerous tight switchbacks. The visitor center is open daily from 8 AM to 4:30 PM. For information, ☎ 505/536-9461.

The **Gila National Forest** encompasses 3.3 million acres, bordering Silver City to the north. The vast wilderness provides countless recreational opportunities, including hiking, fishing, rafting, biking and camping. (See below, under Adventures.)

One of New Mexico's most bizarre landscapes, **City of Rocks State Park** lies 30 miles south of Silver City via US 180 and NM 61. The remains of a several-million-year-old lava flow, a maze of 50-foot-tall rocks stands on a hillside looking much like a city of stone, complete with avenues, residential areas and business districts. In fact, there is some evidence that humans once inhabited the area, but there is no indication they had a hand in the arrangement of the city, since at most every rock is one with the base on which it stands. Camping is available. For information, ☎ 505/536-2800.

Mesa Air, ☎ 800/MESA-AIR, provides service to the Grant County Airport, 25 miles south of Silver City.

Car rental is available at the airport through **Grimes Car Rental,** ☎ 505/538-2142, or in town through **Ugly Duckling,** ☎ 505/388-5813.

For information, contact **Silver City Chamber of Commerce,** 1103 North Hudson Street, Silver City, NM 88061, ☎ 505/538-3785 or 800/548-9378.

Glenwood

Known primarily as a base camp for outdoor enthusiasts heading into the Gila National Forest, Glenwood is a cozy little resort community about 60 miles north of Silver City. Close proximity to **The Catwalk** and **Whitewater Canyon** is the town's major selling point. These are two of the most popular features in the national forest. (See below, under Adventures on Foot/Water.)

The nearby ghost town of **Mogollon** is another popular area attraction. One of the many abandoned mining towns in the region, this little burg boomed between 1912 and 1915, producing more than $1 million in ore each of those four years. A few of the mines in the area are actually still producing, but most of the workers have moved on to other nearby towns such as Glenwood. With only a dozen year-round residents, Mogollon is not completely dead and is now becoming something of an artists' colony. Many of the old buildings have become studios/galleries or antique stores. Tourists usually find the eccentric shopkeepers quite entertaining – and vice-versa.

Mogollon is 16 miles northeast of Glenwood via US 180 and NM 159. The road following the turn-off from US 180 is very steep. Due to tight switchbacks, it is not recommended for trailers more than 17 feet long. Allow at least 30 minutes to drive the last 10 miles to the ghost town.

Adventures

On Foot

The **Box Canyon** area, six miles west of Socorro via US 60, offers some of the best rock climbing in southern New Mexico. Heading west from town, you will see an unmistakable box canyon on your left. Continue past the canyon to the first unmarked left turn. A dirt road curves back around to a small parking area at the mouth of "The Box," as it is commonly called.

Looking northeast from the parking area, the Waterfall Wall, a 40- to 50-foot-high rock face about 100 feet wide, offers approximately 20 good top-rope problems ranging from 5.2 to 5.12 in difficulty. Numerous bolted anchors are accessible by a short trail to the right of the wall.

Further into the canyon, both the east and west walls provide for varied lead possibilities ranging in difficulty from 5.6 to 5.12, with several two-pitch routes. Most routes are bolted, although some require additional protection.

The Box is maintained by the Bureau of Land Management, so camping in the area is permitted and free. The routes, bolts and anchors are well maintained by loyal local climbers, most of whom are students and professors at New Mexico Tech in Socorro.

A detailed climbing guide, *The Enchanted Tower: Sport Climbing Socorro and Datil, NM*, is available through area bookstores, or contact Climbing Guide, New Mexico Tech Student Association, New Mexico Institute of Mining and Technology, Socorro, NM 87801.

Cibola National Forest offers the best hiking and backpacking in the Socorro area. **Magdalena Crest Trail,** between South Baldy Peak and North Baldy Peak of the Magdalena Mountain Range, provides a moderate 11-mile day hike with spectacular views of the surrounding Gallinas, Ladron and San Mateo Mountain Ranges. To find the trailhead, take US 60 15½ miles west of Socorro to the Water Canyon turnoff. Turn left and follow Forest Road 235 for 12½ miles to the marked North Baldy trailhead on the right side of the road. From there, the summit of South Baldy is just a few hundred yards to the west. The trail runs north-south between the summits, dipping in and out of lush forests and grassy meadows. Not well worn, however, the trail sometimes fades away on open grassy saddles and hilltops. It keeps basically to the crest, though, and rock cairns or tree blazes show the way when the path does not. After five miles of relatively level hiking, the trail climbs 500 feet in ¾-mile to the 9,858-foot summit of North Baldy. Break for lunch here and enjoy the panoramic views across wide valleys to distant mountain ranges. Return to the trailhead the same way you came. There is no water along the trail, but hikers with topo maps should be able to locate a number of springs below the crest. Use a Cibola National Forest – Magdalena Ranger District map or the Magdalena and South Baldy USGS 7.5 minute quads for this hike.

In the **Apache Kid Wilderness** of the Cibola National Forest, a 68-mile trail system provides for some very scenic hiking in the rarely-visited but beautiful San Mateo Mountain Range. One of the most accessible trails in the range provides for a strenuous day hike or easy overnighter to the 10,139-foot summit of **San Mateo Peak**. Drive about 45 miles south of Socorro on Interstate 25 to exit 115. Follow the access road to the Forest Road 225/Springtime Campground turnoff. The trailhead is at the campground 13 miles down FR 225. Or, from Truth or Consequences, take Interstate 25 about 20 miles north to exit 100 and continue along the access road on the west side of the interstate to the Forest Road 225 turnoff. From Springtime Campground, follow well-marked Trail #43 for 3¼ miles to the junction with Trail #44, which climbs the last ¾-mile to San Mateo Peak. Both trails are well-maintained and easy to follow, even though the Apache Kid Wilderness trail system is one of the least traveled in the state. The lush forests, beautiful mountain views and sublime solitude (even during summer weekends) of this wilderness make it the perfect trail for those wanting to escape. Several trails branch off from the peak and from Trail #43, offering extended backpacking opportunities, or backtrack to Springtime Campground to finish the trek. Although relatively short at eight miles round-trip, this hike is moderately challenging, climbing nearly 3,000 feet from trailhead to summit. Water is available at several springs along the way. Use a Cibola National Forest – Magdalena Ranger District map and a Vick's Peak 7.5 minute USGS quad for this hike.

The **Organ** and **Franklin Mountains**, just east of Las Cruces, comprise 54,000 acres of public land administered by the Bureau of Land Management. The **A.B. Cox Visitor Center**, nine miles east of Las Cruces via University Drive and Dripping Springs Road, offers information on all recreational pursuits in the area, including biking, hiking, camping and four-wheeling. A 1½-mile trail from the visitor center leads into a narrow juniper- and oak-filled canyon with high sheer walls ending at **Dripping Springs**. In the late 1800s and early 1900s, the canyon was the site of a mountain resort and a tuberculosis sanitorium. The ruins of these enterprises and of an old stagecoach stop lie near Dripping Springs at the end of the trail, adding historic interest to an already beautifully scenic hike. Water is available at the springs, but you're better off bringing your own. Water found in the canyon must be boiled or treated before use.

US 70, through San Augustin Pass, accesses the east side of the Organ Mountains and **Aguirre Spring Campground**, 20 miles northeast of Las Cruces. Two good hiking trails begin at this picturesque mountain campground. **Pine Tree Trail** is a five-mile loop below the rugged crags of the Organ Mountains. The trail wanders through boulders, ponderosa pines and dry stream beds to a primitive camping area at the far end of the circuit. Climbing nearly 1,000 feet, this hike can be moderately strenuous during the heat of summer, but the views afforded of the Tularosa Basin and even distant Sierra Blanca Peak are worth it. There is no reliable water along this trail or at Aguirre Spring Campground, so be sure to fill a bottle or two before setting out.

A six-mile trail through **Baylor Pass** connects the east and west sides of the Organ Mountains. From Aguirre Springs Campground, a well marked trail climbs 1,000 feet to the summit of a pass named for the Confederate general who used it strategically in the capture of Union soldiers in 1861. Views from the west side of the pass look down on the Mesilla Valley and Las Cruces, 2,500 feet below. The trail ends 2,000 feet below the summit at Baylor Canyon Road.

Primitive camping is allowed along this trail, which takes about four hours to walk one way. There is no water available on this hike.

For information, contact **Bureau of Land Management – Mimbres Resource Area**, 1800 Marquess Street, Las Cruces, NM 88005, ☎ 505/525-4300.

There are more than 1,400 miles of hiking trails designated on the **Gila National Forest** map, ranging in length and difficulty from the easy one-mile loop at **Gila Cliff Dwellings National Monument** to multi-day backpacking routes across the **Continental Divide**.

Next to the Cliff Dwellings Trail, **The Catwalk**, through Whitewater Canyon, is the most popular day-hike in the forest. From Glenwood, take NM 174 five miles east to a picnic area and trailhead at road's end. Officially, The Catwalk is Forest Service Trail #207. It follows an old water pipeline through a steep narrow canyon to a picturesque waterfall about three miles from the trailhead. The actual trail is a series of steel bridges and walkways bolted onto the sheer rock walls of the canyon and suspended over Whitewater Creek – thus, the name. This is a moderately strenuous hike as the trail climbs more than 1,000 feet from start to waterfall. After that, Trail #207 continues for miles into the Gila Wilderness, affording spectacular backpacking opportunities. Or you can turn around and return to the picnic area to complete this interesting day-hike.

If you continue on Trail #207, it eventually joins **Crest Trail #182** in Hummingbird Saddle near Hummingbird Spring. Trail #182 reaches the saddle from a trailhead at Sandy Point, accessed via US 180 and NM 159 from Glenwood. From the junction with #207, Crest Trail skirts the east side of 10,895-foot Whitewater Baldy, the highest peak in the Gila National Forest, and continues along the ridge to the 10,770-foot summit of Mogollon Baldy, passing over the 10,533-foot summit of Center Baldy on the way. Countless other trails descend off Crest Trail, affording numerous return routes, but by sticking to the two trails already mentioned, this makes a moderate three- to five-day backpacking adventure, depending on your choice of trailhead. Water is available at several springs along the way, but must be boiled or treated before drinking. Use the Gila Wilderness and Gila National Forest maps, as well as the Grouse Mountain, Holt Mountain and Mogollon Baldy 7.5-minute USGS quads for this hike. For information, contact Gila National Forest, Supervisor's Office, 2610 N. Silver St., Silver City, NM 88061, ☎ 505/388-8301.

On Wheels

The Magdalena Mountains of the **Cibola National Forest** provide numerous mountain biking opportunities in the Socorro area. Take US 60 west about 15 miles from town and exit left onto Forest Road 235. Follow it 4½ miles to the Water Canyon Campground and park there. FS 235 continues from the campground, offering a steep and strenuous nine-mile ride on rocky double-track to the summit of **South Baldy Peak**. From there, several exciting single-track descents are optional. Forest Service Trail #10 leaves from the north side of the peak, following Copper Canyon to FS 406 and back to Water Canyon Campground. About one mile back down FS 235, FS Trail #11 turns off to the left, making a three-mile single-track loop that rejoins FS 235 2½ miles above the campground. The ride from the campground to the summit gains 3,750 feet over nine miles. Both the single and double track descents are steep and highly technical. Intermediate to advanced riders in excellent shape will find this ride difficult, but exhilarating. Use a Cibola National Forest-Magdalena Ranger District map or the Magdalena and South Baldy Peak 7.5-minute USGS quads for further trail details.

Novice or intermediate riders might better enjoy a ride from Magdalena south into **Hop Canyon**. Park at the Cibola National Forest-Magdalena District Ranger Station, County Road 114 and US 60 intersection, then ride CR 114 past Kelly ghost town to Forest Road 101 and up into the canyon. This route follows seven miles of generally unmaintained dirt roads that are loose or even washed out in sections and eventually peter out, becoming Forest Service Trail #25. Elevation gain from Magdalena and the end of FS 101 is 1,400 feet. Ride as far as is comfortable, or until the road gets too steep, then turn around and enjoy the semi-technical downhill return to town. If you wish to explore the ghost town or Kelly Mine, obtain a visitor's pass in Magdalena before beginning this ride. (See above, under Touring.) Maps used for this route are the same as for the South Baldy Peak ride.

The **Organ** and **Franklin Mountains**, just east of Las Cruces, offer numerous mountain biking and four-wheeling opportunities. A six-mile biking/hiking trail through **Baylor Pass** provides a connection between Aguirre Spring Campground, on the east side of the range, and Baylor Canyon Road, on the west side, where a car shuttle or a 14-mile coast down into Las Cruces ends the ride. The first two miles of this trail climb 1,000 feet. Intermediate to advanced riders will find this ride moderate to difficult. (See above, under Adventures on Foot.) **Westside Road** is the most popular jeep trail in the area. It runs southward along the west side of the range from the end of Soledad Canyon Road in Las Cruces until it rejoins Interstate 10, 15 miles outside of town. For information, contact the **Bureau of Land Management-Mimbres Resource Area**, 1800 Marquess Street, Las Cruces, NM 88005, ☎ 505/525-4300.

The **Gila National Forest** offers more than 1,490 miles of trails open to mountain biking, from moderate double-track forest service roads to technical single-track circuits. Remember that biking is prohibited in wilderness areas, and use a Gila National Forest map to locate numerous riding opportunities.

One of the favorite rides among Silver City locals is a 20-mile loop which begins in town and eventually gains the crest of the **Continental Divide**. Ride out Cottage San Road until the pavement ends and the road forks in three directions. Take the left fork, Forest Road 853, and continue three miles to the Continental Divide Trail marked on your right. This single-track climbs steeply to the top of Bear Mountain and then follows a rolling ridgeline for five miles until crossing Forest Road 506. A right turn heads downhill to an intersection, where another right turn sends you past the Little Walnut Campground and back into Silver City. More than 2,700 feet are climbed during this circuit (topping out at 7,800 feet), which requires a strong set of lungs, strong legs and at least intermediate riding skills. This ride could take four hours or all day, depending on individual fitness. The Gila National Forest map and the Silver City 7.5-minute USGS quad both show this route.

An easier 12-mile loop begins the same as the Continental Divide route but takes a left turn down Forest Road 862 before reaching the single-track section of that ride. FS 862 parallels the **Silver City Range** for five miles until dropping down to join US 180. A right turn onto the pavement will take you back to town. Total elevation gain is only 700 feet on easy double-track, so novice and intermediate riders should complete this ride in about two hours. Use the maps mentioned above to find this route. For information, contact Gila National Forest, Supervisor's Office, 2610 N. Silver St., Silver City, NM 88061, ☎ 505/388-8301.

BIKE SERVICE & SALES

Desert Cycles, 105 Plaza, Socorro, ☎ 505/835-4085.
RideOn Sports, 525 Telshor, Las Cruces, ☎ 505/521-1686.
Gila Hike and Bike, 103 East College, Silver City, ☎ 505/388-3222.

On Water

The **Rio Grande River** slices right down the middle of New Mexico and parallels the eastern border of this section of the state. Although not as wild as up north, this stretch of water does provide good to excellent fishing as well as excellent flat water canoeing.

Elephant Butte Lake State Park, seven miles north of Truth or Consequences off Interstate 25, opened in 1965. Covering nearly 70,000 acres, it is the largest park in the state system. The reservoir from which the park takes its name is also the biggest body of water in New Mexico, stretching 40 miles with more than 36,000 surface acres and 200 miles of shoreline. Add year-round balmy temperatures and it's no wonder that this is also New Mexico's most popular state park. In fact, for three days each year during the Memorial Day weekend, the park becomes the second largest population center in the state, the temporary residence for more than 100,000 visitors.

Watersports are, of course, the big draw here with fishing the most popular year-round activity on the lake. Largemouth, smallmouth, striped and white bass, as well as walleye, crappie, bluegill and catfish, are the most consistent pole-benders in these waters. Motor and sail boating are also four-season possibilities, along with scuba diving, windsurfing, jet skiing and water-skiing – with heavy wet suits during winter months. Two paved and three gravel ramps provide lake access to boats and there are numerous sandy launching areas for smaller vessels or jet skis. Swimming, when the weather warms, is also extremely popular. Roughly half the lake's 200-miles of shoreline consists of sandy beaches, with several areas designated "swimmers only."

Birdwatching is another year-round park activity. More than 20 species of ducks have been spotted in the park during fall and spring migrations. Birdwatchers have also spied osprey, bald eagles, great blue herons and egrets, plus hundreds of other species. A visitor center at the park headquarters can provide a birding list as well as literature on the park. The visitor center also displays fossils found in the area, including a tyrannosaurus rex jawbone, and features interpretive exhibits on the geology, history and ecology of the park.

Camping is available at a number of developed and primitive sites around the lake. An extensive network of unpaved roads provides access to most of the southwest shoreline, but the eastern shore and most of the upper half of the lake can only be reached by boat.

Boat and jet ski rentals are available at **Marina del Sur**, 101 South Highway 195 at the state park entrance, ☎ 505/744-5590 or ☎ 505/744-5567, **Rock Canyon Marina**, 3310 Rock Canyon Road, ☎ 505/744-5462, and **Long Point**, Long Point Road, ☎ 505/744-5557.

Fishing licenses and general supplies are available at Marina del Sur and Rock Canyon Marina as well as from several shops in Truth or Consequences.

Desert Bass Fishing Guide Services, PO Box 799, Elephant Butte, NM 87935, ☎ 505/744-5314, offers guided fishing trips on Elephant Butte and other waters in the Southwest.

Para-sailing rides are offered through **Sports Adventure**, at Marina del Sur, ☎ 505/744-5590, and Long Point, ☎ 505/744-5557.

For information, contact Elephant Butte State Park, PO Box 13 Elephant Butte, NM 87935, ☎ 505/744-5421.

Caballo Lake State Park, 14 miles south of Truth or Consequences off Interstate 25, is a good place to get away from the crowds at Elephant Butte. Even though the area does not provide as many services as its northern neighbor, the lake, more than 12 miles long and one mile wide, offers just as much for watersports enthusiasts who bring their own toys. Anglers on the lake routinely hook walleye, catfish and bass. There is also a popular fishing area below the dam where tall cottonwoods shade the river. Take exit 59 off Interstate 25 to reach the visitor center and marina on the west side of the lake. Camping is available. For information, ☎ 505/743-3942.

Farther down the Rio Grande, 21 miles south of Truth or Consequences off Interstate 25, **Percha Dam State Park** again widens the river for recreational as well as flood control purposes. Percha Dam is not nearly as large as its relatives upstream, but the park offers a peaceful riverside atmosphere. Anglers cast their lines from the banks, content to fish beneath the tall shade trees lining the river since the reservoir really never widens enough for boating. The riverbanks also provide a number of sandy beaches near picturesque picnic areas. Camping is available. For information, ☎ 505/267-9394.

The **Gila National Forest** has more than 360 miles of sparkling mountain streams, including the **Gila River**. Trout fishing is good to excellent on almost every stream in the area, although certain wilderness sections are closed to fishing to protect the native and endangered Gila trout. Check with the ranger station for information on how to recognize this rare species. Several alpine lakes in the region are stocked with rainbow trout and provide marvelous casting opportunities. **Lake Roberts**, 25 miles north of Silver City just off NM 15 on NM 35, is the most easily accessible. **Snow** and **Wall Lakes** are the most popular backcountry fishing holes. To reach Snow Lake, travel north from Glenwood on US 180 to NM 159, where a right turn leads east into the mountains and through the ghost town of Mogollon. Not far on the other side of the ghost town, NM 159 becomes a dirt road, actually Forest Road 28. Follow it about 10 miles from the end of the pavement until the road forks. Take the right fork, Forest Road 142, leading to the lake. Wall Lake is accessed by traveling north from Winston on NM 52 and then west on NM 59, which terminates at Beaverhead. From there, Forest Road 150 follows a rough 4WD trail to the lake. A Gila National Forest map is essential when traveling backcountry routes.

A section of the **Gila River** between the NM 15 bridge, 25 miles north of Silver City, and near the town of Cliff, 25 miles northwest of Silver City via US 180, is extremely popular in early spring with area river rafters, kayakers and canoers. The runoff period from mid-March through May provides the most reliable water levels, with 750 cubic feet per second about the minimum required to run the river in a raft. Smaller vessels, drafting only two or three inches, can make the trip with the river as low as 200 cfs. This 32-mile stretch usually takes about five days to run, passing through some of the most rugged and scenic country in the Southwest. The river is Class I most of the way, with a few sections of Class II and III rapids to make the trip exciting. The standard takeout point is at the confluence of the river and Turkey Creek. Forest Road 155, via NM 293, comes to an end just below that point. A second takeout option is nine miles downstream at the town of Gila. For information, contact: Gila National Forest, Supervisor's Office, 2610 N. Silver St., Silver City, NM 88061, ☎ 505/388-8301.

Where to Stay & Eat

Accommodations

SOCORRO

Most of Socorro's motels are located on California Street/US 85, the business loop off Interstate 25. Unfortunately, there's not much to get excited about here. Best Western's **Golden Manor**, 507

North California Street, ☎ 505/835-0230 or 800/528-1234, may offer the nicest rooms in town. **Super 8**, 1121 Frontage Road, exit 150 off I-25, ☎ 505/835-4626 or 800/800-8000, and **Motel 6**, exit 147 off I-25, ☎ 505/835-4300, are other options.

Bosque Birdwatchers RV Park, located just outside the wildlife refuge on NM 1, ☎ 505/835-1366, offers RV camping with limited hookups.

TRUTH OR CONSEQUENCES

Despite T or C's past as a resort community and the current popularity of Elephant Butte Lake State Park, all accommodations in the area are pretty basic and fall into the budget-to-moderate range. **Super 8**, 2701 North Date Street, ☎ 505/894-7888 or 800/800-8000, offers the most reliably clean and comfortable rooms in town. At the lake, **Elephant Butte Resort Inn**, NM 195, ☎ 505/744-5431, provides simple contemporary rooms.

More than 100 campsites at Elephant Butte State Park feature RV hookups.

RV'ers may also opt for the **KOA Campground**, 15 miles south of T or C at the junction of Interstate 25 and NM 152, ☎ 505/743-2811. Several pull-through sites with full hookups overlook Caballo Lake.

LAS CRUCES

Las Cruces has more than 30 hotels, motels and RV parks to accommodate every traveler's budget. **Holiday Inn de Las Cruces**, 201 East University, ☎ 505/526-4411, provides the fanciest digs in town. Southwestern architecture, tiled floors and antiques represent Las Cruces' Spanish heritage. After a margarita or two at the patio-style cantina across from the beautifully landscaped indoor pool, it's easy to feel you're relaxing on the porch of some grand villa in the south of Spain.

The **Las Cruces Hilton**, 705 South Telshor Boulevard, ☎ 505/522-4300, offers contemporary luxury in a seven-story hotel, featuring bright airy suites and guest rooms with mini-bars. There is also an attractive pool, exercise/weight room and terrace restaurant.

The newly remodeled **Days Inn**, 2600 South Valley Drive, ☎ 505/526-4441 or 800/DAYS-INN, has nice rooms for travelers on a moderate budget and features an indoor heated pool, sauna and restaurant.

Budget accommodations are available at **Motel 6**, 235 La Posada Lane, ☎ 505/525-1010, or **Budget Inn**, 2255 West Picacho Avenue, ☎ 505/523-0365. Motel 6 features a pool.

Bed and breakfast aficionados should check into **Meson de Mesilla**, 1803 Avenida de Mesilla, ☎ 505/525-9212. This elegant modern adobe features 13 rooms with Victorian furnishings and private baths. A tranquil courtyard and lawn afford good views of the Organ Mountains.

RV travelers will find full hookups and services at **Bob Lily's RV Park**, 301 South Motel Boulevard, ☎ 505/526-3301, or **RV Dock**, 1475 Avenida de Mesilla, ☎ 505/526-8401.

DEMING

Deming offers standard roadside lodging along Interstate 10. **Holiday Inn**, exit 85, ☎ 505/546-2661, provides the nicest rooms in the area. **Motel 6**, Interstate 10 and Motel Drive, ☎ 505/546-2623, is probably the least expensive.

LORDSBURG

Lordsburg motels cater largely to travelers on Interstate 10. Two Best Westerns, **American Motor Inn**, 944 East Railroad Avenue, ☎ 505/542-3591, and **Skies Inn**, 1303 South Main, ☎ 505/542-8003, offer the most agreeable rooms in town. Less expensive accommodations are found at **Budget Inn**, 816 East Motel Boulevard, ☎ 505/542-3567.

A handful of roadside diners and fast food joints line the Interstate.

SILVER CITY

If you're visiting Silver City to experience its Old West mining town atmosphere, you'll want to reserve a room downtown at the historic **Palace Hotel**, 106 West Broadway, ☎ 505/388-1811. Established in 1882, this Victorian inn was the finest of its day. Completely restored to its original elegance, it remains the fanciest digs in town. In traditional European style, 22 guest rooms range from doubles with shared bath down-the-hall to three-room suites with full private baths. All rooms are decorated with authentic 19th-century furniture and many feature elegant four-poster beds. There is a skylit garden room on the top floor, a game room with pool and poker tables, and a small library. A continental breakfast is included in the standard room rate.

A number of roadside motels line US 180 as it passes through Silver City. Moderate accommodations can be found at **Super 8,** 1121 East US 180, ☎ 505/388-1983 or 800/800-8000. Less expensive rooms are available at the **Drifter Motel,** 711 Silver Heights (junction of US 180 and NM 90), ☎ 505/538-2916, or across the street at **Copper Manor,** (same owners and phone numbers as Drifter). Since 1959, **Bear Mountain Guest Ranch,** 505/538-2538, has been the first choice of outdoor enthusiasts. The ranch's more than 160 acres offer wonderful hiking, biking and birdwatching opportunities, and the innkeepers often lead informative wildlife, archaeology and plant-identification tours on the property. A two-story ranch house and several adjacent cottages provide 15 guest rooms with beautiful wood floors, French windows and stone fireplaces. Since guests are expected to enjoy the numerous outdoor activities available on the ranch, there are no TVs in the rooms. A hearty ranch breakfast (included) is served each morning. Lunch and dinner are also available in the main house or a picnic lunch can be provided by the kitchen staff. To reach the ranch, go west on US 180 about half a mile from downtown, then turn right on Alabama, which becomes Cottage San Road. Three miles down the road, just past the first cattle guard, turn left on Bear Mountain Road. Continue half a mile to the Ranch.

Sapillo Crossing Guest Ranch, junction of NM 15 and NM 35, ☎ 505/536-3206, offers the best access to the hiking, biking, and fishing opportunities of Gila National Forest, located as it is within the actual forest boundary, about halfway between Silver City and Gila Cliff Dwelling National Monument. The Outlaw Bunkhouse features 16 rooms, half with queen-sized beds and half with two longboy twin beds. All rooms represent the true rustic atmosphere of an Old West ranch. There are no phones or TVs. Guests are served a bountiful country breakfast in the White Buffalo Lodge, which also features a dry goods store, tack shop and recreation room. Evenings find guests slurping coffee around an authentic cowboy campfire, where on Friday nights country/western singers provide entertainment for starlight dancing or plain old relaxing. Sapillo Crossing also offers a horse barn, and wrangler Tom Steel will lead groups on backcountry rides extending from a half-day to three days. Call ☎ 505/536-3209 for reservations. Guests may also bring their own mounts since the ranch has numerous fenced pastures and plenty of room in the barn.

RV travelers in the area should head for **Silver City KOA**, 11824 US 180, about five miles east of town, ☎ 505/388-3351. Pull-through sites with full hookups are available year-round.

GLENWOOD

Los Olmos Guest Ranch, ☎ 505/539-2311, is really the only place to stay in Glenwood. A quaint bed and breakfast, the ranch offers 14 stone cabins picturesquely situated on eight acres under sprawling oak and elm trees. All cabins feature cozy fireplaces and some sleep up to six people. Each morning, guests are treated to a chuckwagon-style breakfast in the ranch's main lodge.

Restaurants

SOCORRO

A number of fast food joints line California Street and, regrettably, their billboards line Interstate 25 for miles in either direction. **Val Verde Steak House**, 203 Manzanares Avenue, ☎ 505/835-3380, offers steaks, seafood and southwestern dishes in a fine dining atmosphere. The restaurant is located in the historic 1919 Val Verde Hotel, listed in the National Register of Historic Places.

Good New Mexican food with a new-age flair is available at **Coyote Moon Café**, five miles north of town, exit 156 off I-25, ☎ 505/835-2536. Aside from the familiar tacos, enchiladas and such, several vegetarian dishes are available, including a truly unique green-chili salad. The famous **Owl Bar & Café**, nine miles south of Socorro, is the only thing of interest in the little town of San Antonio just off I-25. If you're passing through on the way to Bosque del Apache, it is on the left at the intersection of US 380 and NM 1. Stop in for a "best-in-the-world" green-chili cheeseburger and an order of fries.

TRUTH OR CONSEQUENCES

For the most part, T or C restaurants offer the typical highway diner and fast food fare. **Damsite Restaurant**, Englestar Route, ☎ 505/894-2073, is a better alternative. Located six miles north of town in an old adobe overlooking Elephant Butte Lake, the restaurant serves steaks, fish and Mexican food along with some of the best sunsets in the area. In town, **La Cocina**, 220 North Date, ☎ 505/894-6499, serves good Mexican food. **Los Arcos**, 1400 North Date, ☎ 505/894-2600, serves good steaks and seafood.

LAS CRUCES

Of more than 100 restaurants in the Las Cruces area, **La Posta de Mesilla**, on the plaza in Mesilla, ☎ 505/524-3524, is the most famous. Located in the old Butterfield Stage Station, this restaurant features tacos, tamales, burritos and rellenos in a 300-year-old building with exotic plants and caged birds. La Posta has been featured in countless national magazines and has been a favorite local eatery for more than 50 years.

The **Double Eagle**, on the plaza in Mesilla, ☎ 505/523-6700, offers the finest dining in the valley. Duck à l'orange, quail, lamb chops and swordfish are served in an elegantly restored adobe building that is listed on the National Register of Historic Places.

Nabe's Coffee Bar and Newsstand, 2001 East Lohman, ☎ 505/523-9339, offers a light menu of pastries, soups, sandwiches and salads, as well as cappuccinos, lattes and decadent desserts. Nabe's is open from 7 AM to midnight.

DEMING

Visitors dining in Deming can't be too picky. The customary fast food joints and locally owned roadside cafés line the Interstate 10 business spur through town. **Si Señor**, corner of Pine and Silver Streets, ☎ 505/546-3938, serves a good Mexican breakfast, lunch and dinner.

SILVER CITY

Dining in Silver City is somewhat limited. There are, of course, a number of fast food joints and roadside diners along US 180 and NM 90. Those looking for a little more should try **Jalisco Café**, 103 South Bullard, ☎ 505/388-2060. Using fresh ingredients daily, Jalisco's serves the best Mexican food in the area and their tamales and burritos are widely heralded.

The Red Barn Family Steakhouse and Lounge, in the Copper Manor Complex, US 180 East, ☎ 505/538-5666, offers a full menu of steaks, chicken and seafood, as well as a salad bar. For fine dining in the area, drive seven miles north of town to Pinos Altos via NM 15. The **Buckhorn Saloon,** next to the old opera house, ☎ 505/538-9911, resides in a beautifully restored adobe dating to the 1860s. Victorian elegance coupled with huge stone fireplaces and classic Old West charm makes dining here a special experience. Escargots and fried mushrooms whet appetites, while trout, scallops, steaks or pastas are among the expertly prepared main dishes.

Camping

Approximately 90 miles west of Socorro, a small isolated campground at the **Datil Well National Recreation Site** offers several campsites with water, pit toilets, picnic tables and grills in the lush pinon and juniper of the Cibola National Forest. Take US 60 north from Datil less than one mile. Signs to the campground make it easy to find.

Water Canyon Campground, 20 miles west of Socorro via US 60 and FS 235, provides several sites with pit toilets, fire rings and picnic tables.

South of Socorro about 60 miles or 30 miles north of Truth or Consequences, via I-25 and FR 225, **Springtime Campground** is a lovely spot with shelters, picnic tables and pit toilets.

Elephant Butte Lake State Park, seven miles north of Truth or Consequences off Interstate 25, offers more than 200 developed campsites and 100 RV hookups. Most sites have shelters, picnic tables and grills. The park also has several playgrounds, dump stations and modern restrooms with showers. Primitive camping is also permitted around the lake.

Both **Caballo Lake** and **Percha Dam State Parks,** south of T or C off Interstate 25, offer shaded camping areas with picnic tables, grills, restrooms and showers.

Aguirre Spring Campground, 20 miles northeast of Las Cruces via US 70, offers beautiful views out over the Tularosa Basin and 55 sites with picnic tables, grills and pit toilets. There is no water at the campground. Plan to bring your own.

Camping facilities at **Rock Hound State Park,** 15 miles southeast of Deming via NM 11 and NM 141, include 29 campsites with shelters tables and water as well as a visitor center, restroom and shower. A number of sites feature RV hookups. Located near Columbus, just three miles from the Mexican border, **Pancho Villa State Park** offers 90 campsites with shelters, tables, water and RV hookups. There is also a dump station, restroom and shower, as well as a visitor center.

The **Gila National Forest** provides 18 developed campgrounds, seven of which have drinking water and toilets. **Scorpion Campground** is the closest to the Gila Cliff Dwellings National Monument, offering 20 sites with picnic tables, grills and pit toilets. During summer, drinking water and flush toilets are available. There are no trash cans at any of the national forest campgrounds. Be prepared to pack out your garbage.

City of Rocks State Park, 30 miles south of Silver City via US 180 and NM 61, features 52 sites with picnic tables, grills and water. Restrooms and showers are available in the park.

Northwest New Mexico

The extreme northwestern part of New Mexico at first appears to be nothing more than sandstone and scrub grass, mostly flat terrain, dry, rocky, and hot. Closer inspection reveals multi-colored rock formations sprouting from desert-like flats, gnarled juniper and pinyon trees, few people, and thousands of acres of rugged, undisturbed nature. The region encompasses part of the vast Navajo Reservation, which will be covered as a single entity in a later chapter. Part of this corner of the state is not Navajo land, but includes a rich mix of cultural influences; this is the region we are concerned with here. Modern and ancient Hispanic cultures are strong forces in this region and, although it is not strictly Navajo Indian land, many Navajo people and other Indians do continue to live here. The New Mexico state tourism office has dubbed the area "Indian Country." It includes reservation lands belonging to Zuni, Acoma, Laguna, and Ramah Navajo tribes. All share a land that has revealed incredible archaeological treasures and continues to add the seasoning of ancient history to a fine mix of sometimes subtle natural beauty and adventurous opportunities.

Four rivers flow into the San Juan River in this area. The Pine and Piedra flow into the San Juan at Navajo Lake and near Farmington the La Plata and Animas empty into it, all flowing toward Utah. Other thirsty streams and dry river beds fill only during storms, rising dramatically and suddenly in flashes of thunder and lightning, only to drain abruptly when the sun returns, which it does reliably. Then the cracked and parched earth returns to grassland – spiky tufts clinging to life under the harsh, purifying sun.

To the south, the remnants of an ancient volcano break the flat horizon with disquieting lava tubes and an improbable ice cave at the El Malpais National Recreation Area. The Bisti Badlands, south of Farmington, offer otherworldly forms, jagged towers and mushroom-shaped rock sentinels guarding the fossilized remains of dinosaurs and ancient sea-bed life.

Aside from the readily apparent Navajo influence here, Apache and Pueblo tribes continue to leave marks on the striated, multi-hued mesas and buttes. Many ancient dwellings are still buried under sands swept by time. Other ancient and modern structures are visible and can be visited. The Anasazi, in particular, have left their mark here, and the ruins of these community-centered people are among the very best preserved of the entire Southwest. Even today, modern Indians follow largely isolated rural lifestyles, coming into the area's two major towns, Gallup and Farmington, only to do their business. They then return to their independent, family-centered, agrarian ways that have endured for centuries amidst the hot, dusty windswept prairies and box canyons.

Northwest New Mexico

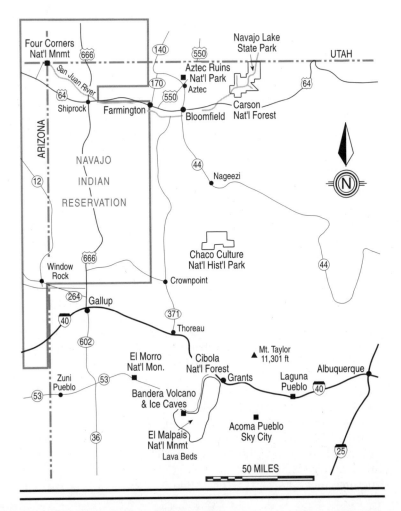

The areas covered in this chapter range in elevation from 5,000 to 8,000 feet. If you're coming from lower elevations, expect to tire easily the first few days and exercise special caution when exploring the outdoors until your body adjusts to the lowered oxygen level in the air.

The arid climate makes dehydration a possibility. If you're going to partake in outdoor summer activities, particularly hiking or backpacking, make sure you have adequate water supplies. Winters can be rough, too, with occasional heavy snows and cold weather. You will need warm layered clothing.

Touring

The suggested route to follow begins west of Albuquerque, on Interstate 40, working westward to Gallup, and then north through Chaco Canyon, Bisti Badlands, Farmington, and Aztec toward the Colorado state line. As for exploring modern Indian pueblos, not federally regulated ruin sites, remember that these are private properties and you are a guest. Many pueblos consider it sacrilegious to record a religious dance on film, or even to photograph parts of the village. Always ask at the tribal office before taking photographs or video recordings. You may be asked to pay a fee for the privilege, or your request may be refused. Pay special attention to whether you are intruding on pueblo residents' privacy. If a site is marked as being off-limits, don't test the system. Exploring a kiva in any pueblo village is also forbidden.

Northwest New Mexico encompasses a corner of the large Navajo Reservation. For complete information on these areas see below under The Navajo Reservation & Hopiland.

Laguna Pueblo

This small, mostly nondescript, modern pueblo community comprised of several small villages is approximately 25 miles east of Grants, close to exit 114 on I-40. There's not much to see here except for the **San Jose de Laguna Mission Church**, which was built in 1699 by the Spanish. Inside the church are some elaborate decorative touches, including a hand-carved pine altar and large religious murals.

For information, contact **Laguna Pueblo**, PO Box 194, Laguna NM 87026, ☎ 505/552-6654.

Acoma Pueblo

One of the most unusual and telling Indian sites in all the Southwest is the Acoma Pueblo. According to Acoma legend, this unusual cliff-top community, called the Sky City, which is still occupied at least part-time by a dozen families, has been here for 1,400 years. This would make it older than many Anasazi ruins, although other experts estimate the age of the original mortar and adobe structures to be only 900-1,000 years old. Regardless of the actual dates, the Acoma community is one of the oldest in North America and functions to this day without running water or electricity. At first, the absence of modern touches may make you feel far removed from trivial cares, although your blissful reverie atop the cliffs might be interrupted by a resident cranking up a noisy generator so the family can watch *Beavis and Butthead* on TV.

The pueblo's distinctive location, high on a steep, rocky outcrop, suggests a fear of invasion that these early settlers lived with, lending veracity to the theory that warfare, not drought and famine, was a primary cause for the dispersion of the Anasazi.

The only way to see the pueblo today is on a guided tour led by a tribal member. You are driven up the only road to the site, at the top of the 357-foot mesa, a narrow track built by a movie company in the 1960s. For thousands of years before the road was built, the only access to the city was by precipitous footpaths carved into the soft sandstone cliffs.

In the Sky City narrow streets are lined with crooked rows of multi-story adobe houses. There is an ancient cemetery and the impressive **San Esteban del Rey Mission**. The church was built with walls nine feet thick, according to the instructions of the Spanish governor of New Mexico in 1640, and is still in use today. Outside, potters and jewelers offer their wares on folding tables, while below the panoramic view of the valley unfolds. Mount Taylor, capped in snow, is far to the north. Enchanted Mesa, another large rock outcrop rising from the flat, sandy ground and the original site of the pueblo, is closer, to the northeast. Surrounded by corn and bean fields, it offers a view little changed from the earliest days of occupation. After an hour or so at Acoma, you can ride back to the small museum and Visitor Center at the base of the mesa, or walk down a steep, cramped, well-worn track, with steps and hand holds chiseled out of the vertical rock walls.

A somewhat jarring modern accompaniment to the ancient pueblo is a nearby bingo hall featuring electronic video gambling.

The Acoma Pueblo is 12 miles south of I-40, off Exit 102. Signs lead to the site. For information, contact **Acoma Tourist Visitor Center**, PO Box 309, Acoma, NM 87034, ☎ 505/252-1139 or 800/747-0181.

El Malpais National Monument

This 262,000-acre valley, covered in black lava rock, was declared a National Monument in 1988. The entrance to the park is 18 miles southeast of Grants on NM 117. The National Monument includes the area to the south and west of Grants.

The name of this place means "badlands" in Spanish, and the lava rock that characterizes the landscape today is the result of several thousand years of geological activity generated by live volcanoes. The molten lava hardened into the sharp rocks you see today, among which are all sorts of geological oddities, including natural bridges, arches, sandstone cliffs, and lava caves. Also found throughout the region are numerous Anasazi ruins.

Places of interest here include the **Sandstone Bluffs Overlook**, 10 miles south of I-40 on NM 17, and seven miles farther south on NM 17 is **La Ventana**, a graceful sandstone arch that is the largest such formation in New Mexico.

The **West Malpais Wilderness** and the **Chain of Craters** area are remote parts of the park where you can see giant lava tubes, including one 17 miles long, and wildlife such as mule deer and wild turkeys.

For information, contact the **Bureau of Land Management/National Park Service El Malpais Information Center**, 620 East Santa Fe Street, Grants, NM 87020, ☎ 505/285-5406, or the Grants Chamber of Commerce (see below, under Grants).

Grants

Grants was a big uranium boom town not so long ago, but today it's just another stop on the interstate, featuring chain motels and fast food. The **New Mexico Museum of Mining** is located here, at 100 Iron Street, Grants, NM 87020, ☎ 505/287-4802, in the same building as the Chamber of Commerce. This is the only museum in the world dedicated to uranium mining. You can take an elevator down into the mine shaft that once provided uranium ore for atomic weapons and power plants. After the tour of the mine, there are dioramas and interpretive exhibits outlining the geological and mining history of the region, with an outline of the economy from the time of the Anasazi through the period when Grants was known as the "Carrot Capital of the World," followed by the brief uranium mining boom days. When you're finished touring the museum you can get area-wide information from the Chamber of Commerce.

For information, contact **Grants/Cibola County Chamber of Commerce,** PO Box 297, Grants, NM 87020, ☎ 505/287-4802, or 800/748-2142.

El Morro National Monument

El Morro was America's first National Monument, dedicated in 1906 by President Theodore Roosevelt. It is 43 miles southwest of Grants, via NM 53, or 56 miles southeast of Gallup via NM 32 and NM 53. Carved into the 1,278-acre monument's centerpiece, the 200-foot-tall Inscription Rock, are centuries-old petroglyphs and the names and messages of travellers who passed this way between 1605 and 1904. The oldest rock carvings are attributed to ancestors of today's Zunis, possibly from the time when the mesa top was inhabited by as many as 1,500 people. The village here was abandoned around 1400, but the etched carvings of animals, hand prints, and abstract designs remain, although their meanings are not known. Spanish explorers were the next known visitors to the area, and one of the names carved is that of Don Juan de Onate, the first Spanish colonizer of New Mexico, dated 1605. As late as 1774, Spanish friars, soldiers, and travellers scratched their names into the rock, probably when they stopped here to enjoy the rare, precious water they found in a rock pool kept filled with run-off from the mesa above. The last set of names are those of US soldiers who surveyed this area in the mid-nineteenth century after it was acquired from Mexico.

Atop the bluff are the ruins of two Zuni pueblos and, at its base, accessed by an easy half-mile trail, are the inscribed names and artwork, as well as the natural water hole that attracted Indians, Spanish explorers, and Anglo soldiers so long ago. A Visitor Center includes a small museum featuring artifacts from pueblo history, and there are picnic areas and a campground close by.

For information, contact **El Morro National Monument**, Ramah, NM 87321, ☎ 505/783-4226.

Bandera Crater & Ice Cave

This site, 25 miles south of Grants on NM 53, contains a privately owned volcano. You can hike to the top of the cone and peek inside, then visit a refreshingly cool volcanic sink where water that flowed through collapsed lava tubes has remained frozen for hundreds of thousands of years, thanks to the insulation of lava rock.

The early ranchers who discovered the ice cave were able to store food in it and, because of the constant 31° temperature, the collapsed lava tube also provided a cool place to escape the parching heat of the surrounding desert badlands.

You can walk into the cave and see the translucent green ice that survives year-round, even during oppressively hot summers.

Next to the ice cave is an extinct volcano known as the Bandera Crater, a 1,000-foot-deep cone that is believed to have blown its top more than 5,000 years ago. A maintained trail to the crater rim provides a panoramic view of the immense lava fields that remain from the volcano's active days. Also at the site is a trading post, snack bar, and picnic area.

For information on Bandera Crater and Ice Cave, ☎ 505/783-4303.

Zuni Pueblo

Nearly 8,000 Zunis live here at the largest pueblo community in New Mexico. The town of Zuni, situated 35 miles south of Gallup on NM 53, looks like many small towns in these parts. Its dusty, dirt streets and simple frame houses belie the ancient traditions that continue to exist in the revered presence of a rainmaker, various war gods, and a sun priest, who runs sacred solstice ceremonies,

At the same time, Catholicism is a significant influence woven into this world view that combines old and new. In the 360-year-old mission church here, **Our Lady of Guadalupe**, there is an altar, a statue of Our Lady of Guadalupe, and a crucifix. But these are flanked by huge, shaggy, mounted bison heads. On the inside of the six-foot-thick walls of the church are 50-foot murals depicting the Zuni religious cycle. These include 24 life-size, masked kachinas, representing ancestral spirits who bring rain, ripen corn, make hunting successful, and bestow happiness and prosperity, among other desirable circumstances.

The church had been abandoned in the mid-1800s. Renovations began in 1966 and were completed in 1972. That same year, the murals were started by Zuni artist Alex Seowtewa. The artist, who now works with his sons Kenneth and Edward, hopes the ongoing, part-federally sponsored project to return the church to its original 19th-century condition will be completed before the end of the decade. The goal is to preserve the vibrant Zuni culture that traces its roots to the ancient Anasazi and even farther back in time. Visitors who have stopped here to admire the work have included Mother Teresa and the late Jacqueline Onassis. The church is open to the public for tours only on Saturdays. ☎ 505/782-5531 for information.

Outside the church, in the streets of Zuni, the scent of fresh baked bread wafts from traditional clay ovens called *hornos*. Many of the foundations below modest-looking homes have been here for 500 years or longer.

Zuni crafts are highly regarded. Artisans are known for silver inlay jewelry and intricate fetishes that represent animals and birds thought to bring numerous varieties of good luck. Arts and crafts are available from local shops or from the tribal-owned Pueblo of Zuni Arts and Crafts Center, ☎ 505/782-5531.

Permission from tribal authorities is needed to visit two local historic sites: the ancient ruins at the village of **Hawikuh**, the original townsite, 12 miles south of present-day Zuni, and the **Village of the Great Kivas**, which contains three unexcavated pueblos 19 miles north of town.

For information, contact **Zuni Pueblo**, PO Box 369, Zuni, NM 87327, ☎ 505/782-4481.

Gallup

Gallup is a big city (population 20,000) to the rural Navajos and other Indians who do business here, but it is not, shall we say, the jewel of the Southwest. It does have a downtown **National Historic District** consisting of around 20 buildings, but the main allure for travellers is probably its nearly 2,000 motel rooms, many of them left over from the days when Route 66, which passes through here, was the main route connecting Chicago with the Southwest and ultimately the Pacific Ocean. It also has close to 50 restaurants, though probably few that you would travel out of your way to reach. Gallup also appeals to Navajos who come here to drink (alcohol consumption is prohibited on the reservation, although changes in this policy are under consideration). Because so many Indians do come through here, it's a good place to shop for Indian jewelry and crafts. It is also close to a lot of beautiful and interesting places, including El Morro National Monument and Bandera Volcano and Ice Caves. An outdoor **Indian market**, held downtown on Saturdays, is a good place to buy authentic crafts directly from Navajo and Zuni artisans. If you do end up spending a night here, try to visit the **Red Mesa Arts Center**, 105 West Hill Street, Gallup, ☎ 505/722-4209. It's a community-run center for promoting regional arts.

For additional information, contact **Gallup-McKinley County Chamber of Commerce**, PO Box 1395, Gallup, NM 87305, ☎ 505/722-2228, or **Gallup Convention & Visitors Bureau**, PO Box 600, Gallup, NM ☎ 505/863-3841 or 800/242-4282.

Chaco Canyon

Chaco Canyon was once the center of a far-flung trading universe that stretched throughout the Southwest and all the way to Mexico. Situated between two long, dusty, rutted dirt roads, it was at one time perhaps the primary Anasazi community. Today it is a federally protected site that offers some of the most sophisticated ruins and least compromised ancient environments anywhere in the Southwest.

Chaco is still remote and inaccessible, 72 miles southeast of Farmington, 95 miles south of Durango, and 115 miles northwest of Santa Fe. The nearest town is tiny Bloomfield, 60 miles north, where you can find gas, food and not much else.

There are no food, gas, lodging or repair services at the park. The closest services are 24 miles north, on NM 44 at Blanco or Nageezi, or 20 miles south at Seven Lakes, where you can find gas, tire repairs, and a telephone.

The northerly entry road to Chaco Canyon veers south for 24 miles from Blanco or Nageezi, southeast of Farmington. The southerly road connects with Grants, which is 80 miles south of the park.

Both entries are over rugged dirt tracks that turn to impassable mud in wet weather. Even under the best conditions, the roads will test the springs and shocks in your car as you bounce over ruts and washboard tracks. The difficult condition of these roads is probably the main reason why Chaco is not completely overrun with tourists. In addition, park facilities are modest, consisting of a small museum, a water spigot, cold water bathrooms, and a shadeless campground nestled among sandstone outcrops, complete with petroglyphs. It takes a few hours just to drive here off the main roads. The following are the only routes into Chaco Canyon.

❑ Travel north from Crownpoint (north of I-40) on NM 371 for 4½ miles to Tribal Route 9. Go east 13½ miles to NM 57 and 20 miles north on a very bad road to the park.

❑ Travel south for 16 miles from Blanco on NM 57 to the intersection with NM 45, and then another eight miles or so to Chaco.

❑ Travel 24 miles south on NM 45 from NM 44 at Nageezi.

In good weather these roads are not beyond the capability of most passenger cars, but it is always wise to phone the park, ☎ 505/988-6716 or 505/988-6727, for updated reports. Do not attempt these roads in wet weather, nor without a full tank of gas, food, and water. You will probably want to spend at least a full day wandering around the short trails to the exceptional ruins or, if you want to stay for longer hikes, you will need to be prepared to camp out. Bring your own firewood; none is available at the park. Wood gathering is prohibited, and it does tend to get cold at 6,200 feet. Temperatures are often below freezing in winter and in the 50's during summer.

At all times in the park, remember that it was established to preserve and protect outstanding archaeological sites for everyone to enjoy. Stay on designated trails and follow the signs. Do not walk on or climb any walls. Do not enter rooms off the trail. Park only in developed lots. Leave all artifacts, including even the smallest pottery shards, where you found them. The Archaeological Resources Protection Act of 1979 is strictly enforced. Federal penalties can be as severe as a $5,000 fine and five years in jail for disturbing archaeological remains.

Chaco culture flourished between 900 and 1200 AD, and remains of 13 major ruins comprised of more than 2,000 sites have been found in this stark, high desert. The known sites provide evidence of Indian architecture and artifacts, clay pots bearing distinctive black and white geometric designs, and jewelry fash-

ioned of turquoise and obsidian, suggesting the history of a complex community system more evolved than the Mesa Verde cliff
dwellers of neighboring Colorado.

With only simple visitor services available, the big tourist
hordes stay away, which makes a far more personal experience of
the ancient Anasazi possible. This is an acknowledged World Heritage Site, certifying Chaco's cultural and historic significance.

The Visitor Center runs a short film about the lives of the area's
ancient inhabitants, along with exhibits of pots, ornamental turquoise objects, and tools recovered from the ruins. Trail maps are
available, along with required backcountry permits, which are free.
A 10-mile loop road leads to various ruin sites around the mile-
wide canyon, now a rocky, dusty desert, but once an urban hub for
the Anasazi.

Evidence of religious beliefs is found in numerous petroglyphs
and fading, colorfully tinted drawings, called pictographs, emblazoned on stones believed to mark ceremonial spots. Atop the
Penasco Blanco Ruins, a pictograph of a star, a crescent moon, and
a hand print was discovered in 1972 beneath a 20-foot-high preci-
pice. Scientists think the long-concealed painting illustrates a su-
pernova that occurred in 1054 A.D. – also chronicled by Chinese
astronomers who reported its visibility in daylight for two years.
At **Fajada Butte,** a sizable spiral is carved into the sandstone, 400
feet over the bottom of the canyon. Three giant rocks rest against
the engraved surface and for approximately 1,000 years, until the
stone slabs recently moved almost imperceptibly, a thin beacon of
sunshine entered the space between the rocks and illuminated the
petroglyph exactly at noon on the summer solstice.

Archaeologists are not in complete agreement about the fate of
these skilled people. Some say too much wood was used to con-
struct roof beams and rafters for elaborate, multi-story dwellings.
Depleted of tress, the soil could no longer hold water and was
washed away, making it impossible to grow life-sustaining crops.
This could have led to the swift degeneration of Chaco culture and
of other nearby related Indian communities. Scrub grass that may
have remained was probably eaten by domestic livestock brought
into the area by white men who began to settle here in the late
1870s, decimating the remnants of ground cover. Others believe
that warfare led to their disappearance. Now, the ancient voices are
stilled and only occasional breezes sing above parched desert.
Chacoan culture was at its most highly evolved levels around 1,000
years ago, with the development of complex, two- and three-story
buildings. During the following 100 years the burgeoning canyon
community expanded to include upwards of 400 settlements, sup-
porting a population of 5,000-10,000 people, and fourth and fifth

stories were added to existing dwellings. Yet, within only another 200 years, during the 1300s, Chaco Canyon had been abandoned.

Europeans were building stained-glass basilicas while these primitive Indians in yucca-fiber sandals were living in remote Chaco Canyon, but no other North American clan left such detailed masonry construction, sophisticated irrigation schemes, or complicated networks of trade highways. Seventy-five neighborhoods have been conclusively linked to Chaco Canyon, extending over approximately 1,200 miles of precisely arranged trade routes fanning out like spokes of a wheel, each separated by no more than a day's travel.

In the ruins, seeds buried in pots and preserved in the bone dry climate are identical to types of beans, corn, and squash that originated in Mexico. Characteristic black and white pottery, turquoise, chalcedony, obsidian, shell artifacts, and yucca fiber clothing and baskets strongly imply connections with far away populations in Mexico and Central America.

Pueblo Bonito, dating from 900-1200 A.D., is the biggest and most impressive ruin in Chaco Canyon. It comprises some 800 rooms layered four stories high and surrounding 37 kivas, which are circular pits that were probably the sites of gatherings or religious observances. This single ruin could have accommodated several hundred people at one time. Most structures here were remodeled at various times and increasingly sophisticated layers were added to previous crude designs. These techniques may be observed at Casa Rinconada, Chetro Ketl, Pueblo del Arroyo and Pueblo Alto, which are smaller ruins around the perimeter of the loop road. Even smaller ruin sites may be reached by following easy hiking trails of one-half to five miles.

Chacoans mastered construction of free-standing masonry walls. They had no metal tools nor draft animals, not even wheels for transporting building materials. They had no written language, so only the carvings and drawings remain to tell their story. Yet for 300 years this was the nucleus of an expansive economic, spiritual, and cultural community spread over 30,000 square miles. Then the Chacoans vanished.

For information, contact **Bloomfield Chamber of Commerce**, 224 West Broadway, Bloomfield, NM 87413-5903, ☎ 505/632-0880, or **Chaco Canyon Park Superintendent**, Star Route 4, Box 6500, Bloomfield, NM 87413, ☎ 505/632-2278.

Farmington

Farmington is among the biggest towns in the Four Corners, with a population of 34,000. It is one of the main trade centers for the Navajo Nation and serves as a regional center for oil, gas, and coal exploration. Though it is not the most scenic or unusual place, it does have a number of motels, fast-food restaurants, and gas stations, which makes it a possibility for a pit stop or an overnight stay. There are a few interesting places to visit here.

Farmington Museum, 302 North Orchard, Farmington, ☎ 505/599-1174, has exhibits detailing the area's various cultures, history, and environment, including a replica of a 1930s era trading post, as well as hands-on exhibits for children.

B-Square Ranch, 3901 Bloomfield Highway, Farmington, is a 12,000-acre ranch, wildlife preserve, and experimental farm owned by the family of a former Governor of New Mexico, Tom Bolack. Tours of a collection of mounted animals from all over the world (☎ 505/325-4275), or of an electro-mechanical museum (☎ 505/325-7873) featuring old telephone, farm and electrical equipment, are by appointment only.

Angel Peak Recreational Area, 15 miles south of Bloomfield on NM 44, offers a 40-million-year-old geological formation surrounded by silent, pastel-shaded, eroded badlands. Angel Peak is the dwelling place of "sacred ones" to the Navajo people, and facilities include camping and picnic sites. No water or other services are available, and the last six miles of the road are gravel and dirt.

Bisti Wilderness, 36 miles south of Farmington on NM 371, is accessed by seven miles of dirt roads on the east side of the highway. This is one of the weirdest landscapes in the Southwest. The mushroom-shaped rocks, spires, petrified wood, and plant and animal fossils create an otherworldly, remote backcountry. There are hardly ever any people here, just you and the rocks. Wonderful photo possibilities are early in the morning or late in the afternoon, but the area is best avoided in midday heat. The harsh desert climate has eroded shale and sandstone into bizarre hoodoos that look something like toadstools. The hoodoos occupy a 4,000-acre area of dry, deep arroyos that were once home to dinosaurs. There are no maintained trails through this sandy wilderness and it's easy to get lost in here. Make sure you have plenty of drinking water and pay attention to where you're going so you can find your way out; no one else is likely to be anywhere nearby to offer help.

Farmington Aquatic Center, 1151 North Sullivan, Farmington, ☎ 505/599-1167, is a year-round facility with an indoor Olympic-sized pool, one three-meter and two one-meter diving boards, a children's playground and a 150-foot double-loop water slide.

Farmington's **Four Corners Regional Airport** is served by **United Express**, ☎ 505/326-4495 or 800/241-6522, with connections to Durango, Cortez, Denver or Grand Junction, CO; **Mesa Airlines**, ☎ 505/326-3338 or 800/637-2247, with connections to Albuquerque and major New Mexico cities; **America West Express**, ☎ 505/326-4494 or 800/235-9292, with connections to Phoenix, Flagstaff, Bullhead City, Kingman, AZ, or Palm Springs, CA.

Car rentals, including some four-wheel drives, trucks and vans, are available at the airport from **Avis**, ☎ 505/327-9864 or 800/331-1212; **Budget**, ☎ 505/327-7304 or 800/748-2540; **Hertz**, ☎ 505/327-6093 or 800/654-3131; **National**, ☎ 505/327-0215 or 800/227-7368. Also in town, **Ugly Duckling Rent-A-Car**, 2307 East Main, Farmington, ☎ 505/325-4313; **Emergency Rent-A-Car**, 1812 East 20th Street, Farmington, ☎ 505/327-2277; **Enterprise Rent-A-Car**, 627 Industrial Avenue, Farmington, ☎ 505/327-1356 or 800/325-8007.

Twenty-four-hour taxi service is offered by **K.B. Cab Co.**, ☎ 505/325-2999.

For information on weather and road conditions, ☎ 505/325-7547 or 800/432-4269. Additional tourist information is available by tuning to 530 on AM radio, or by contacting the **Farmington Convention & Visitor Bureau**, 203 West Main, Farmington, NM 87401, ☎ 505/326-7602 or 800/448-1240.

Salmon Ruins

Salmon Ruins, ☎ 505/632-2013, is between Farmington and Chaco Canyon, just west of Bloomfield on US 64. A museum here displays artifacts from Chacoan settlements of the 11th century and there are ruins of an 11th- to 13th-century apartment complex here. At the center's Heritage Park you can learn how to fling a dart-like weapon called an "atlatl," used for hunting by the Anasazi before the bow and arrow was introduced. Other displays include life-size replicas of a pit house complex, a Navajo forked-stick hogan, a sweat lodge, as well as Native American structures representing thousands of years of human occupation of the San Juan Valley. There is also an ice-age pond, an archaic sand dunes campsite, Ute and Jicarilla Apache "wickiups" and teepees.

Aztec Ruins National Monument

Travelling east on US 64 to Bloomfield, then eight miles north on NM 44 to the town of Aztec – named an All America City in 1963 and still proudly boasting of that quaint fact – is the Aztec Ruins National Monument and Museum, ☎ 505/334-6174, on US 550, north of Farmington. The ruins here have absolutely nothing to do with the Aztecs from Mexico. This was an Anasazi village at one time, connected by road to Chaco Canyon. Today it is the site of the world's largest reconstructed kiva and a small, easily toured cluster of pueblo ruins. The nice thing about these ruins is their manageable size and their proximity to the highway. Rather than mounting an expedition, you can drive right up to this sight, wander around for an hour or two, and be on your way. Some people enjoy a short visit to the **Aztec Museum & Pioneer Village**, 125 North Main, Aztec, NM 87410, ☎ 505/334-9829. Eleven permanent displays include historic items from San Juan County, and there is an oil and gas exhibit. The Pioneer Village consists of 10 replicas of late 1800s structures, including a jail, school, church and general store.

Aztec is one of those small western towns that was practically deserted for a long time, but is now starting to make a comeback based on tourism. Several galleries and shops may be of interest. You can walk through the entire small downtown area in around 15 minutes.

For additional information, contact **Aztec Chamber of Commerce**, 203 North Main Avenue, Aztec, NM 87410, ☎ 505/334-9551.

Trading Posts

An interesting aspect of northwest New Mexico if you're seeking souvenirs and art is the various trading posts. These have traditionally provided commercial goods to isolated Indian residents from the reservation, often in trade for a rug or a piece of jewelry, which would then be offered for sale. Among the most popular items available are collector's pieces, one-of-a-kind items, Navajo folk art, antique carvings, sand paintings, gourd rattles, prayer fans, herbs and sweet grass used in traditional ceremonies, jewelry, pottery, and rugs.

NORTHWESTERN NEW MEXICO
TRADING POSTS & PAWN SHOPS

Tanner's Indian Arts, 1000 West US 66, Grants, NM 87020
☎ 505/863-6017.

Navajo Trading Company, 232 West US 66, Gallup, NM 87305,
☎ 505/863-6131.

Richardson's Cash Pawn, 222 West US 66, Gallup, NM 87503,
☎ 505/722-4762.

Tobe Turpin's Indian Trading Company, 1710 West 2nd, Gallup, NM
87305, ☎ 505/722-3806.

Indian America, 3310-30 East US 66, Gallup, NM 87301, ☎ 505/
722-4431 or 800/748-1912.

Zuni Craftsmen Cooperative (located on West NM 53 in Zuni
Pueblo), PO Box 426, Zuni, NM 87327, ☎ 505/782-4425.

Jewel Box Pawn Shop, 2400 West Main, Farmington, NM 87401,
☎ 505/325-5693.

Navajo Trading Company, 126 East Main, Farmington, ☎ 505/325-
1685.

San Juan Silver & Pawn, 200 West Main, Farmington, ☎ 505/325-
7144.

The Indian Den, 211 West Main, Farmington, ☎ 505/325-7144.

Fifth Generation Trading Company, 232 West Broadway, Farmington, NM, ☎ 505/326-3211.

Bob French's Navajo Rugs (15 miles west of Farmington on US 64),
PO Box 815, Waterflow, NM 87421, ☎ 505/598-5621.

Hogback Trading Company (20 miles west of Farmington), 3221 US
64, Waterflow, NM 87421, ☎ 505/598-5154.

Big Rock Trading Post, 3761 US 64, Waterflow, NM, ☎ 505/598-
5184.

Thomas Harley Trading Company, 103 South Main Avenue, Aztec,
NM, ☎ 505/334-8738.

Trading posts are found virtually all over northwest New Mexico and, of course, the big spot for this sort of stuff is trendy Santa
Fe; smart shoppers browse through this area too, often finding the
same items offered at a fraction of the price. Of course, it is also easy
to get ripped-off at one of these places. Unless you know exactly
what you're looking for, the best insurance is to shop with reputable dealers.

Aside from trading posts, there are many pawn shops in the
area that play a special role in the region's jewelry-driven economy.
Here you'll find something other than the usual array of pawn shop
goods such as stereos, musical instruments, and guns. Instead,
these shops are filled with jewelry, sculpture, and sometimes even
intricate silver horse gear. Items taken in pawn are generally

authentic and of unusual value, including squash blossom neck-laces, belts, and wide cuff bracelets with large turquoise stones.

INFORMATION SOURCES

For specialized maps and brochures, contact these sources:

BLM Maps: Intermediate Scale Maps, PO Box 1449, Santa Fe, NM 87504, ☎ 505/988-6000.

City Maps, County Maps, and State Highway Maps: New Mexico State Highway and Transportation Department, 1120 Cerrillos Road, Santa Fe, NM 87501, ☎ 505/827-5412.

National Forest Wilderness Maps: USDA Forest Service Office, 517 Gold SW, Albuquerque, NM 87102, ☎ 505/842-3292.

State Parks Brochure: State Parks & Recreation Division, NM Natural Resources Department, PO Box 1147, Santa Fe, NM 87504, ☎ 505/827-7465.

Topographic Maps: US Geological Survey Distribution Center, Federal Center, Building 41, Denver, CO 80225, ☎ 303/234-3832.

Adventures

On Foot

This area is not particularly known for its hiking trails, but there are a few good ones. Numerous hiking trails can be found in the vicinity of Mount Taylor, an extinct volcano northeast of Grants, off NM 547. **Gooseberry Springs Trail** leads to the top of the 11,300-foot mountain. In the same area, south of Grants, you can hike across the lava fields in **El Malpais National Monument** or along the length of the **Big Lava Tube**. Bring water and forget about these hikes in summer. It's way too hot then. The best times are spring and fall.

Trails are often uneven and steep. Make all necessary preparations before starting out. Extended exposure during extreme weather can be dangerous. Carry first aid gear. Brief, violent summer thunderstorms or sudden winter snowstorms are always a possibility. Plan ahead for all contingencies. Help is likely to be far away.

An interesting hike is a 7½-mile trail once used as a thorough-fare between Zuni and Acoma pueblos. The trailhead is 18 miles south of I-40 on NM 53. Before you set out, it's a good idea to get a trail map from the BLM/Park Service office in Grants (see above, under Grants). Extremely sharp lava rocks can cut your feet right through your shoes, and the high iron content of the rocks makes compass readings unreliable. Leave word with the ranger station about your intended route, in case something goes wrong, or you might end up another fossil before you're found.

El Morro National Monument includes a steep two-mile, one-way trail to the mesa top and ruins. The trail is only open from April to December.

McGaffey Recreation Area, 15 miles east of Gallup on I-40, then 10 miles south on NM 400, offers several hiking trails through ponderosa pines and around the mesa. **Strawberry Patch Trail** starts at the base of the campground, south of McGaffey Lake, and leads to a fire tower with panoramic views of the area. For information, contact the Cibola National Forest Office (see below, under In Snow).

Chaco Canyon National Historical Park has eight self-guiding trails to major ruins on the canyon floor. Four backcountry trails lead from the canyon to more remote sites. Registration at the backcountry trailheads is required. Camping and fires are not permitted. All trails and ruins are closed from sunset to sunrise.

Extremely rugged hiking trails are found in the **De-Na-Zin Wilderness**, south of Farmington on NM 371 to the intersection of County Road 7500 East. This is BLM land so you can camp here for free, but there are no services, no trees, and there is no water. For information, contact the local office of the BLM, 1235 La Plata Highway, Farmington, NM 87401, ☎ 505/327-5344.

Angel Peak and **Bisti Badlands** offer rugged hiking, with some trails through Angel Peak, but none in the Bisti. It is approximately a two-mile hike east of the parking area at Bisti to reach the first concentration of really weird-looking geology.

On Wheels

El Malpais National Conservation Area offers good terrain for biking, but bikes are prohibited from El Malpais National Monument, which the conservation area surrounds. A rather lengthy 35-mile tour, that can be very hot in the summer, is a one-way ride around the border of the West Malpais Wilderness. It starts off of NM 53, 25 miles south of Grants, at the intersection of County Road 42. You ride south on the county road, within sight of

Bandera Crater and past immense, solidified lava flows. Approaching the Continental Divide, you can see the cinder cones that comprise the Chain of Craters. It's a smart idea to have shuttled a vehicle to the intersection with NM 117, approximately 45 miles southeast of Grants, in advance. Otherwise you have to ride back across the lava beds. For further details, contact the BLM/NPS Information Center in Grants (see above, under Grants).

The Mount Taylor area offers superb trails for the highly skilled mountain biker. Trails in the Zuni Mountains are also good for biking, but you need to be careful not to violate private property. For information, contact Cibola National Forest, Mount Taylor Ranger District, 1800 Lobo Canyon Road, Grants, NM 87020, ☎ 505/287-8833. The office can also provide information on McGaffey Recreation Area. Many of these trails are suitable for biking and hiking. Also try jeep trails through areas of Cibola National Forest.

Six-Mile Canyon is 20 miles east of Gallup. Start riding at the Giant rest stop, 14 miles east of Gallup, and ride six miles parallelling the interstate. Follow the signs north into Six Mile Canyon, a steep climb, followed by an exhilarating downhill run back to the interstate.

Chaco Canyon is great for biking around the canyon floor. Most trails are open to hikers only but the **Wijiji Backcountry Trail** is open to bicyclists.

San Juan College, ☎ 505/326-3311, off 30th Street in Farmington, has a marked mountain bike trail offering sandy washes, arroyos, hilly jumps, steep climbs, and many side trails, including one connecting to Farmington Lake, which has its own trail network.

The **Glade Run Trail System**, north of Farmington, offers 40 miles of rolling desert roads and trails reserved for mountain bikes and small off-road vehicles. Motor vehicles seem to be more popular with local residents, so weekends can be a bit noisy and crowded. Try this on a weekday. Contact Farmington Convention and Visitor Bureau for information. **Pinon Mesa**, three miles north of Farmington's 30th Street on the La Plata Highway (NM 170) has many unmarked trails.

For a real adventure, ride into **Bisti Wilderness** or **Angel Peak Recreational Area**. There are dirt and gravel roads through each area, though fewer in the Bisti than around Angel Peak, which is traversed by numerous oil and gas roads winding through the scenic badlands.

Mountain bike sales & repairs are available from the following Farmington shops: **Havens Bikes & Boards**, 2017 East 20th, ☎

505/327-1727; **Cottonwood Cycles**, 3030 East Main, ☎ 505/326-0429; **Gardenswartz Sports**, 910 East Main, ☎ 505/325-6700.

On Water

Bluewater Lake State Park, 20 miles west of Grants on I-40, then six miles south on NM 412, contains a 2,350-acre lake stocked with catfish and rainbow trout. The lake is used for swimming, water-skiing, and boating, and there is a marina, café, and store. It's a popular spot for ice fishing in winter. Camping is available. For information, ☎ 505/876-2391.

Zuni Lakes, on the Zuni Reservation, offer fishing on nine lakes, all reportedly well-stocked. A tribal permit is required, along with a state fishing license. The lakes include **Ojo Caliente Lake**, 20 miles southwest of Zuni, **Black Rock Reservoir** and **Eustace Lake**, two miles north of Zuni. There is also a string of three **Nutria Lakes**, 18 miles northeast of Zuni. For information, contact the Zuni Fish & Wildlife Office, ☎ 505/782-5851.

McGaffey Recreation Area (see above, under Adventures On Foot), 11 miles southeast of Fort Wingate on NM 400, offers picnicking, camping, and fishing at McGaffey Lake. **Ramah Lake**, another fishing spot, is 20 miles farther south on a gravel and dirt road. For information, contact the Cibola National Forest, Mount Taylor Ranger District (see below, under In Snow).

Thirty-eight miles east of Farmington, via Highway 64 and NM 511, is New Mexico's largest reservoir, **Navajo Lake**. The 150 miles of shoreline fed by three rivers (San Juan, Piedra, and Pine) provide fine lake fishing for German or rainbow trout, salmon, bass, bluegill, crappie, and catfish. Also boating, swimming, waterskiing, windsurfing, camping, and picnicking attract 250,000 recreational users annually to the 15,000-acre reservoir and adjacent **Navajo Lake State Park** (1448 NM 511 #1, Navajo Dam, NM 87419, ☎ 505/632-2278 or 505/632-1770, or Navajo Dam Enterprises, Star Route INBU #6, Navajo Dam, NM 87419, ☎ 505/632-3245). There are three marinas with docks located at the Pine, Sims Mesa, and San Juan River Recreation Areas.

For water activities on Navajo Lake, **Rubber Duckie Rental Company**, San Juan Marina, Navajo Lake, Arboles, CO 81121, 970/883-2343, rents Sea-Doos and pedal boats.

Just below the Navajo Dam is what many believe to be the best trophy stream fishing in the state. Catch-and-release waters are located a quarter-mile downstream from the dam. The four-mile stretch known as the **Quality Waters** is carefully regulated to protect the large rainbow, cutthroat, and brown trout that swim in this stretch of the San Juan River, making it one of the top 10 trout streams in the country. Only barbless hooks and artificial lures are permitted and you are only allowed to remove one trout (of at least 20 inches) from this special catch section per day. Year-round fishing is available in an additional 12 miles of open water.

Jackson Lake, off the La Plata Highway north of Farmington, has good trout fishing year-round.

Morgan Lake, 20 miles west of Farmington on US 64, on the Navajo Reservation, is open year-round for bass, crappie, and catfish. A special fishing license is required from the Navajo Tribe, 602/871-6451. The lake is also known for windsurfing in the ever-warm 83° water, kept that way by heated releases from the mammoth Four Corners Power Plant, situated on the lake shore.

LOCAL FISHING GUIDES & OUTFITTERS

Born-n-Raised on the San Juan River, Inc., PO Box 6430, Highway 173, Navajo Dam, NM 87419, ☎ 505/632-2194 or 505/632-0492.

Duranglers, at Navajo Dam, ☎ 505/632-5952.

Four Corners Guide Service, PO Box 6322, Navajo Dam, NM 87419, ☎ 505/632-3566 or 800/669-3566.

Heath Guide Service, 6209 Doe Street, Farmington, NM 87401, ☎ 505/325-1635.

Anthony Lee, Navajo Fishing Guide, PO Box 124, Bloomfield, NM 87413, ☎ 505/326-0664, specializes in location scouting for fishing expeditions.

Rizuto's Hackle Shop, 4251 East Main, Farmington, NM 87401, ☎ 505/326-0664.

Rizuto's Fly Shop, 1796 Highway 173, Navajo Dam, NM 87419, ☎ 505/632-3893.

Rocky Mountain Anglers, at Navajo Dam, ☎ 505/632-0445.

San Juan Troutfitters, PO Box 243, Farmington, NM 87499-0243, ☎ 505/327-9550 or 800/848-6899.

Sportsman Inn, at Navajo Dam, ☎ 505/632-3271.

State fishing licenses are available from these outfitters or from local sporting shops for one day, five days, or the whole fishing season. For information and rates, phone **New Mexico Game & Fish Department**, ☎ 505/827-7911.

On Snow

Compared with other areas of the High Southwest, there's not much snow in this area, except on **Mount Taylor**, where you can snowmobile or cross-country ski on the area's primitive roads. For information, contact Cibola National Forest, Mount Taylor Ranger District, 201 Roosevelt Street, Grants, NM 87020, ☎ 505/287-8833.

In Air

Farmington International Balloon Festival, held in late May, features races and rides in hot air balloons.

Four Corners Aviation, 1260 West Navajo, Farmington, NM 87401,. ☎ 505/325-2867, offers charter flights.

Southwest Safaris-Flightseeing, PO Box 945, Santa Fe, NM 87504, ☎ 505/988-4246 or 800/842-4246, actually offers FAA-approved natural history tours of the entire Southwest, based in New Mexico. The trips range from one-day to overnight expeditions and you may arrange to visit many major sites. After you land, you can continue exploring the backcountry in a ground vehicle or by raft.

Eco-Tours & Cultural Excursions

Gallup Inter-Tribal Ceremonial. This yearly gathering is one of the largest Indian events in the world, representing 50 or more tribes from all over North and Central America. It is held for a week in mid-August at Red Rock State Park. The park is one mile north of I-40, four miles east of Gallup.

Activities include indoor and outdoor marketplaces featuring the work of more than 1,000 artists. You can buy directly from them at wholesale prices. The market is considered by some to include the best selections of Indian art, produced by the most accomplished artists and at the best prices. A special ceremonial showroom offers sales displays of traditional and contemporary Indian fine arts. In all, more than $12 million worth of Indian arts are on display. Nearby, Indian artists will demonstrate various techniques.

Ceremonial activities include two nights of competitive drumming and dancing, including the top 400 Indian dancers in the

United States, Canada, Mexico, and Central America. There are three nights of ceremonial Indian dancing, non-competitive traditional dancing, and three afternoons of all-Indian professional rodeo, featuring 500 participants competing in nine different events. Indian foods are all here for you to experience, such as barbecued mutton, Navajo tacos, and frybread, a greasy, doughy item that can only be described as a donut with no hole and no sugar. A big event is a Saturday morning parade through Gallup, America's only all-Indian, non-mechanized event. Participants wear elaborate traditional clothing, heavy on beads, bones, and feathers, as they dance to the beat of rhythmic drumming, wending their ways through Gallup's streets. Make reservations early if you want to stay in Gallup for this event. Motel rooms in town sell out far in advance.

For information, contact **Inter-Tribal Indian Ceremonial Association**, PO Box 1, Church Rock, NM 87311, ☎ 505/863-3896 or 800/233-4528.

From Memorial Day to Labor Day, except for the days of the ceremonial, Indian dances are performed each night at 7:30 PM at Red Rock State Park, ☎ 505/722-3839.

In addition, all of the Indian pueblos have feast and festival celebrations scheduled throughout the year. Contact pueblo offices for dates, or **Indian Country Tourism Council**, PO Box 1, Church Rock, NM 87311, ☎ 505/863-3896 or 800/233-4528.

Another Indian event is the monthly **Crownpoint Weavers Association Rug Auction**, PO Box 1630, Crownpoint, NM 87313, ☎ 505/786-5302, held in Crownpoint, on NM 371, 30 miles north of Thoreau at Exit 53 on I-40. Crownpoint is on the southeastern corner of the Navajo Nation, and it is very much part of the reservation in spirit and style. Rug sales are more of a festival than a simple auction. The community of 1,000 residents increases by 50% or so on auction nights, as casually dressed travellers hob-nob in the Crownpoint Elementary School gymnasium with traditionally clothed Navajo women wearing velveteen shirts and elaborate turquoise jewelry. Outside the gym, vendors from nearby Acoma and Zuni pueblos sell pottery, jewelry, and kachina dolls representing various spirit gods.

On any auction night you can see cars in the parking lot bearing license plates from far away. People come for the rugs, which are among the most beautiful you can find in Indian country. Bright geometric designs in shades of deep red and blue stand out against backgrounds of white, brown, gray, and black, combining traditional patterns with modern touches. A three-by-five-foot rug takes an average of 160 hours to produce. Prices vary from $10 for the smallest rug to more than $3,000 for elaborate tapestries covering 60 square feet. Part of the fun is the reaction of the standing-room-only crowd to high-priced bidding duels between aggressive buyers.

The first auction here was in 1964 and the events have grown in popularity since then. Initially, if 50 rugs were sold, the night was considered a success. Today, it is not unusual for 400 rugs to change hands on a single night. The system works because weavers and buyers get a better deal here than they would at a trading post or gallery. You can preview the rugs on the afternoon of the auction, from 3 PM to 6 PM. Auctions are held from 7 PM to 11 PM. Don't forget to pick up a free auction card at the door if you think you might be bidding.

Zuni Mountain Tours, Box 5114, Thoreau, NM 8732-9408, ☎ 505/862-7769, offers all-inclusive one- to five-day tours to Chaco Canyon, El Morro, Zuni, Acoma, and Old Route 66.

For one week in the middle of every August, Farmington is host to the **Connie Mack World Series Baseball Tournament** at Ricketts Park, ☎ 505/327-9673. Teams from the US and Puerto Rico compete here, with many pro scouts in attendance.

Farmington's **Lion's Wilderness Park** is the site of an outdoor summer musical drama, *Anasazi, the Ancient Ones*, ☎ 505/326-7602 or 800/448-1240, performed Wednesday through Saturday nights. A second production may alternate on certain nights. Phone for information and schedules.

Indian Land Adventure Tours are arranged by Global Travel and Tours, 1400 South Second, Gallup, NM 87301, ☎ 505/722-2264 or 800/748-1600. These include customized scenic and historical itineraries visiting trading posts, pueblos, shopping areas, historical downtown Gallup, or other far-flung sites such as Canyon de Chelly, the Grand Canyon, the Petrified Forest, and the Painted Desert. Also, there are special charters and transportation to and from Albuquerque.

Desert Southwest Tours offers a retro-journey in a four-door 1955 Cadillac towing an Airstream trailer. The trips follow fabled Route 66 from Albuquerque through New Mexico and into Arizona, and can be tailored to a five-, seven-, or 14-day itinerary. You don't have to stay in the Airstream. Arrangements can be made for overnight stops at bed & breakfast inns along the way. Other backroad trips, bypassing interstate highways for more scenic and culturally appealing routes, visiting such sites as Acoma Pueblo, Sedona, the Grand Canyon, Monument Valley, Arches, Canyonlands, Mesa Verde, and the San Juan Mountains, are available in a fleet of restored vehicles. These include a 1950 Buick Roadmaster, a 1953 Ford Fairlane, and two 1956 Cadillacs. For information, contact **American Dream Safaris**, PO Box 556, McPherson, Kansas, 67460-0556, ☎ 316/241-5656 or 800/552-2397.

The Culture of the Southwest is the name of a 10-day, nine-night tour that includes visits to Grants, Acoma Pueblo, Chaco Canyon, and Aztec Ruins, as well as Santa Fe and Taos. The focus of the trip is wildlife and native cultures, enlisting expert guides, lecturers in wildlife biology, anthropology, archaeology, and Southwest art. For information, contact **Abercrombie & Kent**, 1520 Kensington Road, Oak Brook, IL 60521, ☎ 708/954-2944 or 800/323-7308.

Where to Stay & Eat

This was once a booming travel area when Route 66 was popular, but nowadays many travellers just zip right through on the interstate. There are many chains represented along the interstate corridor, and independent businesses are sometimes just bare-bones operations. There are, however, some special places a little off the beaten track, if you know where to go.

Accommodations

GRANTS

Here you'll find mostly chain motels and mom & pop operations. The best one in town is probably a Best Western, **The Inn**, 1501 East Santa Fe Avenue, Grants, NM 87020, ☎ 505/287-7901 or 800/600-5221. It has an indoor pool, a restaurant, and a sauna.

The lone guest ranch in Northwestern New Mexico is situated in the shadow Mount Taylor. **Mt. Taylor Ranch and Guest Lodge**, Box 229, Cubero, NM 87014, ☎ 505/552-6530 or 800/432-2237.

GALLUP

Plenty of chains are represented here and at least one independent hotel is definitely worth a try.

Holiday Inn, 2915 West US 66, Gallup, NM 87301, ☎ 505/722-2201 or 800432-2211, has a pool and a restaurant and accepts pets.

The Inn Best Western, 3009 West US 66, Gallup, NM 87301, ☎ 505/722-2221 or 800/528-1234 has a pool and a restaurant.

Rodeway Inn, 2003 West US 66, Gallup, NM 87301, ☎ 505/863-9385 or 800/228-2000, has a pool, restaurant and accepts pets.

El Rancho Hotel, 1000 East US 66, Gallup, NM 87301, ☎ 505/863-9311 or 800/543-6351. George Washington did not sleep here, but Ronald Reagan did. And so did lots of other movie stars, including Burt Lancaster and Betty Grable, though not necessarily together. The place was built by the brother of director D.W. Griffith in 1937 to accommodate those very stars while shooting films on location in the area. There is an excellent collection of Indian crafts on display in the lobby, including fine old Navajo rugs. You'll also see mounted deer and elk heads, a wooden Indian and, of course, autographed photos of the stars, including John Wayne, Humphrey Bogart, and Katherine Hepburn.

ZUNI

This area is generally not known for its dining and accommodations, but things are changing. Although this is far off the beaten track, there are some hidden gems out here.

The historic **Vogt Ranch Bed & Breakfast**, PO Box 716, Ramah, NM 87321, ☎ 505/783-4362, may be the most interesting place to stay in all of northwestern New Mexico. It will appeal to those seeking a cultural lodging experience, rather than an antiseptic, undistinguished chain motel episode. This cozy, antique-filled, two-bedroom house was built in 1915 by the present owner's grandparents, who ran a sheep ranch here. Grandpa was also a photographer, newspaper editor, publisher, and the first superintendent of nearby El Morro National Monument, a position he held for 26 years.

He built his house out of stone extracted from nearby Anasazi Indian ruins in the days before this variety of recycling was discouraged by the federal government. Experts claim the ruins contained 26 rooms, and one of the things they found there, along with corn cobs and pottery, was a skeleton, which was reburied elsewhere. The property was originally used as a guest house starting after World War II and operated until 1965. It was reopened as a B&B in 1986.

The stone house today contains a collection of Anasazi artifacts, a 1915 upright piano, and a substantial collection of Southwestern books. The wood plank floors are covered in Navajo rugs, and the kitchen has a woodburning stove. One of the bedrooms has a Zuni fireplace and the other has a wood stove. Both rooms have private baths. The owner does not live in the house, but comes in the morning to prepare your breakfast of blue corn pancakes, muffins, bacon, eggs, and fruit. Otherwise, you're on your own out here.

The privacy and serenity are exquisite; there's no TV, and Gallup is 40 miles north. Grants is 54 miles east. The location is ideal for exploring the area, with nearby hiking, biking, bird watching, and Anasazi sites, as well as Ramah Lake. It's probably a good idea to bring some food if you're planning to stay a few nights, but there's a good Mexican restaurant a mile away in Ramah. You can get a pizza 21 miles west in Zuni. El Morro is 11 miles east of the ranch on NM 53, and El Malpais is 20 miles farther east on the same road.

Vogt Ranch is one mile southeast of Ramah, on NM 53, between mile markers 34 and 35. The ranch generally closes between January and March. Reservations are highly recommended.

Zuni Mountain Bed & Breakfast, Box 5114, Thoreau, NM 87323-9408, ☎ 505/862-7769, is a new place, also offering guided tours (see above, under "Eco Tours & Cultural Excursions") to various regional sites of interest.

FARMINGTON

Chains and small mom & pop motels can be found here. The safest bets are the chains.

Comfort Inn, 555 Scott Avenue, Farmington, NM 87401, ☎ 505/325-2626 or 800/221-2222, has free continental breakfast and an outdoor pool.

Farmington Anasazi Inn, 903 West Main, Farmington, NM 87401, ☎ 505/325-4564, is unimpressive from the outside, but comfortable inside, with Southwestern furnishings enlivening the typical Farmington motel experience. It also has a passable restaurant.

Holiday Inn of Farmington, 600 East Broadway, Farmington, NM 87401, ☎ 505/325-2545, has a fitness room, heated outdoor pool, and free airport courtesy van.

The Inn Best Western, 700 Scott Avenue, Farmington, NM 87401, ☎ 505/327-5221, has rooms with refrigerators, indoor pool, jacuzzi, saunas, fitness center, and courtesy airport transportation.

La Quinta Inn, 675 Scott Avenue, Farmington, NM 87401, ☎ 505/327-4706 or 800/531-5900, offers free local phone calls.

Several bed & breakfasts have recently opened in Farmington. These include the following: **Casa Blanca**, 505 East La Plata Street,

☎ 505/327-6503; **Silver River Adobe Inn**, 3151 West Main, 505/325-8219 or 800/382-9251.

Twelve miles west of Farmington on US 64, then 35 miles south on NM 44 to Nageezi, is where you will find the only accommodations near Chaco Canyon. **Chaco Inn at the Post**, PO Box 40, Nageezi, NM 87037, ☎ 505/632-3646, is a modest and friendly Navajo-run B&B.

AZTEC

Accommodations in this small town have long been pretty basic motels; they look like 1950s motor courts. But one is nicer than the others. **Enchantment Lodge**, US 550 West, 1800 West Aztec Boulevard, Aztec, NM 87410, ☎ 505/334-6143, has a heated pool, morning coffee, and a picnic area. It is within walking distance of Aztec Ruins.

New in town are two establishments.

Miss Gail's Inn, 300 South Main, Aztec, NM 87410, ☎ 505/334-3452, is an 11-room bed & breakfast.

Step Back Inn, 103 West Aztec Boulevard, Aztec, NM 87410, ☎ 505/334-1200, looks a bit like a nursing home on the outside, but it is close to the Aztec Ruins and downtown.

NAVAJO LAKE AREA

The two motels at Navajo Lake are **Abe's Motel & Fly Shop**, 3391 NM 173, Navajo Dam, NM 87419, ☎ 505/632-2194; and **San Juan River Lodge**, 1796 Highway 173, Navajo Dam, NM 87419, ☎ 505/632-1411.

Restaurants

GRANTS

For the most part, local cuisine will probably not win awards here, but it won't break the bank either. If you're hungry, try the **Iron Skillet**, I-40 at Horizon Boulevard exit, west of Grants, ☎ 505/285-6621. It's open 24 hours. Add the experience here to your ongoing saga of "salad bars of the Southwest."

For Mexican food try **Monte Carlo Restaurant and Lounge,** 721 West Santa Fe Avenue, Grants, ☎ 505/287-9250.

A step above average and out of time is the **Dinner Bell Café,** ☎ 505/287-5100, on old Route 66 in Milan, three miles north of Grants, off I-40. It's the oldest café in town, complete with booths and tables dating to the 1950s. Although the menu is not exotic, featuring burgers and sandwiches, you can get a solid, square breakfast or lunch for around $6. Homemade soups and pies fill out the bill.

GALLUP

For the most part there's more of the same uninspired cuisine in Gallup, with lots of fast foods represented and other highly suspect eateries. However, one must eat, and for standard, rib-sticking Route 66 road food, the best of the lot includes **Peewee's,** 2206 East US 66, ☎ 505/722-5159, or **Roadrunner Café,** 3014 East US 66, ☎ 505/722-7309. **The Ranch Kitchen,** 3001 West US 66, ☎ 505/722-2537, has been "specializing in southwestern cooking for over 40 years!" Not only does this place offer a salad bar, the de rigueur gift shop features Indian arts & crafts, as well as gifts from Mexico. **The Eagle Café,** 220 West US 66, ☎ 505/722-3220, is another old standard serving burgers, ribs and fajitas.

A new gallery area is starting to transform the neighborhood of old houses around West Hill Street. **Desert Dreams,** 106 West Hill Street, Gallup, ☎ 505/863-4616, combines a coffee shop serving decent Mexican food, sandwiches, and pastries, as well as good coffee from Guatemala, Costa Rica, Mexico, and Ethiopia, with a new-age bookstore and gift shop. It's a comfortable place to sit and relax with no pressure.

Shush Yaz Trading Co. and A-OK Café, 214 West Aztec, Gallup, NM 87301, ☎ 505/722-7027, fax 505/722-2005, combines six generations of Indian trading, dating to 1875, with a small café serving breakfast and lunch. Try blue corn pancakes for breakfast. They serve some of the best Navajo food around, including Navajo tacos, or A-OK tacos combining chicken, poblano and avocado, guacamole and beans, or squash, corn, potato, onion, and beans, all served with rice and jicama. The lamb sandwiches are tasty, there's a special soup daily, and, of course, frybread. There's also a small bakery attached serving fresh fruit and berry cobbler, gingerbread or chocolate cake daily and sometimes cardamom coffee cake.

As for the trading post, there's a large selection of art, as well as Pendleton blankets and Navajo squaw skirts at the lowest prices around.

La Barraca, 1303 East 66 Avenue, Gallup, ☎ 505/722-5083, serves homemade Mexican food that is extremely popular with locals but a well-kept secret. Specialties include a superlative mild green chili sauce, seedless chili rellenos stuffed with cheddar cheese and dipped in egg batter, enchiladas, tacos, and burritos.

For the hot stuff, try **Genaro's,** 600 West Hill, Gallup, ☎ 505/863-6761. It serves the hottest salsa in town and huge servings of smothered burritos, and sopapillas stuffed with beef, beans, cheese, and tangy guacamole, chili rellenos, and posole, which is chunks of pork cooked with hominy. Take sauces on the side if you're sensitive to hot, hot food.

Fifteen miles east of Gallup on I-40, then three miles south on NM 400, is another real find, **The Lost Oasis Café,** Bear Springs Plaza, Fort Wingate, ☎ 505/488-6640. The sunny, flower-decked dining room, with large windows and central fountain occupied by a salamander and goldfish, is truly a sanctuary of Nouveau Southwestern cuisine. Offerings include elk medallions, buffalo steaks, and seafood jambalaya, with a focus on traditional New Mexican flavorings added to unusual foods. This translates into elk marinated in green chili, cilantro and lime, or charbroiled swordfish topped with salsa and pineapple. Mexican food specialties are also excellent. The café serves breakfast, lunch, and dinner, as well as Sunday brunch, and occasionally offers weekend dinner shows with live music.

ZUNI

Blue Corn Restaurant in Ramah at the Cowboy Stopover on NM 53, 40 miles southeast of Gallup or 20 miles east of Zuni, may be worth the drive for lunch or dinner. You can smell roasting red peppers as you walk in, and meals start with a big basket of red and blue corn chips with homemade salsa. Dishes include red pepper enchiladas covered in a cilantro cream sauce, beef Normandy, apricot stuffed chicken breast, blue corn crab enchiladas, and chili-lime chicken. For dessert try the kiwi-strawberry tarts in a puff pastry.

There are only a couple of restaurants in Zuni and the best one is **Chu Chu's Pizzeria,** on NM 53, ☎ 505/782-2100. The gent who runs the place learned how to make pizza in New York City.

FARMINGTON

As for dining, from the visible glut of franchise operations along Farmington's main drag, it appears that local tastes run to fast food. There are a few decent places to eat, though. **The Trough**, ☎ 505/334-6176, behind the Country Palace Bar, two miles east of Farmington on US 550, serves enormous western-size steaks, pork chops, and seafood. The ambience is casual, the portions are filling, and the food is edible, which is more than can be said for many dining options in these parts.

For Mexican food try **Señor Pepper's**, ☎ 505/327-0436, located at Farmington's Four Corners Regional Airport. There's not all that much air traffic here, so this place is mainly supported by locals. One popular dish, Steak Mazatlan, was once featured in an issue of *Bon Appétit*. This place also offers Sunday brunch.

Coyote's, at the Anasazi Inn (see above), serves three meals a day. It offers acceptable Mexican food and an all-you-can-eat catfish special on Friday nights.

Something Special Bakery & Tea Room, 116 North Auburn Avenue, Farmington, ☎ 505/325-8183, is hidden away several blocks off Main, serving good home-cooked lunches and baked goods. Dinners are served on Friday only.

The **Farmington Convention and Visitor Bureau** (see above, under Touring-Farmington) can give you the complete roster of places to stay and dine in town.

Camping

There are numerous commercial campgrounds throughout this region, but for anything close to adventure, the public camping areas are more likely to deliver the goods. Listed below are some of the most scenic.

Two campgrounds are in the Mount Taylor Recreation Area, close to I-40. These are the primitive **Lobo Canyon Camp** and the **Coal Mine Campground**, which can accommodate large recreational vehicles. Both are off NM 547, north of Grants.

Bluewater Lake State Park (see above under Adventures On Water) has RV hookups and tent sites, a dump station, and showers.

There is a small, primitive campground at **El Morro National Monument**. Water is available, but not RV hookups.

Red Rock State Park is four miles east of Gallup on NM 566. The campground has 130 spaces, some for tents, some with hook-ups. It also has a dump station, showers, laundry, general store, and a post office.

The Zuni tribe operates several primitive campgrounds down rugged dirt roads in the hilly park lands near the Zuni Lakes.

McGaffey Recreation Area, in the Zuni Mountains, 15 miles east of Gallup on I-40, then south 10 miles on NM 400, has two campgrounds, **Quaking Aspen** and **McGaffey**, a few miles farther south on NM 400.

Chaco Canyon's Gallo Campground has 64 sites with picnic tables, fireplaces, cold water bathrooms, but no showers. Drinking water is available at the Visitor Center, one mile away.

Angel Peak Recreation Area, in the Naciemento Badlands, offers 16 paved campsites with fireplaces, tables, and porta-potties, but no water or other services.

Pine River Site, Sims Mesa Site, or **San Juan River Recreation Area**, all at **Navajo Lake State Park**, offer 200 spaces, eight full hook-ups, 50 electrical hook-ups, picnic tables, rest rooms, and a dump station. The **Cottonwood Campground**, also at the park, has elaborate facilities for the handicapped, including elevated fishing platforms and paved trails.

For those campers caught tentless in Northwest New Mexico, camping equipment and sporting goods may be rented in Farmington from the **San Juan College Outdoor Program**, ☎ 505/599-0221.

Index